DIGITAL FOUNDATIONS

INTRO TO MEDIA DESIGN

WITH THE ADOBE CREATIVE SUITE

XTINE BURROUGH & MICHAEL MANDIBERG

New Riders | AIGA

Digital Foundations: Introduction to Media Design with the Adobe Creative Suite
xtine burrough and Michael Mandiberg
www.digital-foundations.net

New Riders
1249 Eighth Street
Berkeley, CA 94710
510/524-2178
510/524-2221 (fax)

Published in association with AIGA Design Press

Find us on the Web at: www.newriders.com
To report errors, please send a note to errata@peachpit.com

New Riders is an imprint of Peachpit, a division of Pearson Education.

Project Editor: Michael J. Nolan
Development & Copy Editor: Rose Weisburd
Production Editor: Hilal Sala
Proofreader: Jill Simonsen
Indexer: Cheryl Landes
Cover/Interior design: Michael Mandiberg and xtine burrough
Layout Team: Patrick Davison and Tara Romeo

ISBN 13: 978-0-321-55598-4
ISBN 10: 0-321-55598-8

9 8 7 6 5 4 3

Printed and bound in the United States of America

Dedications

xtine dedicates this book to her parents, Viola and Bill, who remind her of the importance of net gains, silver linings and standing up straight (after all, standing tall is an exercise in alignment); to Christopher James, who believed in xtine before she knew how to stand tall as an artist; to her fellow yoginis who always stand tall in tadasana; and to paullester, who supported x during her darkest moments of writing and editing, when standing up straight seemed impossible.

Michael dedicates this book to the artists who raised him: his parents Linda and Joe. He is especially proud of growing up in a woodshop and a house covered in quilts, learning to sew, and how to measure twice and cut once. He also dedicates this book to Uncle David, for persevering in his craft; to Stephen for helping him learn how to teach even the most obstinate, and to his late grandparents for providing a world full of art, music, ideas, and imagination.

In Gratitude

We would like to thank our many colleagues who have encouraged and inspired us to write this book. The Eyebeam crew: Steve Lambert, Jeff Crouse, Amanda McDonald Crowley, Liz Slagus, Emma Lloyd, Robert Ransick, Stephanie Hunt, John S. Johnson and Susan Short. Our fellow faculty members at CSU Fullerton, including Paul Martin Lester, Tony Fellow, Rick Pullen, Coral Ohl, Cindy King, Mark Latonero, and Henry Puente. And our colleagues at the College of Staten Island, City University of New York, including Jeanine Corbet, Cynthia Chris, David Gerstner, Janet Manfredonia, Ed Miller, Sherry Millner, Jason Simon, Matthew Solomon, Francisco Soto, Valerie Tevere, Cindy Wong, and Ying Zhu. We would also like to thank Brian O'Connell, Valerie Tevere, Liz White, and David Jimison for teaching draft versions of this book, and providing invaluable feedback from the classroom.

Many thanks to our peers for their influence on us and their feedback, which helped shape the book: Ernest Larsen, Tom Igoe, Adam Hyde, Marisa Olson, Brooke Singer, Tiffany Holmes, Mike Bonano, Andy Bichlbaum, Peter Duyan, Josh Duyan, Chad Kellogg, Kevin McCarty, Haruko Tanaka, Curt Cloninger, Lucy HG, Adam Schwartz, Nancy Hasselbacher, Crystal Adams, Laurie Cella, Michael Hanson, and Julia Steinmetz. A much deserved thank you to our technical editors, Addie Wagenknecht, Brian McNally, Jennifer Michel, Alec Fehl, Cary Powell, and Gabriel Powell.

This book would not have been released with a Creative Commons license if Steve Lambert had not reminded Michael that he was contractually obligated by the Eyebeam OpenLab to do so, and encouraged us along the way. Michael probably would have gotten around to realizing this anyway, but Steve was the catalyst. Steve, Mushon Zer-Aviv, Alex Galloway, dana boyd, Cory Doctorow, Mark Tribe, McKenzie Wark, and Nathan Yergler at Creative Commons (who repeatedly reminded us that Creative Commons can not offer legal advice or opinions) provided great strategic advice on how to convince the publisher to use a Creative Commons license. We would like to thank Nancy Davis, Editor in Chief, for having the vision to see how sharing helps everyone and everything, including the bottom line.

Digital Foundations would not have been possible without the support of the Peachpit and AIGA team. Michael Nolan understood our project from day one, Sue Apfelbaum intuitively knew the importance of bringing aesthetics back to media arts education, Rose Weisburd was worth her weight in gold. She made sure our words were consistent and offered editorial advice along the way. Charlene Will kept our design focused. Hilal Sala made sure we were ready on the day our book was scheduled to print.

Ellen Lupton's books were our role models, and Marita Sturken provided inspiration and early advice. Curt Cloninger was extremely generous in reviewing our initial proposal, and directing us along the right path. Numerous consultants, assistants, and interns worked on this book extensively at various stages, including Mushon Zer-Aviv, Erika Nishizato, Patrick Davison, Tara Romeo, Evan Moran, Danielle Palladino, Carlo Montagnino, and Michele Rose.

We would like to thank our teachers. From grade school through grad school, we were shaped by those who took the time to share. Shout outs to Jerry Mischak for bringing out the big Albers book from the rare books library. Props to Lowell G. Herr and Mike Bolduan for being such disciplined and yet playful role models, and for Clint Darling for playing with fire. Thank you, repeatedly, to Christopher James, Steven Kurtz, Charles Recher, Ellen Rothenberg, and Humberto Ramirez.

Thanks to our students - past, present and future.

Lastly we would like to thank our families, defined in the broadest sense. It may sound like a platitude, but we would not be the people we are, and would not have written this book, without their influence. Thank you for sustaining us, always.

About the Authors

xtine burrough is a media artist and educator. She has worked in a variety of formats, including the web, digital video, photography and letterpress printing. Recent web projects include www.Delocator.net and www.MechanicalOlympics.org, websites that empower online users in the analog world and promote autonomy and interpretation. Delocator is an online tool that assists participants in locating, sharing and supporting locally owned cafés, movie theaters, and bookstores. Through MechanicalOlympics.org, xtine hired members of the Amazon.com Mechanical Turk elastic workforce to interpret and perform Olympic events during the Summer 2008 games. Web viewers and participants voted for gold, silver, and bronze winners based on contestant videos uploaded to YouTube.

xtine has shown or spoken about her work nationwide and internationally. She has participated in international festivals promoting digital art and culture including Futuresonic (UK), Electrofringe (AU), Sonar (SP) and Prog:ME (BR). xtine is an Assistant Professor of Visual Communications at California State University, Fullerton. A complete portfolio of her work can be viewed at www.missconceptions.net.

Michael Mandiberg is an artist, programmer, designer and educator. His work varies from web applications about environmental impact to conceptual performances about subjectivity, to laser cut lampshades for compact fluorescent lightbulbs.

Recent projects include HowMuchItCosts.us, a car direction site that incorporates the financial and carbon cost of driving, the Bright Idea Shade (with Steve Lambert) a Creative Commons licensed flat-pack laser cut lampshade for bare CFL lightbulbs, Stencilano, a stencil-friendly adaptation of the Zapfino font, and TheRealCosts, a Firefox browser plug-in that inserts carbon footprints into web sites that feature directions for air and ground travel.

His work has been exhibited at such venues as the New Museum for Contemporary Art in New York City, Ars Electronica Center in Linz, ZKM in Karlsruhe, Germany, and Transmediale Festival, Berlin. His work has been featured in such books as Tribe and Jana's *New Media Art*, Blais and Ippolito's *At the Edge of Art*, and Greene's *Internet Art*. He is a recipient of grants and residencies from Eyebeam, Rhizome.org, and Turbulence.org/Jerome Foundation.

An Assistant Professor of Design and Digital Media at the College of Staten Island/CUNY, he is currently a Senior Fellow at Eyebeam. His work lives at www.Mandiberg.com, and his design work lives at www.SubsidiaryDesign.com. Raised in Portland, Oregon, he lives in and rides his bicycle around Brooklyn.

Table of Contents

Introduction: read_me!

Digital Foundations

This book was written by two artist educators who teach digital art and design studio foundation classes. While teaching classes that take place in software laboratories, we noticed that many of our students expected to learn to use software, but gave little consideration to aesthetics or art and design history. A typical first day question is, "Are we going to learn Photoshop in this class?"

At first we were tempted to oblige our students' thirst for so-called practical knowledge, but we recognize that in the absence of the visual, theoretical, and historical frameworks, practical knowledge is practically useless. To teach our classes, we used the very best of the software training manuals, and supplemented them with all the visual and historical material that was missing.

After settling for years on books that don't really encapsulate a class, we finally decided to write the book that we think all introductory media design students should be using. For us, a student is anyone actively engaged in learning. A student can be working towards a degree in art, communication, graphic design, illustration, and so on in a traditional classroom setting, or a self-taught found-it-on-the-bookstore-shelf learner.

In the twenty chapters that follow, we have shared small bites of history, followed by visual references, and then digital exercises that explore Adobe's Creative Suite in a manner that brings design principles into the software demo.

Bauhaus

This book is a mash-up of the Bauhaus Basic Course and the Adobe Creative Suite. We have taken some of the visual principles and exercises from the Bauhaus Basic Course and adapted them into exercises for the Adobe Creative Suite.

The Bauhaus was an influential art, design, and architectural school in Germany. It operated from 1919 to 1933, during which time it transformed art education, through its integration of art, craft, architecture, and design, its emphasis on modern materials, and the creation of the Basic Course. The Basic Course was a year-long course in which first year students learned composition, color theory, and how to use a variety of basic materials. When many of the instructors fled Nazi Germany, arriving in the United States and other countries, they brought this education model with them in the guise of the Studio Foundation course.

This book takes its inspiration from the Bauhaus model.

Operating Systems & Version Numbers

The exercises in this book explore the core principles of the Adobe Creative Suite design applications. The focus is on core principles that do not change with every software or operating system version, rather than the "new bells and whistles" marketing devices intended to sell new versions of the product.

While we have written this book using Adobe Creative Suite 4 on Mac OS 10.5, we have written the book to be version-independent. We expect that this book will still be just as useful if you were using Adobe Creative Suite 2 on Windows XP, Photoshop 7 on Mac OS 9, or future versions of the software that will be released in the years to come. Our screen shots are from CS4, but you can find the full set of screen shots for CS3 on the wiki at http://wiki.digital-foundations.net.

Within this book we refer to all keyboard shortcuts using the MacOS protocol. If you are using this book with Windows, simply translate the Command key to the Control key and the Option key to the Alt key. Everything else remains the same.

Using the wiki

We wrote the entire book online at http://wiki.digital-foundations. net and we will be leaving the text online for anyone to use, for free. You will find our exercise files and any work files that you need to download while working on the exercises in this book at the wiki site. You can download all exercise files from the "Download work files" link, and you can also find work files at the start of each chapter online.

Creative Commons

Digital Foundations: Introduction to Media Design with the Adobe Creative Suite is licensed under a Creative Commons Attribution Non-Commercial 3.0 License 2009 by xtine burrough and Michael Mandiberg.

This means that anyone can reprint, reuse, remix and build upon this work non-commercially. This includes translating the book (via the wiki) into other languages, operating systems, or software packages; making screen-casts of each chapter; and augmenting the book with appendixes of visual examples. We encourage you to tag your reprint, reused, and remixed adaptations "digitalfoundations" and let us know about your work by emailing us at remix@digital-foundations.net.

Commercial (for profit) permissions beyond the scope of this license may be available at http://wiki.digital-foundations.net/index. php?title=Licensing or by contacting permissions@peachpit.com.

Early "computers" at work, summer 1949, photograph attributed to NASA.

1 Metaphor

Computer software interfaces are built on metaphors. These metaphors link the digital interface to real-life tools and processes.

An operating system is software that we use to operate the computer. The operating systems we encounter most often are Mac OS, Windows, or Linux. These operating systems use graphical interfaces to enable us to create, move, and delete files, and use other software to edit the contents of those files.

Regardless of the operating system you are using, most share a few central metaphors such as document, folder, file system, and desktop. Before today's so-called "paperless office," office workers created documents on paper, filed them in folders, and organized the folders in cabinets near their desks. The most important or current project folders might have been sitting on their desktops. Of course the original paper system persists alongside the computerized system, as well as in the computer's metaphorical structure.

If the operating system is like your home office, design software is like your studio. The metaphors of design software are built around the tools of the artist and designer: pencils, brushes, palettes, artboards, and photographic equipment. These tools do what you would expect: pencils make hard-edged lines, brushes make hard- and soft-edged areas of color, colors are mixed in the Color panel.

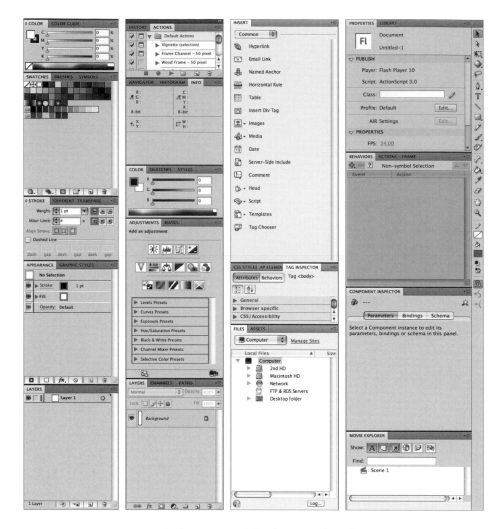

Fig 1.1 – 4 Panels for Illustrator, Photoshop, Dreamweaver, and Flash, respectively.

These metaphors are consistent across the graphical interfaces of operating systems and design applications. For example, the panels and the tools look and behave in the same way — despite subtle application differences — in Adobe's Illustrator, Photoshop, InDesign, Dreamweaver, and Flash. Learning the metaphors and similarities among these application interfaces will be one of the fastest routes to mastering the tools.

EXERCISE
01 Working with folders and files

FIG 1.5 Create a new folder.

Create a new folder

1. To create a new folder on your computer, navigate to the place where you want your new folder to reside (for instance, the Desktop), and from the menu, choose File > New Folder. (Fig 1.5) Most computer users typically store folders in the Documents folder or on the Desktop. As soon as you create a new folder, the operating system temporarily names it "untitled folder". As long as you do not click outside of the folder name, the name area remains highlighted in blue, and is ready for you to type a new name. We named ours "digital_foundations" and pressed the Return key.

2. If you clicked somewhere on the Desktop after creating the new folder, it may seem like you are stuck with a folder named "untitled folder". All folders can be renamed. To rename a folder, click once on the folder to select it, pause, and then either click on the name of the folder or press Return. Once the name is highlighted, you can type on top of the original name to replace it. We renamed our folder "digital_foundations". (Fig 1.6-9)

LEFT TO RIGHT:
FIG 1.6 – 9

untitled folder

untitled folder

digital_foundations

* Finished exercise file available in the Download Materials area of the wiki.

3. Move the new digital_foundations folder you just created to the Documents folder by clicking and dragging it from the Desktop into the Documents folder. (Fig 1.10)

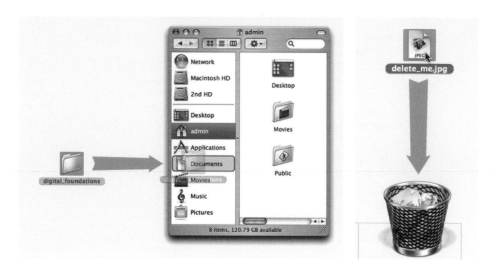

FIG 1.10 Moving a folder into the Documents folder.

FIG 1.11 Moving a file to the trash.

Delete a file

4. Next, we will review three ways to delete a file or folder. (Fig 1.11) Choose one method and delete the new folder you just created. The metaphorical trash or recycle bin appears in most computer operating systems. To delete a document in Mac OS, drag it onto the Trash icon on the Dock.

Another way to move an item to the trash is by selecting the item and pressing Command+Delete. The Command (, ⌘) keys are located directly to the left and right of the spacebar. They are used in most keyboard shortcuts in Mac OS, much like the Control key is used in Windows.

Contextual menus provide yet another way to delete a file. The contextual menus appear by right-clicking the mouse. If your mouse has only one button, Control-click accesses the contextual menu. Contextual menu options change depending on the context in which you click. If you right-click on a folder, you will see a list of actions that can be performed on that folder. This menu is different from the menu that would appear if you right-clicked on a file instead. To delete an item using the contextual menu, right-click on the file and select Move to Trash from the contextual menu. (Fig 1.12)

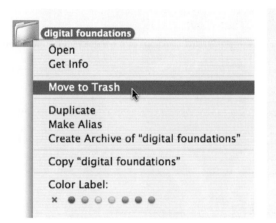

Note:

It is important to remember that there is almost always more than one way to complete any given task. The best method is usually the one that fits most efficiently within your personal work habits.

FIG 1.12 A contextual menu.

Files: vector vs. bitmap

Computer graphics are created in one of two formats: vector or bitmap. Computer files containing these graphics may contain vectors, bitmaps, or both, as we will explore in Chapters 6 and 11.

Note: Illustrator and Flash are the applications most often used to create and modify vector images.

Vector graphics are created by using mathematical algorithms: formulas that describe where points, lines, and planes exist and how these elements relate to one another. Vector graphics can be scaled up to any size and retain their smooth edges. Vector graphics look smooth and crisp at their edges, and they can be easily scaled to any size. Logos are nearly always developed as vector graphics, as a logo has to fit easily on a business card, a web site, and possibly a billboard or bus wrapping.

Bitmap or raster graphics are built from grids of pixels. Each tiny pixel contains a unit of color information. Bitmaps are used for digital photography and scanned images. Bitmap files are not as easily scalable as vector graphics.

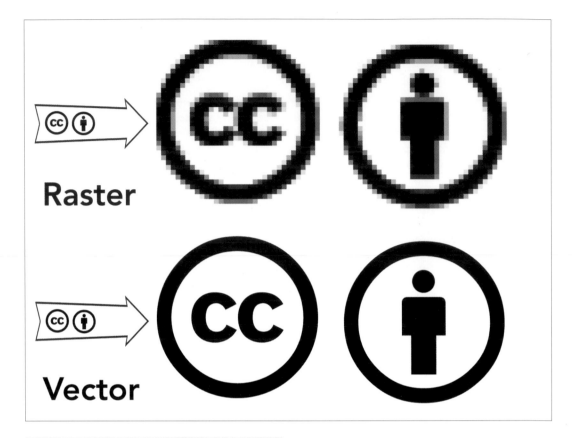

Note:

Photoshop is an application that creates and modifies bitmap graphics, while Dreamweaver is an application that uses them for web page layout.

Vector graphics can be placed into applications that are pixel-based, and bitmap images can be placed in vector-based applications, though a translation process has to take place. This will be covered in later chapters.

FIG 1.13 In the top and bottom images we scaled the same logo to 700 percent. This means we are viewing the images at 7 times their actual sizes. If you enlarge a raster image too much, the pixel grid becomes visible to the human eye. The only possible compensation is to blur the edges. Either way, enlarging a pixel-based image results in a loss of quality. Vector images don't have this limitation. On the other hand, extremely complex vector images take an excessive amount of computer processsing power. The top image is a raster; it is easy to see the individual pixels that comprise the logo as tiny squares of color. In the bottom image, the logo has been opened in the vector-based application Illustrator. Notice that the edges of the lines, letters, and figure are all still rendered as smooth lines.

EXERCISE
02 Creating a new file in Adobe Illustrator

Launch the application

1. In Mac OS, move the mouse to the bottom of the screen so that it appears over the Dock. The Dock displays icons that are buttons which launch various applications in one click. Click the Illustrator icon once and the application will open. If the icon is not in the Dock, you can find the application in Macintosh HD > Applications > Adobe Illustrator or Finder > Menu > Go >Applications > Adobe Illustrator. In Windows OS it is in Start > Programs > Adobe > Adobe Illustrator CS4. (Fig 1.14)

FIG 1.14 The dock may be on the left or right of the screen, or it may be hiding. Move the cursor to the edge of the screen, and it will appear. To change the Dock settings, choose menu > Dock.

Define a new file

2. When Illustrator opens, the Welcome screen appears. Choose the Print Document button beneath the header "Create New" on the Welcome screen. (Fig 1.15)

FIG 1.15 The Welcome Screen appears at the launch of most Adobe applications, and can be turned off by checking the box in the lower left corner, "Don't show again."

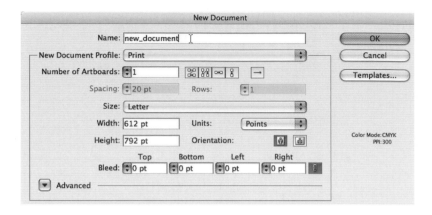

FIG 1.16 New Document dialog box.

When defining a new file, several settings must be taken into consideration. When you choose a new print document (as opposed to a new video document), Illustrator loads some of the default settings — file resolution, document sizes, and so on — appropriate to that particular type of file.

In the New Document dialog box (Fig 1.16), choose Letter from the Size pull-down menu. Letter (8.5 by 11 inches) is a common document size for print media. When we chose a new print document, the Size pull-down menu loaded standard sizes for the medium. If we had selected a web profile, the Size pull-down menu would have loaded standard settings for web design. Click OK.

Note: A dialog box is an interface that pops up when the computer needs information in order to complete a task. To highlight the metaphor, the computer needs to have a conversation with you, hence the word "dialog." For instance, the software needs specific information before creating a new document, such as the size, units, etc. Keep in mind that the dialog box asks questions that must be answered by clicking OK or Cancel before continuing work on the document.

The blank page and your tools

Look around your new document and notice the interface elements. (Fig 1.17) In the center is an Artboard. Analog layouts were created inside the area defined by cropmarks drawn on a board, which was referred to as the Artboard. Illustrator reproduces the analog experience through metaphor.

On the left side of the document area is the Tools panel. Like an artist's or designer's toolbox, the Tools panel holds pens, pencils, brushes, shape tools, and so on.

On the right are more panels. Take notice of the Color panel. Painters mix together individual paint colors on a

FIG 1.17 The default workspace of Illustrator.

palette. In Illustrator, as in the other Adobe Creative Suite applications, you create colors by virtually mixing colors in a panel (read more about this in Chapter 5).

The tools and panels can be moved around the screen, and they can be hidden or shown based on the amount of workspace on the monitor.

3. Show the Layers panel by choosing Window > Layers, then hide the Layers panel by pressing the close Layer panel button in the top left corner. Alternatively, any panel can be shown or hidden by selecting its name from the Window menu.

After quitting and then re-opening a program, panels will assume the same locations as when the application was last closed. This can be a time-saver on a personal computer, but it can be an annoyance in a classroom or lab when the previous user's custom panel configuration appears confusing. Most applications have basic or default workspaces. Reset the workspace layout in Illustrator by choosing Window > Workspace > [Essential]. Before starting each of the exercises, set the workspace to the default or essential settings so that your set-up is consistent with the settings we used while writing this book.

03 Creating a dynamic composition

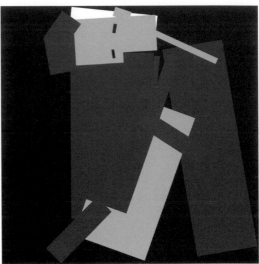

FIG 1.18 *The Poet*, 1911, Egon Schiele, oil on canvas.

FIG 1.19 Compostition created in Illustrator.

Compositions can be static or dynamic. In this exercise, we will recreate the dynamic movement found within a painting. Dynamic compositions are full of energy or movement. Angles are used to create motion. While a flat horizon line is at rest, a triangle is in motion. The repetition of even spacing is easy on the eye, as our minds predict the simple rhythm of an evenly spaced grid. Angles and uneven spacing between objects cause our eyes to move back and forth. This physical movement translates into the perception of movement within a composition. Here, we use a Schiele painting as the guideline for a dynamic composition with rectangles.

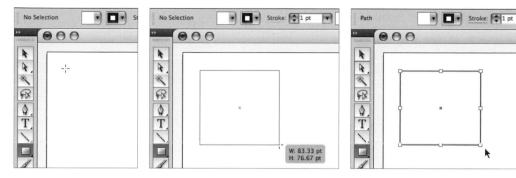

FIG 1.20 Click.　　　FIG 1.21 Drag.　　　　　　FIG 1.22 Release.

1. In Illustrator, click on the Rectangle tool from the Tools panel. Click and drag to draw a rectangle on the page. (Fig 1.20-22)

2. Once the rectangle is created, release the mouse and click on the Selection tool. (Fig 1.23) Objects can only be modified when they are selected. The Selection tool is used to select an object in order to move, scale, or copy it. Click on the rectangle with the Selection tool. Notice that the selected rectangle has square anchor points on each corner and at the midpoint of each line. These anchor points are essential components of the vector art. They determine the contours of the shape by their position in relationship to each other. A rectangle is described by a path that turns at right angles through four anchor points to create four sides and meet itself to close the shape. To deselect the object, click on the Artboard in any area outside of the rectangle.

FIG 1.23 Notice that a tool tip shows up when the mouse hovers over a tool. The tool tip displays the name of the tool and the keyboard shortcut. This is true in most graphics applications.

3. With the rectangle selected, notice how the shape is made. The rectangle is an area filled with color and there may or may not be a line surrounding the edges. The interior color is called the *fill*. The outline is called the *stroke*. White and black are the default color settings for fill and stroke.

4. Look at the bottom of the Tools panel and notice what color is loaded in the Fill icon and what color is loaded into the Stroke icon. The Fill and Stroke icons stack with the active target on the top. To change the fill, it needs to be the top icon. (Fig 1.24)

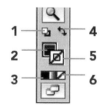

FIG 1.24 1. Reset, 2. Fill; 3: Color; 4: Switch; 5: Stroke; 6: None.

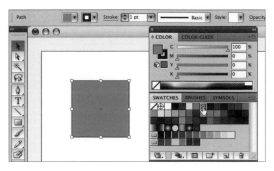
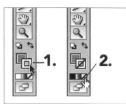

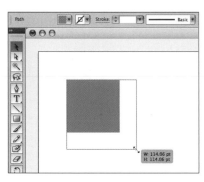
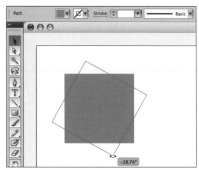

TOP LEFT TO RIGHT:
FIG 1.25 The Swatches panel window.
FIG 1.26 Set the stroke to none.

BOTTOM LEFT TO RIGHT: FIG 1.27 The rectangle scales.
FIG 1.28 The rectangle rotates.

5. While the rectangle is still selected, click once on the Fill icon to reposition it on top of the stroke.

6. Click on the Swatches panel (Fig 1.25), then click on any color. It is assigned to the fill area of the rectangle and it also appears as the color in the Fill icon. The rectangle will change because it was selected before a new color was applied.

7. Click on the Stroke icon to position it on top of the Fill icon. (Fig 1.26)

8. Click on the None icon. This symbol, beneath the Fill and Stroke icons, is a white square with a red diagonal line. Clicking this will remove the stroke from the rectangle. (Fig 1.26)

Tip: Shapes can also be rotated via the Object > Transform > Rotate menu or with the Rotate tool in the Tools panel.

9. With the Selection tool, scale or rotate the rectangle. (Fig 1.27) Scale the rectangle by clicking on an anchor point and dragging toward or away from its center. To rotate the rectangle, position the Selection tool just outside one of the four anchor points at the corners. Don't click yet. Notice that the cursor changes from the usual Selection tool icon

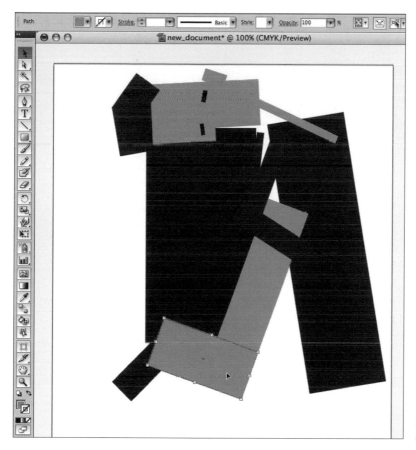

FIG 1.29
A dynamic composition.

(straight, black arrow) to a curved arrow. The curved arrow indicates
that you can rotate the selection. When you see the curved arrow, click
and drag outside of the rectangle to the right or left in order to rotate
the rectangle. (Fig 1.28)

10. When the first rectangle is complete (with the color, scale, and
rotation of your choosing), deselect the rectangle by clicking on the
Artboard. Notice that the anchor points are no longer highlighted.

11. Use the Rectangle tool to begin the process again. Once a rectangle
is made and modified, use the Selection tool to reposition it to the right,
left, or on top of the other rectangle. Re-create the composition with
up to 15 shapes. You should feel comfortable creating a shape and
changing its fill and stroke colors.

LEFT: FIG 1.30 The rectangle postitioned forward.

CENTER: FIG 1.31 Arrange > Send Backward.

RIGHT: FIG 1.32 The rectangle sent backward.

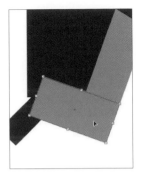

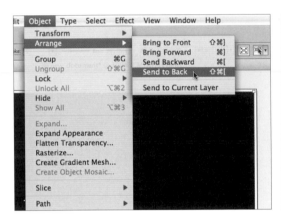

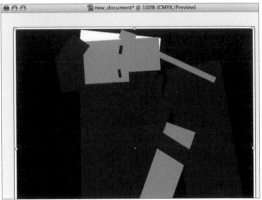

LEFT TO RIGHT:

FIG 1.33 Arrange > Send to Back.

FIG 1.34 A black rectangle has been sent to the back of the entire composition.

12. Arrange the rectangles so that they can be seen as one dynamic composition. (Fig 1.29) Notice that as you create and position each rectangle, they appear stacked on top of each other. (Fig 1.30) While you are creating this composition you may want a rectangle to be "sent behind" another rectangle. Select the top rectangle with the Selection tool, then click Object > Arrange > Send Backward. (Fig 1.31-32)

13. Shapes such as your rectangles can be sent backward repeatedly, or brought forward. Find these commands in Object > Arrange. Any art object can be positioned using these menu items. Finally, while art objects are sent backward or brought forward one at a time (through as many levels of stacking order as there are objects), they can also be sent all the way to the back of the composition or brought all the way to the front of the composition using Object > Arrange. (Fig 1.33)

In this image, a large black rectangle was sent all the way to the back of the composition after most of the dynamic composition was already made. (Fig 1.34)

EXERCISE
04 Saving a file

Choose File > Save As to open the Save dialog box.
(Fig 1.35) Choose a location in which to save your
file. It is common to save files in the Documents folder.
On a Mac, this is located in Macintosh HD > Users >
Your_User_Name > Documents, and can be found on the
left side of the Save dialog box. On Windows Vista, this
is located at Start > My Documents. We created a folder
called "digital_foundations" in the Documents folder. We
will save our work there.

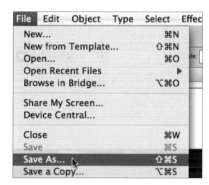

Note:

All actions that can
be performed on
your file are located
in the File menu.

FIG 1.35 File > Save As.

You must name your file when you save it. Follow these
naming conventions:

1. Avoid spaces. Instead, use_underscores_to_separate_words.
Spaces are dangerous in web browsers. Any designer who
plans to work with interactive media should form good habits
by eliminating spaces from her file names.

2. Use lowercase letters. This is also a convention of designers who name files that will be referenced in code. Spaces and
upper case letters will not damage your files, but if you are just
beginning to form good habits, you might as well learn all of
the rules at once.

Reserved Characters

! @ # $ % ^ & * ( ) + = ~ [ ] ' " ? / \ , : ; > <

File Formats

It is very important that file extensions, or suffixes, remain intact. The extension assists the computer operating system. It tells the system the type of file and the application to use when opening the file. This is especially important when bringing a file from one operating system to another (such as moving from a Mac to a PC).

Some important file formats include:

.doc or .docx - Microsoft Word document

.rtf - Rich Text Format, non-proprietary word processing format

.txt - Text only, no formatting

.ai - Adobe Illustrator file

.pdf - Portable Document Format

.psd - Photoshop document

.tif or .tiff - Tagged Image File - format for photographs, saved with lossless compression and used for scanning and printing. This format will be revisited in Chapter 7.

.jpg or .jpeg - Joint Photographic Experts Group - a compressed image file format often used for photographs on the web.

.gif - Graphic Interchange Format - a compressed image file format often used on the web for logos, design elements, and other graphics with low numbers of colors.

.html - HyperText Markup Language - a text file written in the language used to create web pages.

.fla - Flash master file

.swf - Shock Wave Format - exported Flash file for the web.

3. Never use characters such as those in the nearby list, as these reserved characters mean special things to applications and operating systems, and can disable web sites and crash applications.

4. Use a descriptive title, such as xtine_dynamic-comp.ai. Including your full name in a file name is especially important if you are submitting a file in a classroom or professional setting.

5. Make sure the file includes an extension. In this exercise, the file is saved as an Illustrator (.ai) document. The extension is .ai. In other words, the very worst file name that you could use is something like this: "My *best* ever/first file!" Not only does the name include spaces and reserved characters, it also fails to describe the file or format. Other bad names include the likes of "FINAL edit.ai," "final.ai," "composition.ai," and other names that do not specify who made the file or what is in the file. A better model for naming your files includes your individual or group name, a descriptive word about the contents of the file, and a date or versioning system. For example, when we sent a copy of our cover to the publisher on October 20th, we named it *digitalfoundations_cover_1020.ai*.

Native file format for master files

Most applications have a native file format for master files. This format can only be opened in the original program, and should be saved frequently throughout the working process. A copy of a master file is often created in a compressed, non-editable format when the author has finished editing the work. Compressing the file makes it smaller and easier to transfer. These compressed formats are readable by many applications, not just the original program.

An .ai suffix indicates the file is an Illustrator master file. If a logo, for example, was created in Adobe Illustrator, it could be shared with a friend or collaborator as a PDF file, which is viewable in Adobe Acrobat or Preview. These applications are installed on most computers. The exported files cannot be edited and are usually much smaller in file size. If the friend asks for revisions on the logo, the original Illustrator file would be modified. After modification, a new PDF file would be saved and sent to the friend.

Closing and quitting

To close a file in Illustrator, click the red button in the upper left corner of the window, choose File > Close, or press Command+W.

Quit the application by choosing Illustrator > Quit or by using the keyboard shortcut Command+Q. (Fig 1.36)

Key Command:

Command+W closes windows in any application and on the Desktop.

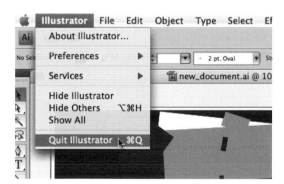

FIG 1.36 Illustrator > Quit.

Google Image Search results for "Bauhaus."

2 Searching and Sampling

The Internet is a treasure trove of photographic imagery. Artists and designers often combine media elements from this visual archive in inventive ways, or use downloaded images as research for their own creative work. While we admittedly live in a copy/paste culture, using a downloaded image from the web has legal ramifications.

Just because you can download an image doesn't mean you may use it! A downloaded image may be protected by copyright laws. Copyright is a legal tool for preserving control over the use of a creative work. Books, poems, music recordings and compositions, photographs, paintings, sculptures, radio and television broadcasts, films, and even dances can be copyrighted.

England initiated what we think of as copyright laws in the early 1700s. The widespread use of the printing press and an increase in literacy rates had resulted in printers commonly reprinting texts without crediting their rightful authors, or paying them. Attribution of proprietary rights in intellectual material has had far-reaching legal and economic implications.

Copyright durations vary by nation. In the United States, the length of a copyright used to be the life of an author plus 50 years; on the 50th year after the death of an author, their works would be released into the public domain. When a work is in the public domain, it is not owned or controlled by anyone. Any person can use the material, in any way, without owing anything to the creator. For works created by corporations, the length was 75 years from the date of publication. In 1998, Congress passed the Sonny Bono Copyright Term Extension Act, which extended copyright by 20 years. This law was authored by a musical-entertainer-turned-Congressman, and was heavily lobbied for by the media industry. The act was nicknamed the Mickey Mouse Protection Act, as Disney lobbied extensively to insure that the law reached back just far enough to protect their copyright over Mickey Mouse. The Act essentially suspended public domain advancement in the United States as covered by fixed term copyright regulations. Copyright law does allow certain types of use of copyrighted material. An image is protected by copyright unless:

1. The use qualifies as fair use
2. The image is in the public domain because the author declares it is, or because it is old enough that the copyright has expired
3. The author licenses it under an alternative model

Fair use is not piracy! Fair use is legitimate and legal use of copyrighted media, as protected by copyright law. Fair use is free speech. Fair use is not file sharing.

Fair use and appropriation

Understanding the key principles of fair use is helpful when thousands of protected images are only a mouse-click away.

Fair use

Tip: For more information about fair use, visit the Stanford Fair Use and Copyright site at http://fairuse.stanford.edu or The Center for Social Media's paper "Recut, Reframe, Recycle" at http://www.centerforsocialmedia.org/resources/publications/recut_reframe_recycle.

Reproduceablity is a central trait of digital media. Unlike lithographs, vinyl records, cassette tapes, videotapes, books, or photographic prints, an exact replica of digital media can be made from a digital copy. This is true for digital photograph files, CDs, MP3s, DVDs, and web sites. From sampling to mashups, collage to subvertisements, contemporary artists and content creators use digital files as source material for the derivation of new works. These works are considered new and original, but they are sometimes built with bits and parts of copyrighted works. In the digital age, new works are often created when more than one existing work is recombined in a new way, providing new visual relationships and new ideas.

Copyrighted content can be used in a new work if permission is obtained from the copyright holder, or if the media use falls into the category of fair use. Under the fair use clause of copyright law, limited copyrighted material can be used for a transformative purpose, such as commenting upon, criticizing, or parodying the initial material. The four significant factors are:

1. The purpose of the derivative work
2. The nature of the derived content: copyright does not limit use of the facts or ideas conveyed by an original work, only the original creative expression
3. The amount of original work used
4. The effect that the new work has on the potential or actual market value of the original

Weighing these four factors in a copyright case is not an easy task, which is why judges have been asked to do so. However, successful commercial media that takes advantage of the fair use clause include "Saturday Night Live" skits, "The Simpsons" cartoons, and Weird Al Yankovic songs. These works all make use of parody, one of the traditional protected purposes. (Fig 2.1)

FIG 2.1 *Maodonna, from 60X1,* Kenneth Tin-Kin Hung, 2001-2008. This net art parody is an example of a work of art protected by the fair use clause of the U.S. copyright laws. Used by permission of the artist.

Another traditional protected purpose is educational use in a classroom. Keep in mind that just because you cannot be sued for using appropriated work for assignments, you should be using it for reasons that advance your education, not just for convenience.

Know that the expectations increase for work done outside of a classroom. For commercial media, your transformation of the source material should be significant. We will explore this in Exercise 3.

The fair use clause also does not mean you may plagiarize. Plagiarism, an ethical offense separate from copyright issues, hides the fact that ideas or content have been copied from somewhere else. Even in cases where no legal violation has occurred, plagiarism is a serious ethical violation that undermines the academic endeavor and destroys the plagiarist's credibility.

Fair use foregrounds that work has been copied and uses the original work as a springboard for further development, often citing the creator in an obvious way so as not to put its source into question.

Appropriation

Note:

Ironically, we do not have copyright permissions to show Warhol's paintings or photographs of his Campbell's soup cans in this book! Try an image search if you're curious about viewing this work.

Appropriation is a word used by media artists to describe the visual or rhetorical action of taking over the meaning of something that is already known, by way of visual reference. For example, Andy Warhol appropriated the Campbell's soup can visual identity to make large, iconic silkscreen prints. Warhol's soup cans are an interpretation of the physical object. The visual reference to the original soup can is important, as the viewer needs this information in order to understand the idea that the reference conveys. (Your personal translation of this could range from a feeling associated with something as simple as a popular American icon or comfort food to repulsion at the commodification of domestic life.) By transforming not only the size and graphic palette for portraying the soup cans, but also the place where the viewer will encounter them (an art gallery as opposed to a grocery market), Warhol appropriates the original Campbell's soup cans to create art that relates to popular culture in its iconic form. Appropriation falls into the category of fair use.

Marcel Duchamp was the first known artist to appropriate a common object in his art. This challenged the art community in its definition of what is or is not labeled art. Duchamp believed that declaring an object a work of art was the artist's main role in creating art. In the case of *Fountain*, he took a urinal, turned it on its side, and signed it with his pseudonym, R. Mutt. (Fig 2.2)

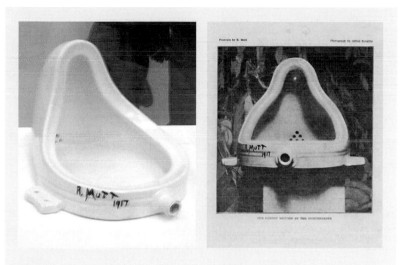

FIG 2.2 *Fountain*, Marcel Duchamp (a.k.a. R. Mutt), 1917, ready-made object photographed by left; David Shankbone and right; Alfred Steiglitz.

In this act of appropriation, the everyday object became something other than what it once was. Duchamp's transformations included the addition of the signature to the porcelain, the change of context from a bathroom to a gallery, and the change in purpose (the status of the urinal before it fell into Duchamp's hands is unknown, but after 1917 no one has used the urinal that R. Mutt signed for the purpose of waste containment). In these ways, Duchamp's use of the urinal foregrounded the viewer's understanding of the urinal as a concept and an object. This foregrounding is one of the central motifs in appropriation. In addition to fair use, many works are in the public domain or are licensed Creative Commons.

Determining what is protected, what is fair use, and what is free to use is part of the cultural producer's job. A few search techniques will make it easier to successfully sort through the vast online image archive.

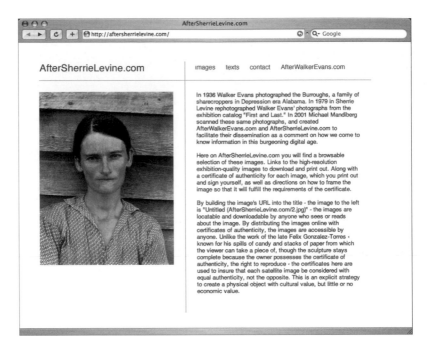

FIG 2.3 AfterSherrieLevine.com, Michael Mandiberg, 2001, web site with high-res scans and certificates of authenticity.

Artists who create new media by way of appropriation often work at the edges of copyright law and fair use. It can be conceptually or politically efficacious to break or side-step societal rules. Authorship and ownership are fluid, abstract concepts. Rule breaking provides visual, political commentary. Furthermore, artists understand that most legal consequences will lead to greater public awareness, positively impacting the work.

In 1979 Sherrie Levine photographed 22 of Walker Evans's Depression-era photographs as a comment on authorship and reproduction. In 2001 Michael Mandiberg made high-resolution scans of these images, and made them available for download and printing on AfterSherrieLevine.com, complete with certificates of authenticity to be signed by the user. (Fig 2.3) The goal was to comment on the transition from analog reproduction to digital reproduction, and the impossibility of controlling a work in the digital age when each digital file (CD, MP3, DVD, etc) is itself the source for making perfect copies of that same file. The second goal was to create an art object that accrues cultural

FIG 2.4 Delocator.net, xtine burrough, 2005, web site.

value by negotiating art history and theory, yet which has little or no economic value. Whereas a certificate of authenticity is conventionally used to preserve the economic value of an art object through a limited edition, here the certificate is used to insure it has none.

Appropriation can be used to reinterpret language, both visually and verbally. Marcel Duchamp's *Fountain* is a visual example of this type of reinterpretation, where the urinal becomes art. Delocator.net, xtine's website for locating and supporting locally owned businesses (launched in 2005) reuses the concept of an online retail store locator to "delocate" away from mainstream, chain stores. (Fig 2.4) The site was originally launched with a database full of Starbucks addresses and an empty set of local cafés on facing sides of a zip code results page. Users from all 50 states contributed to the database so café-goers could find and support neighborhood cafés. In 2006 the site was adjusted to collect locations for independently owned movie theaters and bookstores; other types of businesses will be added as the site grows.

01 Advanced searching in Google

1. Open Google Image Search (http://images.google.com) in a web browser.

2. Type the word "Bauhaus" into the search field and click the Search Images button. The search engine will return all images related to the word "Bauhaus." (Fig 2.5)

Note: This book's examples were created with Firefox and Safari, two free browsers you can download. We recommend you use one of these browsers to follow our tutorials; other browsers, such as Internet Explorer, may have slightly altered interfaces.

FIG 2.5 Google Image Search.

Note: The Bauhaus was a revolutionary arts and design school that operated in Germany from 1919 to 1933. The Bauhaus defined arts education for the 20th century and beyond. You will learn more about the Bauhaus throughout this book.

3. Filter your results by file size. Click on the pull-down menu next to the word "Showing:" near the top of the search results page. You can choose from a range of small to extra large images. Select "Large images" from the pull-down menu. (Fig 2.6) The page will reload showing only images larger than 600 by 800 pixels and smaller than 1200 by 1600 pixels. (Pixels are the basic units of image displayed on screen.)

4. Expect errors! Nearly every search result produces errors. Sometimes errors follow a pattern that can be identified and excluded from the search query. In this case, your results are likely to include images of the 1980s band Bauhaus. Add the word "band" to the search field preceded by a minus sign ("-band") to remove results for the band.

* **Finished exercise file available in the Download Materials area of the wiki.**

5. Results can be limited by searching for a specific phrase. To search by a phrase, enclose the words in quotes. A search for "Bauhaus Dessau" should result in mostly images related to the Bauhaus at Dessau. Dessau, Germany, was the location of the Bauhaus from 1925 to 1932. When you put quotes around your search phrase, Google looks for web pages where that exact phrase appears. Without quotes, Google simply looks for pages where those words both occur, whether they appear together or not. Make sure to reset your image size to "All image sizes" to see the maximum number of search results. (Fig 2.7)

FIG 2.6 Advanced Image Search.

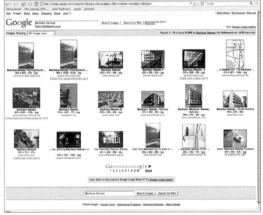

FIG 2.7 The Image Results page.

Advanced Image Search will give you control over additional parameters, such as file type, color mode, and usage rights.

6. The more specific your keywords are, the better your results will be. If you are looking for images of any of Marcel Breuer's steel tubular chairs, try "Marcel Breuer steel chair" as your search term. But if you are looking for an image of Marcel Breuer's famous Wassily armchair, try "Marcel Breuer Wassily chair" as your search term. You could further refine that search by adding any of the following keywords: "original," "leather," "canvas," "brown," "black." If you want to find an original Marcel Breuer Wassily chair in black, you can type "Marcel Breuer black original."

7. Click on one of the images from your search to bring up the Image Results page.

8. Click the "See full-size image" link to load the full-resolution image in its own window. (Fig 2.8)

9. Download the file. You can drag the file to your desktop from the browser, choose File > Save, or right-click the image with the mouse and choose Save Image As. (Fig 2.9) Save the file on your hard drive so that it will be easy to locate. (The desktop or Documents folders are typical storage locations for short working sessions.)

EXERCISE 02 Searching for public domain and Creative Commons licensed content

Public domain images have no licensing restrictions. An image automatically enters the public domain when a copyright expires. As media corporations struggle to control their brands by repeatedly extending copyright terms, less content is able to enter the public domain. The irony is that the copyright was introduced to protect authors from corporate power.

Several alternative licensing models exist, the most popular of which is the Creative Commons license. Creative Commons operates under the tagline "Some rights reserved," and offers a range of licenses with varying degrees of control over whether derivative works and for-profit uses are allowed. (Fig 2.10)

To find out more about Free Culture, public domain, and the Creative Commons, visit http://CreativeCommons.org or http://lessig.org. Lawrence Lessig is one of the founders of Creative Commons and the Free Culture movement.

Wikimedia Commons (http://commons.wikimedia.org) and
Flickr (http://flickr.com/creativecommons) focus partially
or exclusively on public domain or Creative Commons
licensed images. Wikimedia Commons is an archive of
public domain and Creative Commons images. Much
like Wikipedia, it is organized by historical subjects, and
is collectively edited and maintained. Flickr is a photo
sharing site that encourages the culture of sharing through
many of its features, and many Flickr users license their
photographs under Creative Commons.

1. Go to the Wikimedia Commons (http://commons.
wikimedia.org) and search for Walter Gropius, the
founding director of the Bauhaus. (Fig 2.12)

2. View several of the images, and notice that the images
are either in the public domain or licensed Creative
Commons. (Fig 2.13)

Download Markers

- For images & documents:
  - Official CC Markers
  - User Submitted Markers

- For audio:
  - CC Podcast Plugs ⊠

- For video:
  - Official CC Bumpers
  - User Submitted Bumpers

FIG 2.10 Creative Commons markers
available for download and use.

LEFT TO RIGHT:
FIG 2.11 Wikimedia
Commons logo.
FIG 2.12 Image pages
show descriptions and
licensing rights.

BELOW:
FIG 2.13 The licensing
area will show if the
image is copyright
protected or in the public
domain.

Licensing   [edit]

*This image (or other media file) is in the public domain because its copyright has **expired**.*
*This applies to the United States, Canada, the European Union and those countries with a copyright term of **life of the author plus 70 years**.*

⚠ Note that a few countries have copyright terms longer than 70 years: Mexico has 100 years, Colombia has 80 years, and Guatemala and Samoa have 75 years. This image may not be in the public domain in these countries, which
moreover do not implement the rule of the shorter term. Côte d'Ivoire has a general copyright term of 99 years and Honduras has 75 years, but they do implement that rule of the shorter term.

العربية | Asturianu | Български | Català | Česky | Dansk | Deutsch | English | Ελληνικά | Esperanto | Español | Euskara | فارسی | Français | Gaeilge | Galego | עברית | हिन्दी | Bahasa Indonesia | Italiano | 日本語 | 한국어 | Kurdî / كوردی | Lietuvių |
Magyar | Nederlands | Norsk (nynorsk) | Македонски | Bahasa Melayu | Polski | Português | Română | Русский | Slovenčina | Slovenščina | Shqip | Suomi | Sámegiella | Türkçe | 中文(简体) | 中文(繁體) | 粵語 | +/-

FIG 2.14 Flickr.com.

TOP: **FIG 2.15** Flickr Search page.
BOTTOM: **FIG 2.16** Flickr Advanced Search.

FIG 2.17 Flickr search results.

FIG 2.18 Flickr tag cluster.

3. Go to Flickr (http://flickr.com), click Search and then click Advanced Search. (Fig 2.14-16)

4. Type in "Bauhaus," and choose "Only search within Creative Commons-licensed photos." Everything in your search will be CC licensed, though not all will allow derivative works (for example, using the image in a collage) or commercial use.

5. Notice that all of the images in the search are organized by tags. A tag is a word or phrase used to categorize web content. In this case, many images share the tag "Bauhaus." (Fig 2.17)

6. Clicking on a tag will reveal the tag's cluster page. (Fig 2.18)

Types of Creative Commons licenses

Upon setting a Creative Commons license (Fig 2.19), the creator of the work decides if both commercial and noncommercial uses are allowed; if others are allowed to modify the work once it is licensed (derivative work); and, if derivative works are allowed, whether or not the newly modified work also has to be licensed with CC (share alike).

The six types of licenses and a very brief description of each follow. More information can be found on CreativeCommons.org. All CC licenses state that the original author will be given credit, in addition to the following details:

FIG 2.19 Creative Commons homepage.

 1. Attribution Non-commercial No Derivatives (by-nc-nd). This license provides the least freedom to others. The work cannot be used for commercial purposes and derivative works cannot be made. It would be illegal to use this work as part of a collage.

 2. Attribution Non-commercial Share Alike (by-nc-sa). This license allows others to build upon the original work. This work could legally be used in a collage as long as the new work is also licensed in the same manner, with a CC by-nc-sa.

 3. Attribution Non-commercial (by-nc). This license allows others to build upon the original work without having to license it as a CC by-nc. This work could be used, legally, in a collage. However, the resulting work cannot be used for commercial purposes.

 4. Attribution No Derivatives (by-nd). This license allows others to use the work as it is, without making derivative work, for any purpose (commercial or non-commercial).

 5. Attribution Share Alike (by-sa). This license allows others to use the work as it is or in derivative forms, for commercial and noncommercial purposes, as long as the new work is also licensed with the same CC by-sa license.

 6. Attribution (by). This license provides the most freedom to others who want to use the work.

Licensing your own work is easy on the Creative Commons web site. Once the author answers a few simple questions about how the work can be protected or shared, the licensing information is exchanged via e-mail.

03 Searching in stock photography web sites

TOP: FIG 2.20 iStockphoto search.

BOTTOM: FIG 2.21 No one walking around talking on a cell phone has a smile as big as this man!

Another source for imagery is stock photography web sites such as GettyImages.com or iStockPhoto.com. These web sites are full of photographs and vector graphics to be used in advertising, corporate media, brochures, reports, and other design applications.

The advantage of these sites is that they seem to have endless search detail.

On the left is an iStockPhoto image from a search for the term "writer" combined with the term "table."(Fig 2.20) This young woman looks nothing like the two of us as we sat at our computers editing this book on a wiki interface.

The disadvantage is that the photographs have the impersonal feel of an advertisement and often are extremely generic. No one ever looks as happy as a model in an advertisement, and most people feel they are not as physically attractive as the models used in commercial photography. (Fig 2.21) Stock images need to work in a variety of situations to give the buyer flexibility and value. Therefore, it is not surprising to feel a lack of specificity, an overall generic quality, in a stock image.

Stock photographs often look noticeably staged. This inauthenticity is a drawback that requires thoughtfulness on the part of the designer.

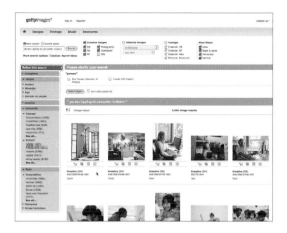

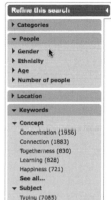

LEFT: FIG 2.22
Getty image search.

RIGHT: FIG 2.23
Refine search.

1. Go to Getty Images (http://GettyImages.com) and search in Creative Images for an image of what you are doing right now. In our case, that is "person typing at computer indoors." You might type "person reading book on couch." Try adding specifics like your hair color or the types of clothes you are wearing. (Fig 2.22-23)

2. Refine your search with their search phrases.

3. Ask yourself if anyone ever looks quite that content, pensive, or photogenic while reading a book unless they are acting for the camera.

One strategy for using stock photography is to radically alter the original image, either through extreme image adjustments in Adobe Photoshop or by tracing the image in Adobe Illustrator. As a transformation to the image, this kind of treatment usually results in using the image under the clause of fair use.

The following illustration was created using a collection of stock photographs as templates for the illustration's content. Notice how any photographic information has been modified and abstracted in an illustrative form. (Fig 2.24)

FIG. 2.24 From the series *Wish You Were Here! Postcards From Our Awesome Future*, Packard Jennings and Steve Lambert, 2007, 6' by 4' giclée prints. CC-BY.

Old Man in the Lehnstuhl and *Portrait of Saskia (Saskia as a young woman)*, Harmensz van Rijn Rembrandt, 17th century, close-up views, oil on wood. These two paintings illustrate symmetry in the human face. Seen from straight on, our faces are symmetrical compositions – eyes evenly balanced, nose and mouth evenly centered in the middle. Seen in profile, the human face is asymmetrical – the sharp contour of nose, mouth, and chin contrast the smooth, hairy back of the head.

3 Symmetry and Gestalt

Symmetrical shapes are identical when flipped across a line of reflection. For example, the human face has intuitive symmetry across a meridian that runs through the forehead, down the nose and mouth, and past the chin. A bicycle viewed from the front has symmetrical handlebars and pedals, along with a frame and wheels that project exactly the same distance to the right and left of its centerline. Symmetry creates stability and balance.

"Positive space" is a term used to describe the shapes added to a composition. "Negative space" is a term that refers to the space around those shapes. In symmetrical compositions, the positive space often contains the active design elements, while the negative space is passive.

The opposite of symmetry is asymmetry. Asymmetric compositions are not identical when flipped across a line of reflection. For example, when you view a face in profile or a bicycle from the side, they create asymmetric compositions. Asymmetric compositions can be balanced or imbalanced. Often, in an asymmetric composition, the negative space is more active as it leads the eye into the positive space.

Using symmetry or asymmetry in a composition is a strategic design decision you should make in order to meet the visual or psychological expectations of your audience.

FIG 3.1 Advertisement for the New York literary journal *The Bookman*, April 1896. The balance in this advertisement is achieved by the airiness of the complete female figure on the left counter-balanced by the density and darkness of the smaller male figure on the right, which is only seen from the waist up. The symmetry is reflected over the y-axis in the center of the composition. The typography is centered across the top and bottom of the composition.

It is essential to understand the relationship that is made between each design element and with the negative space in the composition. Gestalt (German for "shape") psychology provides a theory for the way humans perceive groups of shapes in a composition. The Gestalt principle called Prägnanz (German for "conciseness") is fundamental to understanding that viewers see a group of like objects as a whole unit before seeing the individual parts. Gestalt psychology started in Germany in 1910, and many of the Bauhaus school educators attended lectures by the Gestalt theorists.

Elements that are similar, close together, or arranged with visible continuity appear to belong together. This cross-cultural psychological tendency forms the basis for design decisions. These decisions conceptually connect the presented material to the presentation. For example, a horror movie poster should feel emotionally charged, suspenseful, and frightful, while a logo for a bank should feel secure, safe, and trustworthy to the viewer. In the language of design, the

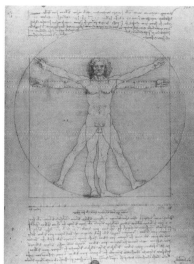

FIG 3.2 *Vitruvian Man*, Leonardo da Vinci, drawing on paper, 1492. Photograph by Luc Viatour, 2007.

FIG 3.3 *Codex Aureus of St. Emmeram*, Scene: Portrait of Abbot Ramwoldus, book painting on parchment by Adalpertus, 1000.

horror poster's composition would express tension (which we will create in Exercise 3) and use asymmetry to produce the frightful feeling. The bank logo might be designed with symmetry and balance (which we will create in Exercise 2) to represent stability and trustworthiness.

In this chapter, we explore laws of proximity (Exercises 3 and 6), continuity (Exercise 4), and similarity (Exercise 5).

Leonardo da Vinci's classic drawing of the human form demonstrates the principle of symmetry in the human body. (Fig 3.2)

Symmetry is achieved in Adalpertus' book painting across both the x- and y-axis. The image is almost a mirror reflection on both axes. (Fig 3.3)

Note: See http://en.wikipedia.org/wiki/Gestalt_psychology#Pr.C3.A4gnanz for images and complete definitions.

01 Creating symmetry and asymmetry with your body

Note: Choose the Essentials workspace from the pull-down menu in the Application bar before working on the following exercises.

Before touching the pencil or mouse, you can exercise these design principles as lessons in weight distribution.

The grid is created by the x-axis along the hips and the y-axis from the toes to the head.

1. Stand straight, with feet hip-width apart and knees slightly bent. This places the body in a balanced, symmetric position.

2. Now that you have achieved symmetry, lift one foot off the floor. Bend the lifted leg at the knee as much as possible without falling over. You will feel less stable and balanced. Your body has achieved asymmetry.

Preview of the remaining exercises

In the following exercises (2–7), each composition will be created within an individual square. (Fig 3.4) All of the exercises are created in a single document, established in Exercise 2. For these compositions the grid is simple: the horizontal and vertical intersection at the middle of each square is the grid. See and "feel" the visual weight that is constructed between the four quadrants (upper left and right, lower left and right) in each composition.

⋆ Finished exercise file available in the Download Materials area of the wiki.

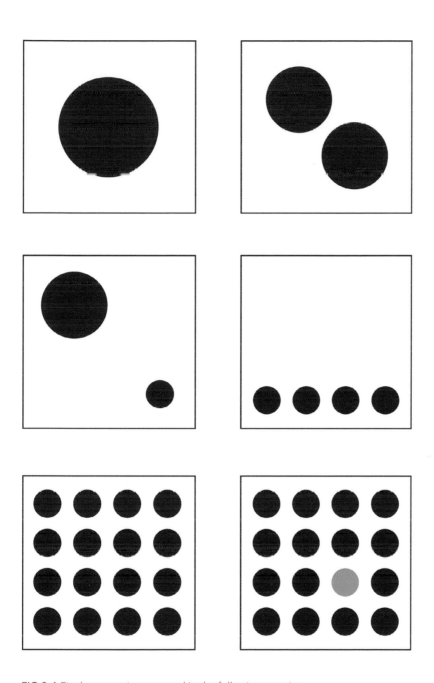

FIG 3.4 Final compostions created in the following exercises.

02 Symmetry with passive negative space

FIG 3.5

In this exercise, the black circle in the center of the composition is the positive space, and the white surrounding area is the negative space. The negative space is not active. It is overshadowed by the active, positive form. The circle is evenly distributed within the composition. It is perfectly symmetric in relation to both the x and y axes, from the left to the right and the top to the bottom. (Fig 3.5)

1. Create a new document in Illustrator (File > New) using the default settings pull-down menu to create a letter-size page in RGB color space.

2. Click on the Rectangle tool to create one square that has a white fill and a black stroke. Set the fill and stroke colors before drawing the rectangle. The Fill and Stroke icons are stacked on top of each other at the bottom of the Tools panel (see Chapter 1 for working with the fill and stroke). Double-click the icon that is on top and select the color you want to use from the Color Picker. (Fig 3.6) After you set the color for the top icon (whether it is the Fill or Stroke icon), click once on the bottom icon and define this color by using the Color panel (Window > Color). The Color Picker and the Color panel are two different ways to fill an object with color.

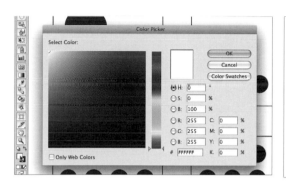
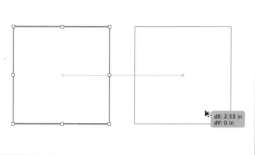

FIG 3.6 The Color Picker dialog box.

FIG 3.7 Duplicate square created by Option-clicking and dragging.

3. With the fill and stroke colors defined, hold the Shift key while dragging the Rectangle tool on the Artboard. The result is a square instead of a rectangle. The square we made was about 2 by 2 inches.

> **Key Command:** While you are working with most of the tools in Illustrator, Command is the hot key for accessing the Selection tool.

4. Although copy and paste are accessible through the Edit menu, we will instead use the Selection tool to duplicate and position five copies of the square.

Hold the Option key and click on the original square with the Selection tool, then drag the mouse to the right. (Fig 3.7) While you are dragging (and still holding Option) also press Shift. Adding the Shift key keeps the movement restricted to a 0-, 45-, 90-, or 180-degree motion. (In other words, you'll position the new square to the right of the original square along the same baseline or x-axis.)

> **Key Command:** The relationship between the Shift key and the Selection tool is two-fold: 1. Shift will constrain the proportions of objects as you drag to resize a shape or image, and 2. Shift keeps the movement of objects aligned vertically or horizontally on the Artboard.

Tip: Click with the mouse and begin dragging before holding the Shift key, and release the mouse before letting go of the key. By holding the Shift key, you can constrain the proportions of almost anything you draw so the image remains symmetrical.

5. Now that you have two squares that are exactly the same, side by side, select both squares at one time by clicking outside them anywhere on the Artboard and dragging over both of them. This is called *marqueeing*. Alternatively, you could Shift-click, or select the first square and then hold Shift while clicking with the mouse to add the second square to the selection. Group the two squares using Object > Group.

Grouped objects can be moved, transformed, and have their colors edited as one unit while their individual properties are maintained. In this case, the squares will be copied and positioned together.

6. Copy the two squares two more times, moving down the page.

7. Use the Selection tool to position the squares into place. Be attentive to the space between the margins of the page and the space between the outlines of the squares. Often it is helpful to view the Artboard at different sizes, both in full size and different percentages of it. You can zoom in or out using View > Zoom In or View > Zoom Out.

8. Use the Layers panel (Window > Layers) to lock the squares on Layer 1. Click on the square between the Eye icon and the layer name in Layer 1. A Lock icon will appear, indicating that the layer is locked. (Fig 3.8) Locked layers cannot be modified until they are unlocked. This is a protective measure that a designer often takes when part of a project is complete and she doesn't want to accidentally select or move objects that are already established.

FIG 3.8 Lock layer.
FIG 3.9 Create New Layer.

9. Once the layer is locked, create a new layer to work on by clicking the Create New Layer icon at the bottom of the Layers panel. (Fig 3.9) Layer 2 will appear above Layer 1. This is the layer that will contain the rest of the vector art objects in this chapter. Be sure that it is active (it will be highlighted) before proceeding.

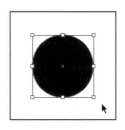

10. Create a black circle in the middle of the top left square with the Ellipse tool. The Ellipse tool might be buried beneath the Rectangle tool in the Tools panel: access it by clicking the Hidden tools triangle in the lower right corner of the active tool. A tear-off menu of more shape drawing tools will become visible. Move the mouse over the Ellipse tool to select it. With this tool, click-drag within the top left square. Hold the Shift key once you begin dragging the mouse so that the ellipse becomes a perfect circle. (Fig 3.10)

FIG 3.10 Hold the Shift key while dragging open the Elipse tool.

03 Symmetry with less passive negative space

FIG 3.11

In this exercise, the two new circles create a balanced, symmetric composition. The visual weight is the same in the four quadrants created by the intersection of the x and y axes; and the circles are reflective over a diagonal line. However, notice the tension between the two circles at the middle of the page. This tension is created when the two active forms are so near to each other that the eye cannot help but notice the negative space between them. The negative space fights for the viewer's attention. Therefore, the negative space is slightly more active than it was in the first exercise. As the two circles are so near to each other, they are perceived by the viewer as one visual element on the page in the foreground space. Our mind's preference for grouping the shapes together is accounted for by the Gestalt law of proximity. (Fig 3.11)

1. Copy the black circle by using the Selection tool to click and drag on the original circle while holding Option, and move the copy into the second square. Keep your finger down on the Shift key to insure the circle does not become malformed while dragging. Drag the new copy into place and release the mouse before releasing the key.

Watch Out: If you are new to using the mouse and the keyboard together, practice using your non-mouse hand to activate key commands while keeping your mouse hand on the mouse. It is ineffective to lift up your mouse hand!

Watch Out: Did your circle turn into an ellipse? Without the imposed constraint of the Shift key, the circle lapses back into an ellipse. When drawing Shift key-constrained shapes, be sure to release the mouse before releasing the Shift key.

2. The new circle should still be selected, with anchor points surrounding the edges of the selected area. Use the Selection tool to reduce the size of the circle by clicking on one of the four anchor points at the edges of the circle and dragging towards its center. Practice holding down the Shift key while reducing the size of the circle.

3. Create another copy of this circle by dragging with the Selection tool while holding down the Option key. Nudge the circle into position by using the left, right, up, and down arrow keys. The arrow keys will move the selected object by just one unit, while Shift+arrow moves the object in increments of 10.

> **Note:** The units of increment that the arrow keys move an object are set in General Preferences (Illustrator > Preferences > General). They are called keyboard increments, and the default setting is 0.0139 inches. All preferences are user-defined. It is often a good idea to check these preferences and make note of them if you are using a public computer, as no two users' preferences are necessarily alike.

EXERCISE
04 Balanced asymmetry

FIG 3.12

In this exercise the two circles create an asymmetric composition. The weight distribution between the four quadrants of the composition is not even, as most of the visual weight is felt in the upper left quadrant. The composition does remain balanced, as the negative space between the two circles activates the viewer's attention and becomes part of the visual weight on the page. The white area is still the negative space; however, the white area between the two circles is within the path of the viewer's eye movement from the top (larger) circle to the bottom (smaller) circle. As our eyes travel along the path from the top to the bottom circle, our way of seeing follows the Gestalt law of continuation. (Fig 3.12)

1. Copy the second circle from the previous exercise and drag it into position in the third square.

2. Make another copy of this circle and drag it to the lower right of the composition.

3. Select the circle and scale it down using the Shift key with the Selection tool.

Asymmetry with imbalanced visual weight

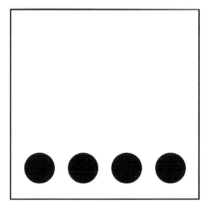

FIG 3.13

In this exercise, the negative space is the white area surrounding the four black circles. The four black circles are asymmetric in regards to the overall composition. The negative space creates more mass than the positive space, and the four black circles pull the viewer's eye to the bottom of the composition. What is also noteworthy about this exercise is that the four black circles are read as a line by the Gestalt law of similarity, where like elements (four circles) are read as a whole shape before being perceived as individual shapes. (Fig 3.13)

1. Copy the smaller circle in the fourth rectangle and move it to the empty composition to the right.

2. Create three copies of the small circle within the composition.

Watch Out: If the Align to Artboard box at the bottom of the Align panel is active, the circles will align to the whole Artboard instead of to themselves. If your circles don't go where you think they should, be sure that this option is not active in the pull-down panel menu.

3. Select all four circles using the Selection tool by marqueeing or Shift-clicking. See Step 5 in Exercise 2 to review both methods of selecting multiple objects.

4. With the four circles selected, view the Align panel (Window > Align). This panel will be used to distribute the four small circles evenly. Click the fifth button from the left under the Distribute Objects part of the Align panel. Hold the mouse over this icon to see a tool tip that displays the words "Horizontal Distribute Center."

If the circles were not duplicated with the Shift key pressed (to keep them on one line), the Align panel can also be used to vertically align the objects across their tops, centers, or bottoms.

EXERCISE
06 Symmetry with patterning

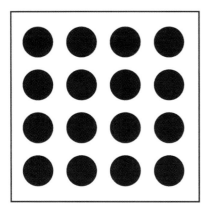

FIG 3.14

In this exercise, 16 circles are repeated to create the perception of a square. Our minds do not need to see the entire contour or edges of the square in order to perceive this alternate shape. The Gestalt law of proximity accounts for our perception of the square, which is in fact made up of individual circles. (Fig 3.14)

1. Select all four of the circles in the row in Exercise 5. Choose Object > Group. Grouping objects is a convenient way for objects to maintain their individuality while acting as part of a set that moves, transforms, and receives color information together. Grouped objects can always be ungrouped with Object > Ungroup.

2. Hold the Option key as you click on the grouped row of small circles and drag it to the next composition. Duplicate the row three more times while adding Shift, so that all four rows of circles have their left and right edges on the same margin lines. Use the Align panel to fix the rows if they aren't organized (try selecting all four rows and using Horizontal Align Left).

3. Select all four rows and click the second button in the Distribute Object section of the Align panel (Vertical Distribute Center).

Key Command: Command+G is the key command for grouping objects. Command+Shift+G is the Illustrator key command for ungrouping objects. Memorizing these simple key commands will streamline the design process once you become more fluent in the software. It's a great idea to memorize them now to save time later.

EXERCISE 07 Defining a focal point within symmetric patterning

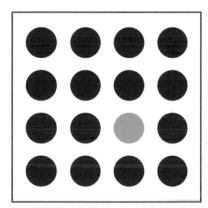

FIG 3.15

In the last exercise, the repetition of the 16 circles created a pattern. In this exercise, the repetition is broken by changing the value and hue of one circle (one part of the whole) in the lower right quadrant of the composition. A focal point is created by the contrast of value and hue. When the contrast between like and unlike forms is as extreme as it is in this exercise, the designer can direct the viewer's eye to a particular part of the composition. Using contrast to create a focal point is an essential design skill. (Fig 3.15)

1. Select all of the circles in Exercise 6, Option-drag them to the final composition. Hold Shift as you drag to move the set of circles along a straight path on one axis.

2. Within the last composition, change the fill color of one of the individual circles to set a focal point. All of the black circles are part of a group. If the group is selected and the fill color is modified, all of the circles are modified. While this is useful, it is not our current goal. Instead, use the Direct Selection tool to select just one circle. The Direct Selection tool can be used to modify a path, an anchor point, or one part of a group of objects. Click inside one of the circles. Be sure to click inside the circle and not on the path around the edge of the circle. We do not want to modify the path; we want to modify the color of the whole circle. If you accidentally colored the path, undo the action with Command+Z.

3. Set the fill color to a color of your choice by using the Swatches or Color panel, or the Color Picker (in Chapter 5 we will delve into color theory). Notice that as the value lightens, the contrast between your colored and black circles increases.

Key Command: Command+Z will undo your last step in virtually all applications of the Creative Suite.

Grid Systems

![dark square]

Lorem ipsum dolor sit amet, consectetuer adipiscing elit. Aliquam sodales lectus sed diam. Nam condimentum ultrices nulla. Duis eget quam ut nibh adipiscing imperdiet. Pellentesque id erat. Etiam sit amet felis. Sed a quam sed elit placerat auctor. Aenean molestie, libero at accumsan mollis, felis ligula iaculis lorem, vel aliquam lectus dolor eget eros. Fusce a diam a pede hendrerit volutpat. Donec et eros non purus vehicula suscipit. Morbi tincidunt mollis augue. Donec ultricies purus eu mi. Mauris at massa a magna aliquet iaculis. Sed eget elit. Praesent pretium, diam sed tempus porttitor, dolor diam sodales pede, ac malesuada nisl diam id metus. Proin rutrum, nibh sit amet egestas hendrerit, odio nisl dapibus tellus, ac pharetra nunc urna

The theoretical grid system we layout in this chapter.

4 Type on the Grid

For many students and educators, the Bauhaus has become a symbolic point of entry to art and design education. In *The ABC's of Bauhaus, The Bauhaus and Design Theory*, Ellen Lupton credits the movement as being "the mythic origin of modernism."

One of the central inventions of the Bauhaus was the use of industrial techniques, such as the grid. Bauhaus founder Walter Gropius and artist László Moholy-Nagy devoted themselves to creating a "universal language" that embraced and mirrored methods of mass production. The Bauhaus put emphasis on the grid as a structure upon which forms can be precisely placed, reflected, balanced, or imbalanced.

For the Bauhaus the grid was not only an organizational structure, but a structure that could be easily multiplied and reproduced. By understanding the relationship between the grid and the organizational requirements of automation and mass replication, the Bauhaus is responsible for a design aesthetic that became popular in the 1920s and is still noticeable today.

Formulating an abstract concept from simple lines and planes is a practice in translating visual cues into language-based meanings. It is the goal of any visual communicator to learn to do this, as both the reader of the message and the generator of visual content.

Note:

The grid is used for creating relationships between the formal elements within the composition and the positive and negative space. Formal elements are all the things that a designer adds to a composition, such as shapes, images, and typography. Negative space includes the white space between those formal elements and between elements and the edge of the document. The grid is the invisible underlying structure that sustains the relationships between all formal elements in print design, interactive design, industrial design, architecture, fashion, and more.

Joseph Campbell has found origins of the grid as far back as the High Neolithic Era (4500 – 3500 BCE). In his book *The Masks of God*, he defines it as "a geometrical organization of an aesthetic field."

FIG 4.2 *The Cardplayers*, Theo van Doesburg, oil on canvas, 1916-1917. The Hague, Gemeentemuseum Den Haag. In this painting, van Doesburg illustrates card players with vertical, horizontal, and diagonal lines and flat fields of color.

FIG 4.1 *Counter-Composition XXI*, Theo van Doesburg, oil on canvas, 1923. Bauhaus members were aware of and influenced by De Stijl.

EXERCISE

01 Using guides to create a grid

1. Create a new Illustrator document (File > New) using the Print pull-down menu. Choose 1 Artboard, letter size, portrait orientation (8.5 by 11 inches, as opposed to landscape orientation of 11 by 8.5 inches), and type the name *the_grid*. (Fig 4.3)

2. Rulers can be turned on or off. They appear at the top and left side of the document window. If the rulers are off, choose View > Rulers. (Fig 4.4) Right-click or Control-click on the ruler to see all of the available units of measurement. Choose inches from the pull-down menu.

The rulers now show that the Artboard measures 8.5 by 11 inches. Sometimes the horizontal rulers load with the origin at the top left edge of the document, but the vertical ruler origin is at the lower left corner of the document. To reposition the ruler origin so that it is located in the same place both vertically and horizontally, put the mouse in the top left corner of the ruler area, where the vertical and horizontal rulers seem to overlap, then click and drag to the top left corner of the page on the Artboard. (Fig 4.5) Clicking and dragging from this area repositions zero on the Artboard. We do this so that we have a constant point of origin to work from and do not have to change values later.

Note: Choose the Designer workspace from the pull-down menu in the Application bar before working on the following exercises.

Key Command: Command+R reveals and hides rulers.

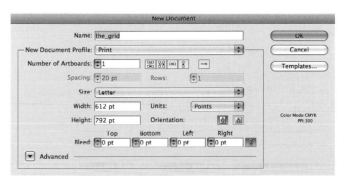

FIG 4.3 Create and name a new document.

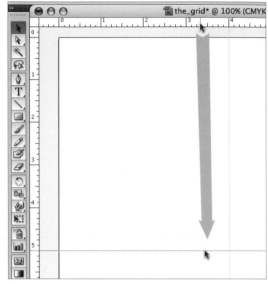

LEFT TO RIGHT:
FIG 4.4 Choose Show Rulers in the View menu.
FIG 4.5 Reposition artboard to zero.
FIG 4.6 Pull guides from document rulers.

3. In this step we will pull guides from within the document rulers.

Click on the Selection tool, then place your mouse cursor within the ruler area at the top of the document. Click on the ruler and drag the mouse downward. A guide will be set in place where you release the mouse. Release the first guide at 5 inches on the ruler against the left edge of the page. (Fig 4.6)

4. Repeat this step for the vertical guide, by pulling from the vertical ruler on the left edge and releasing the mouse at 4 inches on the ruler against the top edge of the page.

Note:

Guides are available in all Adobe Creative Suite applications. They are always pulled from the rulers. Guides are used to create a grid on the page. The grid occurs when two guides (one horizontal and one vertical) intersect. The advantage of guides is that you can create a customized grid on both axes for a quick visual reference when moving or adding objects. Guides will not be printed.

EXERCISE

02 Lines

A line is the result of connecting any two points on a plane. Lines can be thin or thick, bumpy or smooth, dotted or solid, straight or curvy. In this exercise we make a straight, thick, black line. In later chapter exercises, you will create lines by alluding to them with repetitious single forms or by the gaze of the photographically reproduced subjects within the composition. Lines can be used to provide direction, to separate parts of the page, or to support elements on which images or typography rest. Many of the typographic visual references from the Bauhaus include heavy lines that are used to separate areas of the page and provide direction for the viewer's gaze.

1. Press the letter *d* on the keypad to load the default colors into the Fill and Stroke icons at the bottom of the Tools panel. The default colors in any of the Adobe Creative Suite programs are black and white. The letter *d* on the keypad always loads black and white into the color chips in the Tools panel.

2. Click on the Line Segment tool. Clicking and dragging with this tool creates a new line. Holding the Shift key while dragging creates a new straight line. Create a new straight line across the horizontal guide. (Fig 4.7)

3. Release the mouse, and the line will be selected. If you click someplace off of the line and accidentally deselect it, reselect it using the Selection tool. With the line selected, look in the Control panel at the top of the document window. Notice that the line has values associated with it, including a fill color (automatically set to nothing, as signified by the red stripe across a white field), a stroke color (black), and a numeric value indicating the weight of the stroke. Change the numeric value of the stroke weight on the line to 30 by using the pull-down menu or by typing 30 into the value box. (Fig 4.8)

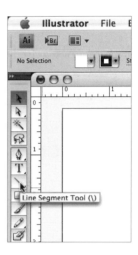

FIG 4.7 Choose Line Segment Tool.

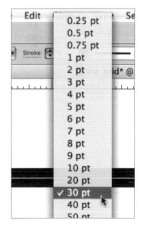

FIG 4.8 Select stroke weight.

4. With the Selection tool, adjust the line so that it begins at about an inch into the page from the left edge. The line may extend beyond the page edge on the right side. Anything that is outside of the page, represented by the black frame of the Artboard, will not be printed.

5. Deselect the line by clicking with the Selection tool anywhere on the Artboard outside of the line's anchor points.

EXERCISE 03 Using the Type tool to create a headline

Headlines are typically larger than body copy and maintain a heavier weight on the page than most other elements. The scale of the headline often relates to the scale of an accompanying photograph or illustration (it may be the same width or half of the width, for example, as a photograph on the front page of a newspaper).

In this exercise, Gill Sans was the typeface used for both the headline and the body copy. The ultra-bold font style creates a weighty headline, and the regular style of the typeface is very easy to read as body copy.

1. Select the Type tool in the Tools panel.

Tip: How to tell Illustrator you are done using the Type tool: 1. Press the Command key and click anywhere outside of the type on the Artboard. The type is now deselected. 2. Press the Escape key on the keypad. Notice your Selection tool is automatically activated. 3. Choose the Selection tool from the Tools panel.

2. Click anywhere on the Artboard with the Type tool. Do not drag. Clicking just one time will change the Type tool into a flashing cursor. When you see the flashing cursor begin typing the headline, "Grid Systems." Illustrator is a smart program, but it doesn't know when you are finished using the Type tool. You have to tell it "I'm done." There are a few ways to do this (see the tip). When you are finished typing your headline, click on the Selection tool. The type is automatically selected as an object and the flashing cursor is gone.

3. Once the type is created, it can be edited by using the Selection tool and the Control or Character panel. If your type is not selected, click on it with the Selection tool.

Note:

Fonts that are installed as part of the computer's operating system, such as Arial and Times, are reliable choices for web design, where font choice must be limited to what users can be expected to have. However, some operating system fonts were not even meant for print use, so print designers must become familiar with the limitations of so-called "system fonts." Fortunately, useful and appealing fonts can be found as part of the Adobe Creative Suite, bought online, or downloaded free. A great way to find new fonts is to search Google for typography collections. Usually, you can find free or almost-free fonts to help you enhance and control your style.

Different fonts are designed for different purposes (for example, display, body copy, or screen). Display fonts (ornamental fonts, such as those that are free to download on http://chank.com/freefonts.php) are not legible enough to be used for body copy, but may be selected for headlines, as they tend to be eye-catching and expressive. Sans-serif type was invented by William Caslon IV (1816) and was reserved, as John Kane writes in his *A Type Primer*, "almost exclusively for headlines." Using a sans-serif font for headlines often commands attention.

Tip: *Holding Shift while scaling type is essential.* It is a very common mistake for beginning designers to forget to hold Shift while scaling type, and the result is not pretty. One of the most significant elements of designing a typeface is the relationship between the various parts of the letter. Skewing those relationships while scaling type destroys the detail that identifies the letterform.

4. In this exercise, we used Gill Sans Ultra Bold for the headline. While the type is selected, choose Gill Sans Ultra Bold (if you have it installed) or any other font of your choice from the Type pull-down menu (Fig 4.9) either from the Control panel or from the Character panel (Window >Type > Character).

5. The font size can be edited by typing a number into the font size box in the Control or Character panel, or by scaling the type with the Selection tool. To scale the type, click on any of the four anchor points at the corners of the selected type object and drag towards (decreases the scale) or away from (increases the scale) the center of the type while holding Shift. In this exercise, the headline is 44 points.

6. Use the Selection tool to pick up the head-

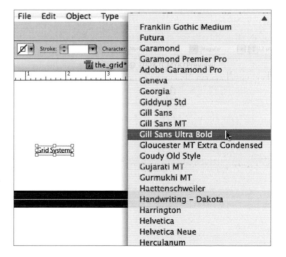

FIG 4.9 The Character pull-down menu.

line and move it so that the baseline (Fig 4.10) is within the black line and the *S* in the word "Systems" is just to the right of the vertical guide.

7. Kerning is the space between the letters in a single word. When you set body copy (for instance, a letter typed in Microsoft Word), you usually do not have to be concerned with kerning. Good body fonts are created to be well-kerned at smaller font sizes (such as 9 – 12 points). However, when working with display text, such as a 44 point headline, the kerning should be studied. Traditionally, the amount of space between each letter should be even.

In this exercise, we will adjust the space between the *i* and *r* in the word "Grid" and the *s* and *t* as well as the *t* and *e* in the word "Systems." Place the type cursor just between the *i* and *r* in the word "Grid." Click when you see that the cursor looks like a single line, which means it was successfully placed within the word.

Once the Type tool is between the *i* and the *r* in the "Grid," use Option and the right or left arrow keys on the keypad to nudge the letters to the left or right. (Fig 4.11) This is the method of manually adjusting the kerning of the display text in Illustrator, Photoshop and InDesign. Repeat this for the *s* and *t* and the *t* and *e* in the word "Systems."

RIGHT: FIG 4.10 The word "baseline" refers to the invisible line upon which typographic letters rest, as shown to the right, in light blue.

BELOW: FIG 4.11 The word "Grid" before and after kerning.

Creating body copy with the Type tool

Body copy is the content of an article, a book chapter, an essay on a web page, and so on. Body copy should be set within a text box in all of the Creative Suite programs. Body copy is usually set in rectangles, and the production artist controls how many columns of text populate a page grid.

The artist should be interested in creating legible body copy. Legible body copy is not too big, too small, too lengthy, too short, too light, or too dark. For a considerable amount of body copy (a full article, for example), the copy should be set in columns between 3.5 and 4 inches in length or 35 to 65 characters. This is the point at which many readers begin to read back over the words that they have already read. A 3.5-inch line of body copy encourages the reader to move to the next line of type at about the time that she is ready to move her eyes from right to left.

Assessing body copy is easy: squint your eyes while looking at the printed body copy. The overall grayscale value of the printed rectangle (body copy) should be about 40 to 50 percent. It should not read as stripes of black against the page. In this exercise, we will consider adjustments that can be made if the copy is too light or dark.

1. Create a new vertical guide at the end of the last *s* in Systems.

2. When you click and drag instead of clicking once and entering text, the Type tool will create a text box. Create a text box at about 7.25 inches (vertically), between the two vertical guides. You can set a guide at 7.25 inches. In the example we have used a paragraph of "dummy" (or placeholder) text that graphic designers have been using since the 1500s. The text begins with the two words "Lorem ipsum," and is often simply referred to as Lorem

Watch Out: If the final product will be printed, the designer should always take time to assess the printed version of the composition. It is incredibly difficult to assess printed typography on the computer screen.

ipsum (e.g., "Put some Lorem ipsum in there for now, we should be receiving the copy in a couple of days"). Lorem ipsum is used as placeholder body copy when the actual text is not available, as its letters are more or less evenly distributed. Looking at "dummy text inserted here, dummy text inserted here" repeated enough times to create a block of body copy draws attention to itself with a noticeable pattern. (Fig 4.12) At the time of writing, lipsum.com was offering Lorem ipsum by the word count, paragraph count, and byte count. Included in the download area of the wiki is a text file with the Lorem ipsum text used here, but if you can see the wiki, then you have access to the Internet. Assuming lipsum.com is still available, you should generate two paragraphs of text there.

3. Copy and paste the Lorem ipsum text from the web to your new text box. We used Gill Sans Regular, set in 11 points.

4. The body copy pasted into the new text box should be left-justified by default. If it is not, use the Control or Character panel to set the justification to the left. The straight alignment of letters at the left of the text box creates a virtual line that extends to the headline, as the left of the text box is aligned with the *S* in Systems. By the property of continuation, a line is made from the *S* to the body copy on the page. While this "line" created by the left margin is not as literal or heavy as the black

dummy text inserted here dummy text inserted here dummy text inserted here dummy text inserted here dummy text inserted here dummy text inserted here dummy text inserted here dummy text inserted here dummy text inserted here dummy text inserted here dummy text inserted here dummy text inserted here dummy text inserted here	Lorem ipsum dolor sit amet, consectetuer adipiscing elit. Curabitur urna ipsum, feugiat eget, bibendum ac, varius ut, est. Vestibulum venenatis, mauris porttitor sodales faucibus, mauris quam pretium sem, pellentesque blandit tortor risus non magna. Donec semper augue et lorem. Maecenas luctus lorem ultrices leo. Nulla facilisi. Aliquam sit amet elit nec sem rhoncus lobortis. Vivamus pharetra fermentum turpis. Sed volutpat. Aliquam lobortis

FIG 4.12 Lorem ipsum text is easier on the eye than four repeated words.

line made in Exercise 2, it is just as relevant to the layout. It provides an intersection with the black line to further define the grid on the page.

5. Leading is the space between lines of type. The body copy is set at 11 points, and the leading is set at 15.2 points. This is traditionally referred to as 11/15.2. Insert the Type tool into any area of the body copy and then press Command+A on the keyboard to select all of the type within this type box. With all of the type selected, press Option and the down arrow key to open the leading. (Fig 4.13)

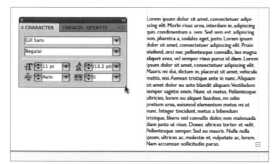

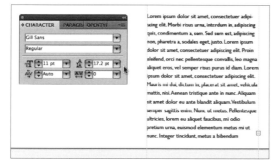

FIG 4.13 In these images, the leading has been adjusted and the text box has been resized in consideration of the margin space at the right and bottom of the composition. Notice how opening or loosening the leading creates a slightly lighter grayscale value when you squint your eyes and look at the block of text.

Note:

Although this did not occur in our exercise, two other typographic problems to look out for are orphans and widows. An orphan is a single word that dangles on the last line of body copy, and a widow is a single word at the top of a new column of text, such as the end of a paragraph carried over to the top of the next column. These are undesirable typographic happenings that create imbalance and draw attention to a place on the page where you don't intend for the viewer to focus.

05 Directing the viewer with color

In this exercise, we will replace the dot over the *i* with a red square. Then we will copy the square to the bottom of the composition, near the start of the body copy. By repeating this form on two parts of the page, we will make a relationship between the headline and the body copy. Red is used intentionally to push the viewer's eye from the headline to the body copy.

Note: Creating outlines of the type will annihilate editing possibilities on the text object. Duplicate the text and leave it in the white space outside of the Artboard for reference or later editing.

1. To create a focal point in the headline, replace the dot over the *i* in "Grid" with a red square. Removing one part of a letter is easy, but the letter must first be transformed from a line of editable text to a group of shapes.

With the Selection tool, click on the "Grid Systems" type, press the Option key, and drag the duplicate copy of the text off the Artboard. Select the original "Grid Systems" type on the Artboard and choose Type > Create Outlines. (Fig 4.14)

The outlined type will be grouped together, so that all the letters would move or be transformed as a group.

2. Ungroup the type by choosing Object > Ungroup. (Fig 4.15)

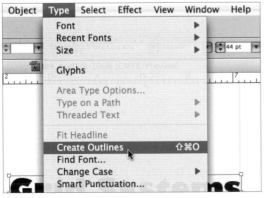

FIG 4.14 Select Type > Create Outlines.

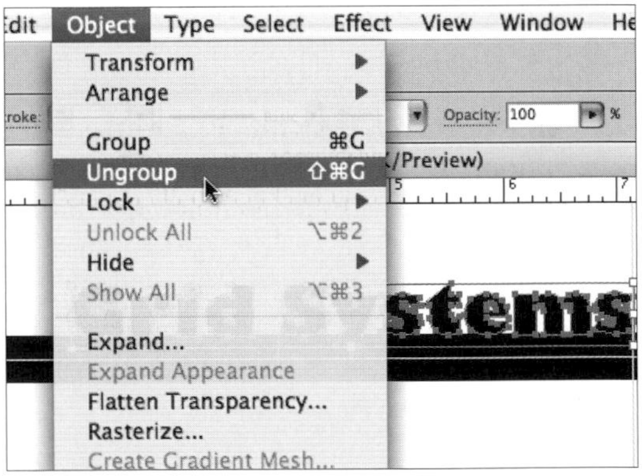

FIG 4.15 Select Object > Ungroup.

3. Use the Direct Selection tool to select and delete the
dot over the *i*. When you click to select, the rest of the *i*
will also be selected, so you need to marquee to get just
the portion you want. Only marquee over the dot. (Fig
4.16) Zooming in on the type will increase the likelihood
of getting this the first time you try it, so don't be afraid to
use the Zoom tool or Command+=. When the dot over the
i is selected, press the Delete key until you see that the dot
over the *i* is missing.

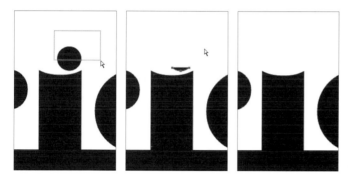

FIG 4.16 Marquee over the top half
of the letter *i* with the Direct Selection
tool, then press the Delete key.

4. With the Rectangle tool, create a square in place of the
dot over the *i*. Change the fill color to a red hue of your
choice by selecting the Color Picker or double-clicking on
the fill box.

5. Duplicate the square and move it to the bottom of the
composition, just above the first word in the body copy,
by using the Selection tool and holding Option while
dragging.

6. While the copy of the square is still selected, double-
click the Scale tool in the Tools panel. Scale the square by
300 percent. (Fig 4.17)

7. Finally, position it above the copy at the bottom of the
page, to the right of the guide.

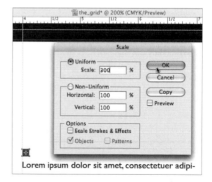

FIG 4.17 With the Scale tool, change
the scale of the letters to 300%.

EXERCISE 06 Adjusting shapes with the Direct Selection tool

1. Click on the top left anchor point of the *d* in "Grid" with the Direct Selection tool. Notice that the anchor point increases in size as your mouse moves near it with the Direct Selection tool. Hold Shift and click on the top right anchor point of the same *d* to add it to the selection.

2. With only the top two anchor points of the letter *d* selected, expand the size of its ascender by using the up arrow key on the keypad. In this exercise, we pressed the up arrow key while holding Shift three times. (Fig 4.18)

FIG 4.18 Expand the ascender of the *d* by using the up arrow key.

Contra-Composition with dissonances XVI, Theo van Doesburg, 1925. Oil on canvas. 100 × 180 cm. The Hague, Gemeentemuseum Den Haag.

5 Color Theory and Basic Shapes

Color has always been present in our natural environment and in art across the world. From the 30,000-year-old Chauvet-Pont-d'Arc cave drawings in southeastern France, where the creators used carbon black and ochre pigments to represent Paleolithic horses, to the Tournament of Roses Parade on January 1, 1954, which was the first national television broadcast in color, color has been a focus of artistic creation.

Artists, mathematicians, and scientists have developed theories of color since the 17th century. Color theories are usually encapsulated in what is referred to as a *color model*. German Bauhaus school educators Josef Albers and Johannes Itten helped define and expand upon the RYB (red-yellow-blue) color model during the years 1919–1923. Albers created a course in color theory that inspired the tutorial in this chapter. College-level art and design students typically complete these color studies using pigment and brushes or Color-Aid paper. However, formal color studies can be executed in the digital environment. In the following four exercises hue, value, and contrast are exploited to achieve various color relationships.

The traditional, analog color wheel utilizes the RYB (red-yellow-blue) color model. In this color model, red, yellow, and blue are the primary hues (what we think of as colors), which can be mixed together to create any other color on the color wheel. (Fig 5.1) Complementary colors are opposite, while analogous colors sit side-by-side on the wheel. A surface appears colored because it reflects some light frequencies while absorbing others. When the pure primaries are mixed together in this subtractive system, the resulting product is black because all light shining on it is absorbed, leaving no light to reflect back to the eye and convey color.

We usually encounter digital media as a projection of light or as a print made with ink. Art may be projected on a screen or uploaded to an electronic device such as an iPod, or it may be printed on an inkjet or a four-color press. There are different color models for various display purposes.

Note: This book was designed and printed in CMYK.

The CMYK (cyan, magenta, yellow, and black) color model is specific to the print industry. Artists and designers often create art for high-volume printing using the CMYK color model to synchronize the digital file with the four corresponding printing inks. Even though it is worked on with digital tools and examined via the projected light of a computer screen, this system is also subtractive, meaning overlapping inks create a darker hue.

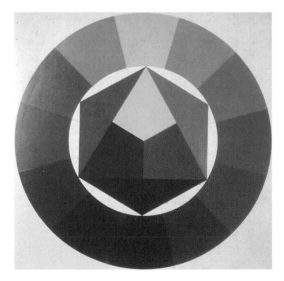

FIG 5.1 *Color Wheel,* Johannes Itten, 1961

Note:

The Pantone company publishes swatch books as a reference to their Pantone Matching System (PMS) ink colors, along with a book that shows how PMS mixtures will look when converted to CMYK, a CMYK reference, and more recently a translation of on-screen color to on-paper color.

You can get a sense of the color selection by simply doing an image search for Pantone, or you can order a color chip system at http://www.pantone.com/. Commercial printers typically keep some Pantone swatch books in their offices and are more than happy to have you visit and use them to choose the color palette for your project. These are helpful if you want to see what the color you specified in your file will really look like when you go to print.

Television screens and computer monitors do not use ink or paint — they use red, green, and blue light. RGB is an additive color model. Colored light is mixed to create hue and value with red, green, and blue as the primary colors. When the primary colors in the RGB model are mixed together, the result is white. (Fig 5.2)

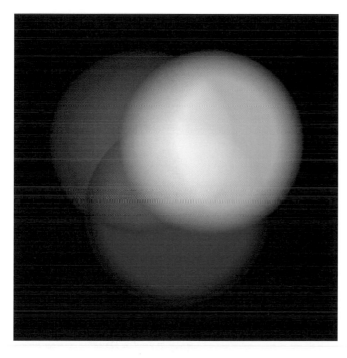

FIG 5.2 (Approximate) RGB color wheel. Since we are printing this book in CMYK, this image does not truly represent an RGB color wheel.

Vocabulary

Hue is color (e.g., red, blue, green, yellow).

Intensity, Saturation, Chroma, and *Brilliance* all refer to how much pigment is in a color, which translates to how vivid a color appears.

Value is measured by how much white or black is mixed with a hue, or it can be registered as the grayscale equivalent of a color.

Shades are a hue mixed with black.

Tints are a hue mixed with white.

Analogous colors are adjacent on the color wheel.

Complementary colors directly oppose each other on the wheel.

FIG 5.3 Stamp featuring *Homage to the Square,* Josef Albers, 1950–1975. Analogous colors are demonstrated on this stamp. Albers began working on this series in 1950 and made over a thousand works addressing the square over the course of 25 years.

FIG 5.4 *Portrait of Madame Manet on a Blue Sofa,* Edouard Manet, 1880, oil on canvas. Complementary colors are used in Manet's painting to create contrast between the blue couch and the orange wall in the background. Notice how Madame Manet's clothes are neutral, creating harmony between herself and the couch.

01 Hue has value!

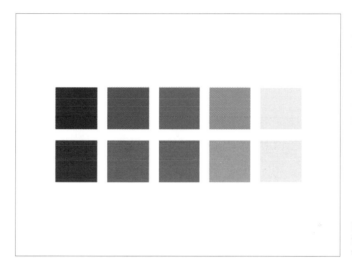

Note: Choose the Essentials workspace from the pull-down menu in the Application bar before working on the following exercises.

FIG 5.5 Gray squares reflect the value associated with each hue.

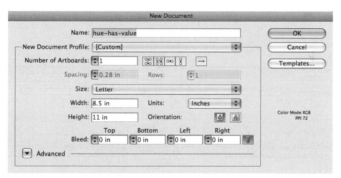

FIG 5.6 Create a new document.

1. Create a new document in Illustrator using the Basic RGB profile. Adjust the settings so the units are measured in inches and choose Letter from the Size pull-down menu. We named our document *hue-has-value*. (Fig 5.6)

2. Using the Rectangle Shape tool, draw five squares on the Artboard. Hold down the Shift key while dragging each square to keep the proportions equal. (Fig 5.7)

3. For each square, choose a fill color of a different hue with different values. Do not use a stroke. Remember to select the shape before you select a new color from the Swatches or Color panel. (Fig 5.8)

4. To select all of the shapes with the Selection tool, either marquee over them (click and drag over all of the shapes from a starting position outside them) or hold Shift and click on each shape. (Fig 5.9)

5. Hold the Option key while dragging the squares to create a duplicate set. If you hold Shift after you begin dragging the mouse, the duplicate copy will move only in 90- or 45-degree movements. (Fig 5.10)

LEFT: FIG 5.7 Draw a square.
RIGHT: FIG 5.8 Choose a fill color using the Swatch panel.

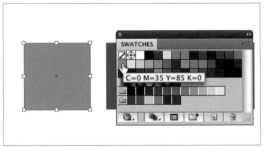

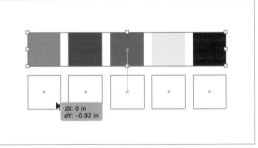

FIG 5.9 Five squares, each filled with a different color.   **FIG 5.10** Duplicate squares.

6. Deselect by clicking on the Artboard, then select one of the duplicate squares with the Selection tool. Click on the Color panel pull-down menu (located in the top right area of the Color panel) and choose Grayscale. (Fig 5.11) This removes the hue from the square and demonstrates the value of the associated hue. Repeat this step for each of the squares in the duplicate set. Observe how each hue has an associated gray value.

7. Rearrange the color-grayscale pair according to the grayscale value, with the closest to white at the right, and black at the left. (Fig 5.12) Select each pair (either by marqueeing with the Selection tool or Shift-clicking on one square followed by the next) and drag it left or right in the grayscale order. Be sure to hold down Shift once you have started to drag the mouse, as this will keep your movement strictly vertical or horizontal.

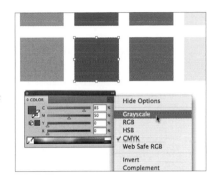

FIG 5.11 Use the Color Panel pull-down menu to covert color to grayscale.

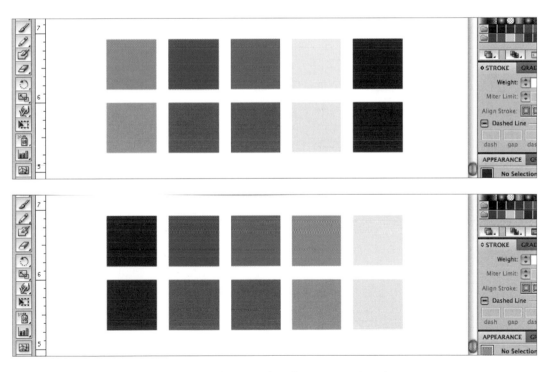

FIG 5.12 Shown above is the illustration before and after of rearranging the color-grayscale pairs according to the grayscale values from dark to light.

02 Top or bottom?

FIG 5.13 Hues with different values relate to the colors around them.

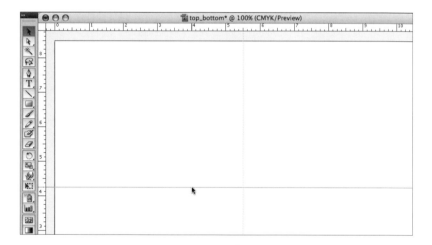

FIG 5.14 Guide set at half page.

1. Create a new file in Illustrator as we did in Step 1 of Exercise 1.

2. Use a guide to separate the page into two halves (top and bottom) by pulling the guide from the top ruler to the halfway point on the vertical ruler. (Fig 5.14) If you don't see your rulers, turn them on by choosing View > Show Rulers (Command+R). Repeat this process to create a second guide that cuts the page in half vertically (left and right).

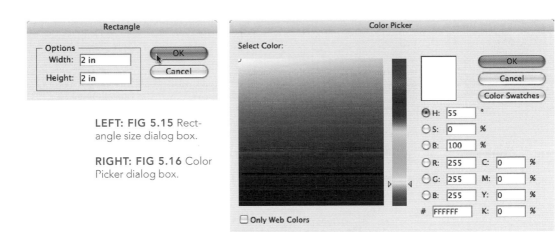

LEFT: FIG 5.15 Rectangle size dialog box.

RIGHT: FIG 5.16 Color Picker dialog box.

3. Create a 2-by-2-inch horizontally centered square on the top half of the page by aligning the bottom of the square to the horizontal dividing line. To make the square exactly 2 inches by 2 inches, double-click on the Artboard with the Rectangle tool to see the Rectangle Options dialog box. Type "2 in" into the horizontal and vertical measurement boxes. (Fig 5.15)

4. Colors have three properties: Hue, Value and Saturation. Hue is the name used to define the color. For instance red, yellow, and blue are hues. Value refers to how much white or black is mixed into the color. Baby blue is a tint, or blue with white in it, while navy blue is a shade of blue that contains black. Saturation is the level of intensity of the color. The color of pale winter tomatoes is less saturated than the color of ripe summer tomatoes.

Double-click on the fill color in the bottom of the Tools panel. The Color Picker dialog box appears. (Fig 5.16) The Color Picker is another location for choosing colors. The Color Picker has controls for all three properties: hue, value, and saturation. Choose a hue on the vertical slider to the right of the color selection area. Then choose a value by moving the color selection circle up or down. The higher you move the circle, the higher the value, and the lighter the color appears. The lower the circle is placed, the lower the value and the darker the color. Choose saturation by moving the color selection circle left or right horizontally. Moving left lowers the saturation, and the color becomes more gray. Moving right raises the saturation value, and the color becomes more intense.

Tip: If the dialog box is set to a different unit of measurement when it first opens, for instance points or pixels, typing "2 in" tells the program to use inches instead of the units of measurement that initially appeared.

TOP TO BOTTOM:

FIG 5.17 Create three color-filled squares.

FIG 5.18 Duplicate three squares overlapping 1 inch of the top squares.

FIG 5.19 New squares have higher hue values.

5. Make sure that the square is selected before choosing a color in this step. Use the Color Picker to choose a hue with a low value for the fill color of the square. Do not assign a stroke.

6. Option-drag your square to the left to create a copy (holding down Shift after you start dragging will restrain it to a movement along the x-axis).

7. Repeat this action to make a copy of the square to the right.

8. Select all three of the squares and Option-drag them down to the right so that 1 inch of the upper left corner of the new squares overlaps with 1 inch of the bottom right corner of the original squares. (Fig 5.18)

9. Give all three of the new squares a different hue with a value higher than the top three: with all three squares selected, double-click on the fill square to bring up the Color Picker. Choose a different hue, and choose a higher value so the color has less black in it. (Fig 5.19)

10. Select the left set of two squares (marquee or Shift-click with the Selection tool).

11. With the two shapes selected, open the Pathfinder panel (Window > Pathfinder). Click the Divide button, the first button under the Pathfinder heading. (Fig 5.20) Dividing two objects creates a new shape at the intersection of the paths. The overlapping space is the 1-inch square. It will become its own whole shape, and the three shapes will remain grouped.

12. Select all three shapes and ungroup them by clicking Object > Ungroup (Command+Shift+G). Now they can be selected and treated individually. (Fig 5.21)

13. Repeat Steps 10–12 with the middle and right set of squares.

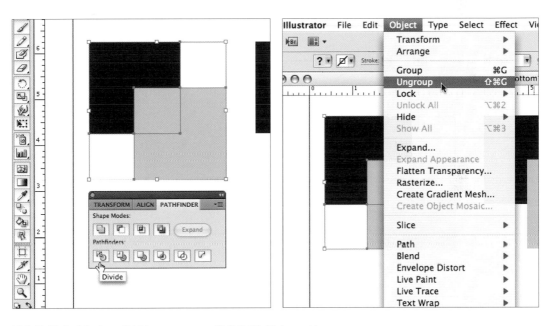

FIG 5.20 Pathfinder > Divide.   **FIG 5.21** Object > Ungroup.

Creating foreground and background depth using hue and value

Now we will continue to work with the file created in Exercise 2 (Fig 5.22) and modify the color of the middle squares, starting with the left square. The purpose of this exercise is to see how hue and value can be used to create space or depth within a color field. You will modify the colors of the middle square to control the perception of it in relation to the other two squares. The middle square will seem to be pulled forward or pushed back in space.

1. For the left set of squares, modify the center square so that it is part of the top square, and both it and the top square are floating above the bottom square. Achieve this by choosing a hue and value that create strong contrast with the bottom square (especially perceptible at the boundary between the two shapes) and little or no contrast with the top square.

2. For the center set of squares, modify the smaller middle square so that it is floating over both the larger squares. This is achieved by choosing a hue and value that creates strong contrast with both of the other squares.

3. For the right set of squares, modify the smaller middle square so that it is part of the bottom square, and both it and the bottom square are floating over the top square. This effect is achieved by choosing a hue and value that create strong contrast with the top square and little or no contrast with the bottom square.

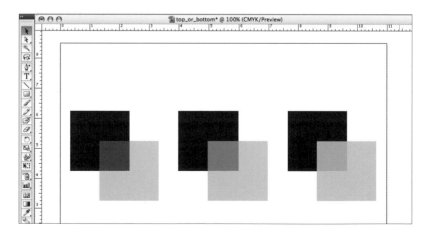

FIG 5.22 File created in Excercise 2.

EXERCISE

03 Interaction of values

1. Create a new document, as we did in Exercises 1 and 2.

2. Use the Rectangle tool to create a 20 percent gray rectangle that covers the whole Artboard, by using the CMYK color sliders to set the K value to 20 percent and all other sliders to 0 percent. (Fig 5.23)

FIG 5.23 CMYK color slider set at 20% K.

3. Open the Layers panel (Windows > Layers). The gray shape should be located on Layer 1. Lock Layer 1 so the gray shape does not move while you are completing the following steps. (Fig 5.24)

4. Create a new layer using the button at the bottom of the Layers panel. (Fig 5.25)

With Layer 1 locked and Layer 2 selected (highlighted in the Layers panel), the following steps will be accomplished on Layer 2.

FIG 5.24 Locked layer.

5. Create two 3-by-3-inch squares on top of the gray background. Fill one with white, eliminate any stroke color, and fill the other with black. Place the squares side by side, so that the left edge of one touches the right edge of the other in the middle of the gray area. If you have trouble getting them to align, try adding a guide by pulling one down from the top ruler. (Fig 5.26)

6. Create one .75- by-.75-inch square in the center of the white square. Fill the square with 50 percent black (middle gray). (Fig 5.27)

7. Option-drag a copy of this square to the middle of the black square with the Selection tool.

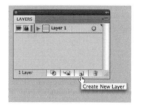

FIG 5.25 Create New Layer.

Note: When values are placed near to or on top of each other, we perceive their values as interacting and affecting one another. It is important to keep this in mind when choosing hue and value combinations, as one value will always influence the appearance of another.

FIG 5.26 Aligned white and black squares.

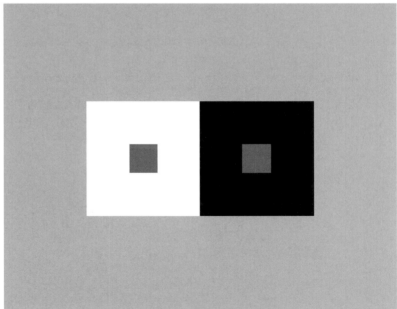

FIG 5.27 Notice how the middle gray squares inside the black and white areas appear to have different values.

EXERCISE
04 Interaction of hues

Now for the magic trick: in the next exercise, three colors appear as four.

1. Re-save your Exercise 3 file with a new name using File > Save As. It is helpful to save a file with a new name before starting to experiment.

2. Shift-click to select the two smaller squares and use the Color Picker or the Color Sliders (Window > Color) to assign the same hue to them. A secondary color, like green, will work the best. (Fig 5.28)

3. Select the larger square on the left (in this example, the white square is selected) and assign it the middle value of one of the primary colors that makes up the secondary color you just chose for the smaller squares. You can use the Color Picker or the Color panel. (Fig 5.29)

4. Select the larger square on the right (in our example, the black square) and assign it a medium value of the other primary color used to make up the color of the small squares. We used the Color Picker this time to choose a rich yellow, the other primary component of our small squares' green hue.

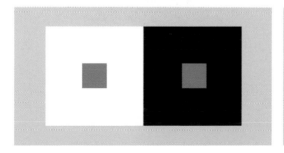

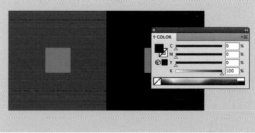

FIG 5.28 Change the color of the small squares.

FIG 5.29 Choose the colors for the large squares.

FIG 5.30 Notice that the two small squares look like they are different colors. They are, in fact, the same color, but the presence of the complementary and analogous colors influences our perception. The complementary color emphasizes the perception of the hues, while the analogous color de-emphasizes the perception of the hues.

The Murders in the Rue Morgue, Aubrey
Beardsley, Illustrations of short stories
by Edgar Allan Poe, 1894-1895.

6 Line Art and Flat Graphics

No matter the weight of the line, from finely etched crosshatching to bold marker or brush strokes, line art is binary: the color is either on the paper or it is not. Line art uses solid colors, and does not include a continuous tonal scale. A newspaper headline is line art, but the photograph below the headline is not line art. Lines and shapes form a composition with a strong figure/ground and negative/positive space interplay.

Line art as has routinely been employed in the commercial arena. (Fig 6.1) Andy Warhol blurred the border between the worlds of commercial and fine art by using line art and flat graphics on paintings to be shown in galleries and museums as a critique of the commercial world that this genre serves. Visible in Warhol's illustrations of Campbell's soup cans are thin, black lines that delineate the top edges of the can and a large, flat field of red-orange on the label.

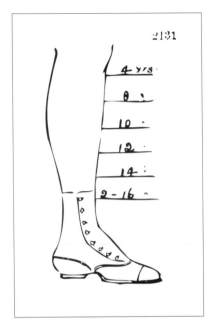

FIG 6.1 The proper length for little girls' skirts at various ages, a diagram from *Harper's Bazaar*, 1868.

Plakatstil is the original flat graphic style used in advertising and poster campaigns. Plakatstil is German for "poster style." Plakatstil is the opposite of decoration. Flat graphics are bold and minimal; often type is large. Lucian Bernhard's 1906 poster design entry to a contest held in Berlin by the Priester Match Company is the first work to embrace this new graphic style. Bernhard was inspired by the industrialization of city life and a desire for rapid communication. In posters such as Bernhard's, or Jim Fitzpatrick's poster of Che Guevara, the color palette is minimal, and the contrast between shapes, values, and intensity is extreme. (Fig 6.2) As a result the message is bold and powerful.

Although line art and flat graphics are especially used for the commercial purposes of logo and identity pieces, the outcome of drawing a single line is as personal as your signature. Artists such as Pablo Picasso and Egon Schiele (see Chapter 1) are often identified by their line quality. Revisit Schiele's work and notice that contrast can be achieved by juxtaposing solid and implied lines as well as lines of varying thicknesses.

The Pen tool

The Pen tool is used for creating lines and shapes. It can be used to to draw or to trace images. In addition to contouring and tracing, the Pen tool is often used to create masks. Using this tool sometimes feels counter-intuitive. The artist has to know where her next point is before plotting it. The forethought that accompanies the use of this tool — visualizing lines, shapes, and space before they exist — can be challenging. In this exercise, you will make quick gesture drawings of lines and shapes with the Paintbrush tool and then recreate them accurately with the Pen tool. With enough practice on top of template layers, you are sure to develop Pen tool intuition.

FIG 6.2 In this political poster of Che Guevara by Jim Fitzpatrick (1968), the portrait is represented as a flat graphic. The contrast between the vibrant red, black, and paper white is intense. The message is quickly understood through a design that is both minimal and powerful.

EXERCISE 01 Gesture drawings on a template layer

Note: Choose the Essentials work-space from the pull-down menu in the Application bar before working on the following exercises.

1. Start with a new Adobe Illustrator print document set to standard letter-size dimensions.

2. To begin, we will set up a template layer with quick gesture strokes using the Paintbrush tool. Select the Paintbrush tool from the Tools panel. Press the letter *d* on the keypad to set the default colors into the fill (white) and stroke (black). Draw a straight line by clicking and dragging with the Paintbrush tool. Deselect the straight line by clicking off of it with the Selection tool.

> **Key Command:** Another way to deselect in Illustrator is to use the Command key to access the Selection tool and then click an empty area of the Artboard.

3. Draw a triangle with the Paintbrush tool. The results of the paintbrush drawings are vector shapes, which are outlined by anchor points that can be modified with the Direct Selection tool.

4. Deselect the triangle and draw the remaining curves pictured at right. (Fig 6.3)

5. Open the Layers panel by clicking in the panel shown in the illustration below or choosing Window > Layers. Double-click the icon for Layer 1 in the Layers panel. Click the Template button and then click OK. The Template feature will lock the layer, so that you will not accidentally modify the paintbrush work. Template layers also dim artwork on those layers (this will be especially evident in Exercise 4). (Fig 6.4)

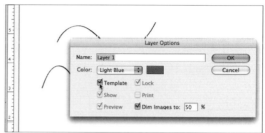

FIG 6.4 The Layer dialog box, with Template selected.

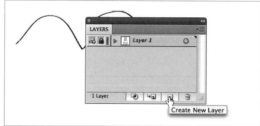

FIG 6.5 The Create New Layer button at the bottom of theLayers panel.

FIG 6.3 Final curves drawn in this chapters exercises: line, triangle, curve, swoosh, hills.

6. Create a new layer in the Layers panel. We will use the Pen tool on Layer 2. (Fig 6.5)

EXERCISE
02 Re-creating straight lines with the Pen tool

FIG 6.6 Variations on the Pen tool.

1. Select the Pen tool from the Tools panel. Click and hold your mouse on the tool to see the additional tools used on vector paths. (Fig 6.6)

The Pen tool plots anchor points each time you click the mouse. Click once on the Stroke icon at the bottom of the Tools panel and set the stroke to red, so that you will see your work when it sits on top of the black template layer. Set the fill color to none.

2. To make a straight line in red, click one time at the beginning of the black painted line. Release the mouse. Move the mouse to the end of the black line. Click one time. In two clicks, the Pen tool creates two anchor points and joins the points with a straight line. (Fig 6.7)

3. Once the line is made, it can be modified with the Selection tool for moving, rotating, or transforming or by the Direct Selection tool, to modify one anchor point at a time. (Fig 6.8) Deselect the line, then use the Direct Selection tool to click once on the anchor point at the end of the line and drag it to increase the length of the line. (Fig 6.9)

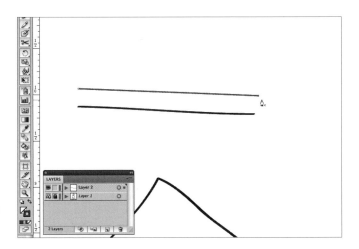

FIG 6.7 Click twice with the Pen tool to make a single line. Do not drag.

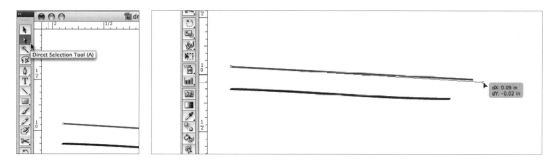

FIG 6.8 The Direct Selection tool.   FIG 6.9 Changing a line by moving a single anchor point.

4. Use the Selection tool to select the line and change the weight of the stroke from the Control panel. Notice how the line can be bold and aggressive with a larger stroke size, or slim and faint with a stroke size that is less than 1 point. Deselect the line when you are finished.

Tip: In Illustrator, the anchor points grow larger as the mouse hovers near them, making it easier to find the anchor points when nothing is selected.

Part A: Re-create the triangle with the Pen tool

1. Click once at one corner of the triangle with the Pen tool. Release the mouse. Click on the next corner of the triangle. Release the mouse. Click on the third corner of the triangle. Release the mouse. The fourth click needs to be exactly where the first anchor point was made. (Fig 6.10)

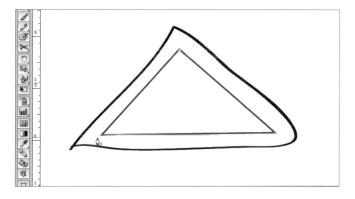

FIG 6.10 A closed vector triangle.

Notice in this image that the Pen tool displays a small circle, symbolizing that the path will be closed and a whole object is made when the last click is made directly on the first anchor point. This is referred to as *closing the path*. When a path is closed, or a shape is whole, it is easy to fill the shape with a color using the Selection tool and the color tool panels. If the shape is not correctly closed, the entire Artboard will be filled.

Key Command: The letter x on the keypad will switch the fill and stroke colors in Illustrator. In Photoshop the same key command switches the foreground and background colors.

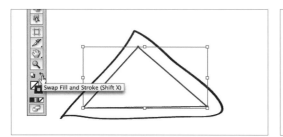

FIG 6.11 Swapping stroke and fill.

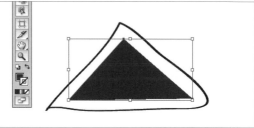

FIG 6.12 The triangle with a red fill, and no stroke.

2. Select the triangle with the Selection tool if it isn't already selected. Click the curved arrow above the Fill and Stroke tools in the Tools panel. The stroke and fill colors switch places. (In this example, the triangle becomes red with no stroke, as opposed to a triangle with no fill, outlined in red.) (Fig 6.11-12)

Part B: Modify anchor points using the Direct Selection tool

Just for practice, use the Direct Selection tool to modify two anchor points at a time. You can also click on one side of the shape with the Direct Selection tool and modify a side. Click on one anchor point of the triangle. Hold the shift key and click a second anchor point (so one whole side is selected), then begin dragging the mouse to move both anchor points at one time. Alternatively, you can marquee over one side of the triangle, and two anchor points will be selected. You can click and drag with the mouse to move these anchor points, or you can use the up, down, left, and right arrows on the keypad.

Shift+Arrow modifies the placement by 10 pixels.

Part C: Create a second shape to add dimensionality

1. Begin by creating a second shape (a parallelogram) using the Pen tool. Plot the first anchor point near the top of the first triangle.

2. Use the edge of the first triangle to help visualize the dimensionality of the second shape. Plot the second anchor point to create a parallel line between the two shapes.

3. Set the third anchor point so the area appears to recede in space, creating a unified perspective between the two shapes.

4. Close the path by using your fourth mouse click to return to the first anchor point. If the shape isn't perfect, you can always go back with the Direct Selection tool to modify individual anchor points. (Fig 6.13)

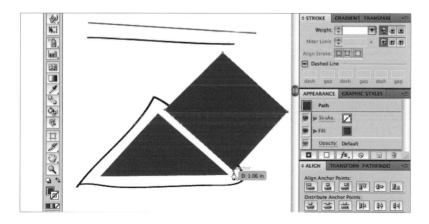

FIG 6.13 A new rectangle alongside our triangle.

Part D: Atmospheric Perspective

Stand outside early in the morning or at twilight and look far down the street towards the horizon. Objects that are further away appear less saturated than those that are near. Atmospheric perspective accounts for the perceptual change that happens to the overall opacity of objects as they recede in space.

1. Select the parallelogram and fill it with the same color you used in the triangle.

2. Open the Transparency panel (Window > Transparency). While the second triangle is still selected, change the transparency to 80 percent. Flat, basic shapes created with the Pen tool can be combined to imply complicated shapes and three-dimensional space by using different transparencies to create a sense of atmospheric perspective. (Fig 6.14)

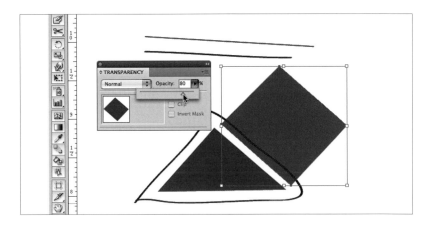

FIG 6.14 Changing transparency.

EXERCISE

03 Curves

Part A: One curve

1. The first curve is created in two points. The first anchor point is made by clicking and dragging the mouse slightly upward to imply the direction of the curve. Do not drag all the way over the curve as if you are using a pencil or paintbrush; this tool does not work like a pencil or paintbrush. Release the mouse. (Fig 6.15)

2. Click once at the end of the curve and drag slightly downward until the curve looks similar to the template. (Fig 6.16)

3. Deselect the curve.

FIG 6.15 Click and drag to place the first curve point.

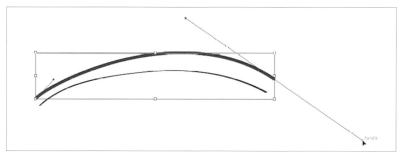

FIG 6.16 Click and drag again to place the second curve point.

Part B: Bezier handles

When you are finished, you will have one curve with two anchor points. Each anchor point will also have bezier handles, which are used to modify sections of the curved line. With the Direct Selection tool you can modify the anchor points, the line segments, and each bezier handle. Every curve has a mid-way point — the bezier handles pull on each side of this point. (Fig 6.17-18)

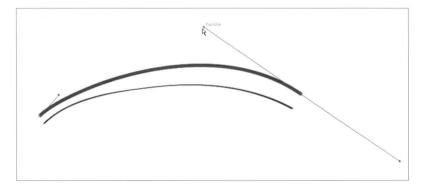

FIG 6.17 Grabbing a bezier handle.

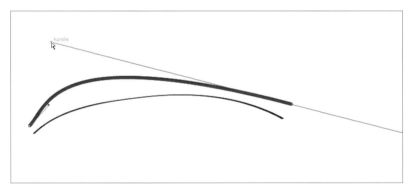

FIG 6.18 Using the handle to change the curve.

Part C: Two curves in a row

1. Click and drag with the Pen tool in the direction of the first curve. Release the mouse. (Fig 6.19)

2. Click at the end of the first curve and drag down with the mouse — this tells the Pen tool the direction of the next curve. Release the mouse. (Fig 6.20)

3. Click at the end point of the last curve and the final curve is made between the last two anchor points. (Fig 6.21)

When you are working with the Pen tool, you have to think ahead of the tool, towards the place where the line changes. Think about where the curve should change directions. This will inform where you click and how you drag the mouse.

Tip: If you're having trouble envisioning where to click with the Pen tool, you can practice envisioning contour on a sketchpad. Practice creating blind contour drawings to gain confidence in this skill.

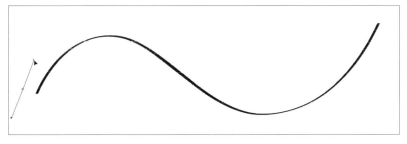

FIG 6.19 Click and drag in the direction of the first curve.

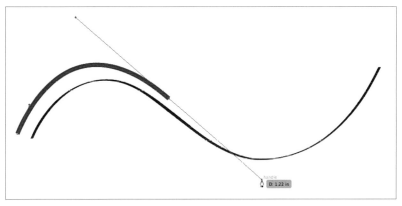

FIG 6.20 Click and drag in the direction of the next curve.

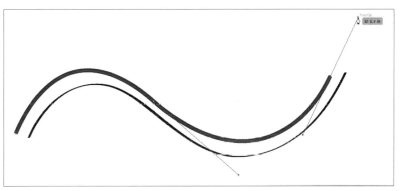

FIG 6.21 Placing the final point.

Part D: Deleting and adding anchor points

You can click on an anchor point with the Direct Selection tool and press the Delete key, or, if the anchor is in the middle of a path, you can use the Subtract Anchor Point tool (Pen Minus) to click on an anchor point you want to delete. You can use the Add Anchor Point tool (Pen Plus) to add an anchor point anywhere on a path after you have finished creating it. (Fig 6.22-23)

Deselect before working on the next exercise.

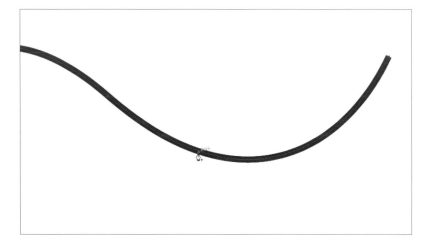

FIG 6.22 The Pen tool can add an anchor point to an existing curve.

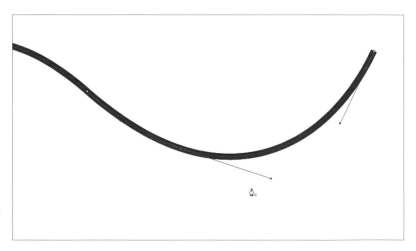

FIG 6.22 Any new points will come with their own bezier control points.

04 Curves and angles

The last sample on the template is an example of a curve next to an angle, next to a curve, next to an angle, and so on. The Convert Anchor Point tool is used to create this juxtaposition. This tool becomes active if you place your mouse near an anchor point while drawing a path. It is also available as a separate tool, hidden beneath the Pen tool in the Tools panel.

1. Use the Pen tool to click once and drag in the direction of the curve at the first anchor point.

2. Click at the second anchor point and drag to finish the first curve.

3. Now place the Pen tool close to the anchor point you just created, wait until you see the Convert Anchor Point tool, then click the mouse. The bezier handle disappears because you no longer have a curve. The Convert Anchor Point tool can be used to convert an anchor point from an angle to a curve or from a curve to an angle. (Fig 6.23)

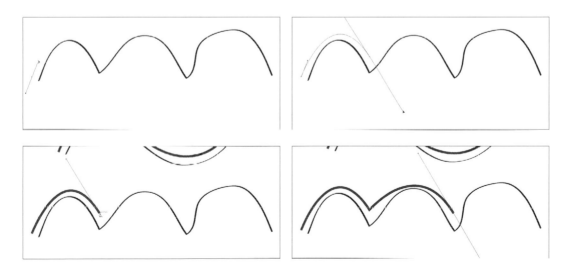

FIG 6.23 Following curves and creating corners by clicking on the most recent anchor point.

4. Click after the next curve and drag the mouse down to create the curve.

5. Click on the anchor point to convert it to an angle.

6. Repeat this process until you trace the template. (Fig 6.24)

By understanding how to create straight lines and curves, and by converting anchor points from curves to angles or angles to curves, you can trace any image.

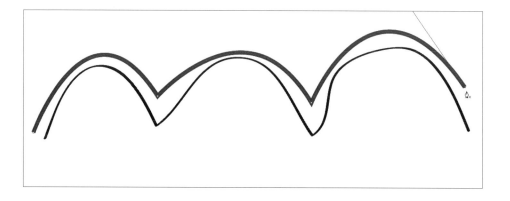

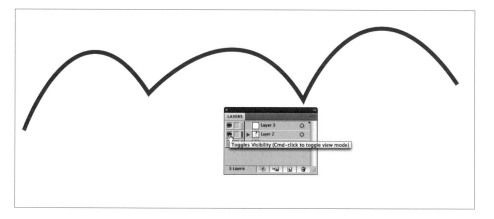

ABOVE: FIG 6.24 The finished curve.   **BELOW: FIG 6.25** With the template hidden.

EXERCISE 05
Tracing an image and creating a clipping mask

The Pen tool is often used in combination with images or vector art to create clipping masks. A mask is used to define which parts of an object or image are revealed to the viewer. They are commonly used on photographic images to hide the background around a figure in the image. A good example of this is a magazine cover or advertisement where the background is completely solid. Alpha channels, layer masks, and clipping masks can be made in Photoshop. We will create masks in Photoshop in Chapters 10 and 11. In this exercise, we will use the Pen tool to create a clipping mask. The Pen tool can be used to mask an object or image in InDesign and Flash, as well. For this exercise, place any image onto the template layer and trace it with the Pen tool on Layer 2. An image of a human figure is a challenge, as it always includes combinations of curves and straight lines. Included on the wiki is a photograph of a hand in front of a flat wall. You can do this exercise using that file or any image of your choice. First the Pen tool will be used to draw a path around the arm, then the resultant path will be turned into a clipping mask to hide the rest of the photograph.

1. Create a new layer and turn off the Eyeball icons of the other two layers to hide them while you are working on this new exercise. (Fig 6.26)

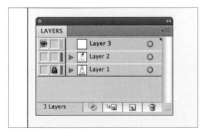

FIG 6.26 The last two layers, hidden.

2. Choose File > Place to place the image of the hand (or your image) on the new layer.

3. Double-click the icon in the Layer panel and click on the Template checkbox. The image will appear dim. Create a new layer above the template layer. (Fig 6.27-28)

4. Use the Pen tool to trace the contour of the image. Remember to start and stop on the same anchor point. Also remember that the path doesn't have to be perfect, as the Direct Selection tool can be used to modify it once it has been created. (Fig 6.29)

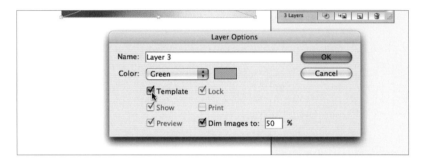

FIG 6.27 Setting the layer to Template.

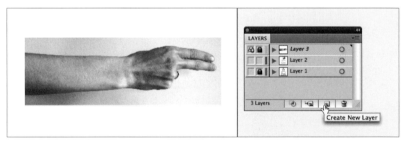

FIG 6.28 Making a new layer.

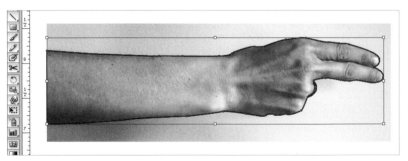

FIG 6.29 Using the Pen tool to trace the image.

5. To transform the path into a clipping mask, you will select both the path and the image. First, unlock the template layer. Use the Selection tool to click on the path first, then hold Shift and click on the photograph. You will see anchor points around the path you just plotted and on the four corners of the placed photograph. Choose Object > Clipping Mask > Make. (Fig 6.30)

6. Modifying the clipping mask or image that is masked is possible, as long as you select just one or the other with the Direct Selection tool. This is not always as easy as it sounds. The most fool-proof way to select the mask and not the image is to use the Layers panel. Expand Layer 2 by clicking on the arrow left of the small thumbnail on the Layers panel. Now you have a group that contains the clipping mask and the photographic image. You can see the mask and the image as separate parts of the layer. (Fig 6.31) A small colored box appears in an area on the right of each path on a layer when that path is selected. Clicking on this area when it is empty will select a path. Click this area of the Layers panel on the clipping mask layer. You will see a blue box in the Layers panel and the anchor points surrounding the mask within the document. Use the Direct Selection tool to modify the mask without altering the photographic image.

Tip: The path that will become the clipping mask should be inside the boundaries of the photographic image. That is, the photographic image should be larger than the path that will be used to mask it. If the path is larger than the entire image, the mask will simply reveal everything, in which case there is no reason to use a mask.

Tip: Be sure to click on the path, then Shift-click the photographic image someplace outside of the path. Shift-clicking inside an area that includes both the path and the image deselects everything!

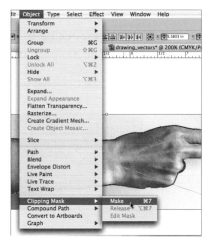

FIG 6.30 Object > Clipping Mask > Make.

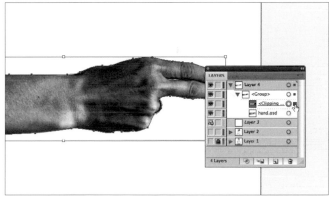

FIG 6.31 Selecting the clipping mask.

7. The Selection tool can be used to move the entire image and mask as one unit, since they are grouped together within the Layers panel. Once a clipping mask has been made, it will remain grouped in the Layers panel unless you release it.

8. To delete the clipping mask, click on it with the Selection tool then choose Object > Clipping Mask > Release. Now both the path that was used as the mask and the image are available as two separate objects. They can be deleted or modified as individual objects. (Fig 6.32)

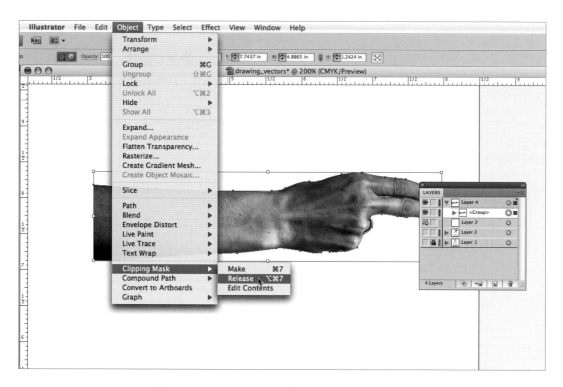

FIG 6.32 Any new points will come with their own bezier control points.

The final scanogram created using the
exercises in Chapter 7.

7 Image Acquisition and Resolution

There are several ways to bring an image into the computer. The two most common are photographic in nature, that is, both methods involve exposing sensors to an item or scene in the real world. The camera or scanner then writes digital data to display that image on the screen. While the sensor technology is essentially the same, a camera is made to capture scenes with depth of field, while a scanner is made to focus on and capture just one flat plane.

Photograms are made by placing objects on sensitized paper, exposing the objects and paper to light, and then processing the paper to reveal the print. A camera is not necessary for the production of this type of graphic image. The first photograms were made by photographic pioneers William Henry Fox Talbot and Anna Atkins in the mid-1800s. This type of contact print can have an uncanny life-like presence that, like an X-ray, reduces three-dimensional information onto a two-dimensional plane without the perspective that a camera lens introduces. This overall focus and flattening of visual information results in a poetic and magical image.

A scanogram is the digital method of producing something like a photogram. It is the image made by placing objects directly on the scanner.

Photograms have been made by photographers, artists, and designers. Anna Atkins created early renderings of natural elements. The avant-garde formal experiments of Man Ray, El Lissitzky, and László Moholy-Nagy are central works of 1920s art and design. Commercial designers such as Paul Rand used the technique for package design and book jackets. The process is fun to explore, and the results are always surprising.

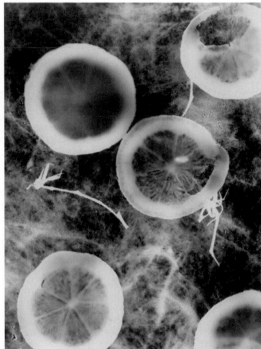

FIG 7.1 A photogram of algae, from the book *British Algae*, Anna Atkins, 1843. This is the first book composed entirely of photographic images.

FIG 7.2 A photogram of lemons, uploaded to Wikimedia Commons in August 2005 by user name Cormaggio.

EXERCISE 01
Creating a scanogram and understanding input resolution

Scanners are optical input devices that use software to send the captured image from the scanning bed to the computer. Though scanning software varies among brands, all scanners operate in the same manner, and all scanning software has the same essential functions. Typically, a scanner is used to create a digital image of something two-dimensional. In this exercise, you will scan a three-dimensional object.

1. Place your object on the scanning bed. If the lid does not close, put a dark piece of cloth around the scanner so ambient light doesn't leak in and interfere with the exposure during scanning (a jacket or dark sweater will work). We are scanning a flower that fell to the ground — it lies flat, so it will be easy to close the lid on the scanner.

2. Open the scanning application.

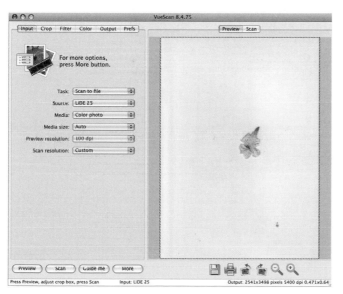

At home we use VueScan, a stand-alone application that seems to work with most scanners. The Epson scanners in our labs are operated through Photoshop's Import feature, located in File > Import > Scanner Name. If you are not sure which software interface to use, please consult your scanner's documentation.

FIG 7.3 The scanner will digitally capture the entire scan bed area. The preview of the flower takes up a small part of the entire scan bed.

Finished exercise file available in the Download Materials area of the wIki.

3. The scanner may automatically create a preview of whatever is placed on the scan bed. If it does not, a preview of the last item scanned may be visible. To create a preview, look for a button labeled with a word like "preview," "view," or "prescan." (Fig 7.3)

4. If your object is smaller than the scan bed, select just the area that you want to scan by marqueeing over the image area. (Fig 7.4-5) You may have to look for a Selection tool in the scanning software's toolset, or you may be able to just click and drag over the preview without changing to a tool. At this point, your selection marks the location of the object on the scan bed. If you lift the lid and move the object, you will have to re-preview in order to tell the scanner where to locate the selection.

5. Choose your resolution. This is the crucial step. Before scanning, the artist must decide upon the file's input resolution.

Note:

WYSIWYG stands for "What You See Is What You Get." We will revisit this term in Chapter 15.

Different output devices require different resolutions to produce quality output. Resolution is the number of pixels displayed per inch (PPI), also called dots per inch (DPI). In 1984, when Apple pioneered consumer WYSIWYG text, a way was needed to translate font sizes on screen to printed output dimensioned in inches. The early Macintosh computer screen used a logical inch made of 72 pixels, or 72 dots per inch. Windows was programmed to assume monitor displays of 96 dots per inch. Printers can easily squeeze 300 dots into an inch, and some go much higher. Knowing what kinds of resolution the intended output device has will help you decide what input resolution to use.

FIG 7.4 Notice the selection edges are very close to the edges of the flower.

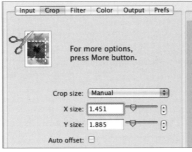

FIG 7.5 Here we cropped the scan area to the edges of the flower. It's almost 1.5 by 2 inches. This is important information, as it will help to determine what resolution to use when scanning the file.

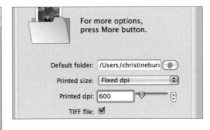

FIG 7.6 We are scanning at 600 dots per inch. We know that we can make a high-quality print on an inkjet printer at 300 dots per inch. Since 300 multiplied by 2 is 600, we will be able to print this scan at close to 3 by 4 inches, or the width and height multiplied by 2.

Printed images are measured in inches

Print resolution is often 300 dots per inch. You can get away with printing at 200 dots per inch in non-commercial situations, but the industry standard for printing on a digital printer is 300 DPI. This may vary by output type, so always ask the printer for the proper file resolution.

Effective resolution

Are you planning to enlarge or reduce a digital image before output? Once pixels are acquired, image data can't be added, so any image enlargement will result in a loss of quality. Reducing an image is no problem, but remember to keep the original file in the largest size and use Save As to create a smaller version.

Effective resolution is the magnification factor multiplied by the printing resolution. You should end up with a number that corresponds to your targeted output device.

For example, if you are scanning a 4-by-6-inch photograph to print it on the full page of an 8-by-12-inch photo inkjet paper at the printing resolution of 300 DPI, you will scan the original image at 600 DPI. The magnification factor is 2, and the printing resolution is 300 DPI. The effective resolution is 300 times 2.

Resolution for screen presentations

Any image that will only be used on-screen, for instance on a web site or in a video, will only need to be saved at screen resolution. Although monitors may vary, 72 dots per inch is a very common screen resolution. Image files saved at screen resolution are much smaller in file size than images that are saved for printing.

Monitors are measured in pixels

For any image that will be used only on-screen and is not intended for eventual printing, the only goal should be to create the number of pixels you want to display. If you want to display a 500-pixel-wide image on a monitor, then scan it so it is 500 pixels wide, and you're done. If your scanning software requires you to choose a DPI or PPI resolution, choose 72 and make sure your scan remains 500 pixels wide.

6. Using the guidelines above, choose a resolution and be sure that the color mode is appropriate (black-and-white line art, grayscale, or color). (Fig 7.6)

7. Select the TIFF file format and name the file. File formats such as JPEG, PNG, and PDF compress the size of the file, and may result in a loss of digital information. File formats such as TIFF and PSD are not lossy, and are therefore better format choices for high-quality scans. In

FIG 7.7 This is our final TIFF file as seen in Apple's image viewer application Preview. We will be opening this file in Photoshop for the next exercise.

VueScan, we set the name and format of the file using the Output tab before creating the scan.

8. The last step is to click on a button that reads something like "scan" in order to actually scan and save the file. Depending on your software, Steps 7 and 8 may need to be switched. Depending on your scanning software, you may have to specify the name and file format in a Save As dialog box after pressing the Scan button.

EXERCISE 02
A brief tour of tools and panels in Photoshop

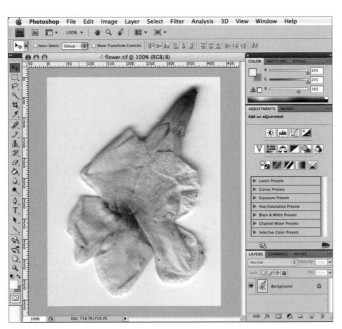

FIG 7.8 The Essentials workspace of Photoshop.

1. Open the scanogram file in Photoshop by dragging it to the Photoshop icon in the Dock or choosing File > Open in Photoshop.

2. Set the default workspace by choosing Window > Workspace > Essentials. Notice that the tools are located in the Tools panel on the left side of the screen. You can view the tools in a single or double column. (Fig 7.8)

Tip: In the Creative Suite programs, panels are accessible from the Window menu. Panels are also docked on the right side of the screen. All panels can be minimized or closed and reopened if needed. As you become familiar with Photoshop, you will be able to minimize and do without certain panels so there is more room for viewing the image.

3. Click once on any tool and notice the Options bar at the top of the screen. (Fig 7.9) As with tools in Illustrator, most Photoshop tools have adjustable values. In Photoshop this is done in the Options bar.

FIG 7.9 This is an image of the Options bar. For this screenshot, the Rectangular Marquee tool was selected. When a different tool is selected, its options are shown here.

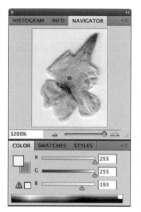

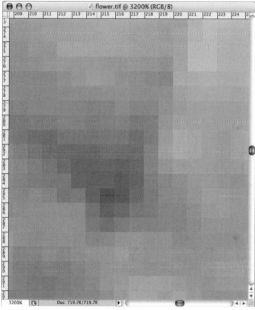

FIG 7.10 The red outline over the thumbnail display indicates the image area you are viewing. Notice the slider is pushed to the right, and in the bottom left corner our magnification is set at 3,200 percent.

FIG 7.11 A pixel is the most basic picture element of the bitmap digital image file.

4. The Navigator panel can be used to explore various areas of an image. An image that has more vertical or horizontal pixels than the monitor will not fit on screen at 100 percent magnification. The Navigator can be used to move around an image that is large or magnified, but you will soon learn shortcut keys to use instead of this panel. Move the slider on the bottom of the Navigator panel all the way to the right to zoom all the way in to the image. (Fig 7.10)

5. Enlarge the view of the image by zooming in, and the individual pixels that comprise the image are in plain view. (Fig 7.11)

Pixel

The word *pixel* is a combination of two words: *picture* and *element*. A pixel is the smallest unit of color information in a digital image.

Bitmap or raster images

A digital file is considered bitmap or raster (two words used interchangeably) if it is composed of a grid of pixels. *Raster* is the German word for "grid." Photoshop is the Creative Suite application that is primarily used to work with raster images.

6. Double-click the Zoom tool in the Tools panel to see the image at 100 percent. It is important to view digital images at 100 percent as this is the "true" representation of the file. This is as good as it gets on the screen.

FIG 7.12 In the Zoom tool options bar, locate the Zoom out button (Zoom tool with a minus sign). Click this and then click anywhere on the image. Keep clicking and you will continue to zoom out of the image. The Actual Size button will display the file at 100 percent. The Fit Screen button will make the image as large as it can be viewed on your screen.

7. Now we'll try some key commands. Zoom in by using Command+= and then use the Spacebar key to access the Hand tool. Hold the Spacebar and use the mouse to click and drag on the image. This moves the image around within the workspace. Using the Hand tool is a more efficient work habit than using the scroll bars.

Key Commands:

Command+0 will change the viewing percentage so the image is as large as it can be on your screen. This hot key works in all of the Creative Suite applications.

Holding the Spacebar on the keypad changes most tools to the Hand tool. This is useful for quick, temporary access to the Hand tool.

03 Image size, file size, and resolution

1. When working with scanned files or files input from a digital camera, the only layer in the Layers panel is the *Background layer*. A layer is like a single sheet of transparency paper. An empty layer is transparent. When a scan or digital photograph is first opened, Photoshop puts it on the *Background layer*. Look in the Layers panel (Window > Layers) and notice that the *Background layer* is locked. Double-click on the words "Background Layer" in the Layers panel to rename it through the Layer Options dialog box. (Fig 7.12) When you rename the *Background layer*, it is automatically unlocked. Unlocking the *Background layer* is a good habit, because you will name it and prepare the layer for further manipulation.

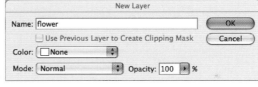

FIG 7.12 Changing the layer's name.

2. The Status bar runs along the bottom of the document window. Click on the area of the Status bar that reads "Doc:" followed by a number in kilobytes or megabytes. This area reports the file size. Here you will see the width, height, and resolution of the image. To see a visual representation of the printed size of the digital file, choose File > Print and notice the print preview. Our print would be very small at the current file settings. (Fig 7.13) Now press the Cancel button to return to standard editing mode.

Tip: Double-clicking a layer's name, thumbnail, and mask thumbnail launches different actions. If you get an unintended dialog box after double-clicking on a layer, press Cancel, then try again by double-clicking specifically on the name of the layer.

FIG 7.13 Print preview.

3. Choose Image > Image Size to see the resolution of the image.

4. Make sure Resample Image is not checked, so that Width, Height, and Resolution are linked together. Notice that the pixel dimensions at the top of the Image Size dialog box are no longer editable fields. The pixel dimensions will not change if a change is made to the editable areas beneath Document Size. Modifying any one of the variables Width, Height or Resolution, results in corresponding changes to the other two variables. We set the resolution to 300 DPI. (Fig 7.14-15) This resulted in a width and height twice as large as the original scan.

5. By using the Image Size dialog box with Resample Image unchecked, you can change the dimensions of the printed image without changing the number of pixels in the file. This is a good thing — in general you don't want to change the number of pixels within the image.

Pixels are created during image acquisition, on a scan bed or within the digital camera. Pixels can de discarded, but the only way to add new pixels is to rescan or re-capture the digital file using a higher resolution. Photoshop cannot add meaningful new image data, it can only interpolate information based on the surrounding pixels, and the result is usually a soft and mushy image.

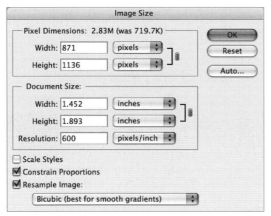

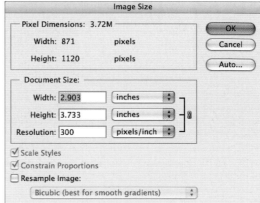

FIG 7.14 Our scan is about 1.5 by 1.9 inches at 600 DPI.

FIG 7.15 Without resampling we change the size and resolution of our image.

6. Click OK. Notice that nothing seems to happen to your file on the screen. This is because there was no change to the actual number of pixels in the file. What changed is the amount of pixels that will be printed in 1 inch when the image is printed. Use the Print preview to examine the result. By nearly halving the resolution, the dimensions of the printed image have doubled while the pixel dimensions of the file are the same. (Fig 7.16)

7. Choose File > Save As to change the format of the file from TIFF to Photoshop (PSD). The name of the file does not have to change, as the change in extension will create a new file. The original scan remains untouched as a TIFF, while the document that was just altered has become a derivative with the same name and a .psd file extension. Always save using the native or master format of the editing application associated with that kind of file. (Fig 7.17)

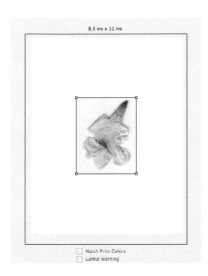

FIG 7.16 The print preview shows that the scan will print at a much larger size than it would have printed before changing the resolution settings in the Image Size dialog box.

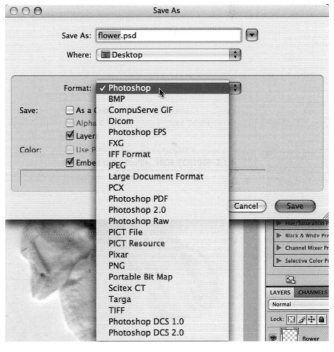

FIG 7.17 Choosing a file format from the Save As dialog box.

EXERCISE

04 From the camera to the computer

Top: FIG 7.18 Image Capture.

Middle: FIG 7.19 Select destination folder.

Bottom: FIG 7.20 After clicking Download Some... small thumbnails of each image appear. In this illustration, the highlighted images have been selected by holding the Command key and clicking once on each thumbnail.

Tip: A card reader will appear on the desktop as an external hard drive. Simply drag and drop the folder of image files from the card reader to the desktop or documents folder. Once images are copied to the desktop, it is safe to delete them from the card.

Digital cameras use memory cards to store file information. To send the images from the storage device to the computer, the camera is connected to the computer via a cable. Alternatively, the memory card can be taken out of the camera and inserted in a card reader connected to the computer to be read like a small hard drive or jump drive.

1. If you connect your camera to the computer with a cable, then you will use an application to read the images. On a Mac, iPhoto may automatically launch; however, our favorite Mac application is Image Capture. If you are using a Mac and don't see Image Capture on your Dock, look in the Applications folder for it. To transfer files from the camera to the computer with Image Capture, connect your camera to the computer (USB or Firewire), launch Image Capture, and press the Download All or Download Some... button.

2. By default, images will be downloaded and saved to the Pictures folder on the Mac hard drive. Use the scroll menu next to Download To to change the location of the files by clicking Other... and then selecting the desktop or a folder of your choice. (Fig 7.19)

3. Download Some... will display thumbnails of each image, and you can choose which images to download by selecting multiple files with Command-click. (Fig 7.20)

4. When you are finished choosing images for download, click the Download button.

5. Quit Image Capture. Open the folder you selected in Step 2 to locate the image files on your hard drive.

Tonal variations created with the source document, *trees_rgb.psd*, during exercises in Chapter 8.

8 Tonal Range

The tonal range is the change in value from black to white. It is the set of grayscale information in an image. Sometimes tonal range must be adjusted so that images have a full range of values in the shadows, midtones, and highlights.

Adjusting the tonal range addresses these common problems:

1. The image is too light or too dark. There may be a lot of detail in the light areas or in the shadows that can be made visible or printable through an adjustment.

2. Contrast is too low or too high. A low-contrast image has a flat tonal range. A high-contrast image has very light highlights and very dark shadows, and very little detail in the midtones.

3. The image displays a color cast — evidence of a hue in areas that should be neutral gray or white.

Watch Out: All monitors are different. If you consistently see a color cast in all your images and in an area you know to be a neutral gray (such as the gray surround in Photoshop's Maximized Screen mode), use the buttons on your monitor to calibrate it until the monitor can display a neutral gray.

FIG 8.1 *View from the Window at Le Gras*, Nicéphore Niépce, 1826, Saint-Loup-de-Varennes, France. Captured on 20-by-25-cm oil-treated bitumen.

Above, in what is the first recorded photograph, the exposure time was eight hours! Notice the limited tonal scale and high contrast between the dark and light values. (Fig 8.1)

The photograph at right was commissioned by the Farm Security Administration (FSA). (Fig 8.2) Florence Owens Thompson looks towards the future with worry, as her children bury their heads into her shoulders. Notice how the range of tonal values expresses the details in Florence's face and on the blanket on her lap. The FSA (1935–1944) was part of the New Deal, a set of programs initiated by Franklin Delano Roosevelt to stimulate and revitalize weak economies. Starting in 1935, the FSA hired photographers, such as Lange, Walker Evans, and Marion Post Wolcott to document America during the Great Depression.

FIG 8.2 *Migrant Mother*, Dorothea Lange, 1936. Silver gelatin print, Library of Congress, Prints & Photographs Division, FSA/OWI Collection, [LC-USZ62-95653].

01 Minor adjustments to the original file

1. For this exercise, open any image from your digital camera or scanner in Photoshop. You may also use the file on the wiki called *rgb-trees.psd*.

2. If the image needs to be rotated or cropped, make this adjustment now. To rotate the entire document 90 degrees (clockwise or counter-clockwise) or 180 degrees, choose Image > Rotate Canvas > and select the amount of rotation from the submenu.

3. To crop the image, use the Crop tool to click and drag around the area of the photograph that you intend to keep. The Crop tool displays the cropped area by setting a dark gray cast on the parts of the image that will be cropped out of the scene. Use the anchors along the side edges of the crop box to adjust where the crop box is located in relationship to the image. When the crop area looks appropriate, press Return on the keypad or click on the checkmark in the Options bar to commit to the crop operation.

Crop tool:
You can rotate the Crop tool's marquee area by placing the mouse just outside one of the corners. It will change into a curved arrow to indicate rotation. Once you press Return, the Crop tool will rotate and crop the image.

If it seems like the Crop tool is sticking to the edges of your image, click and hold on an anchor then hold down the Control key, which temporarily turns off "snapping" (a feature in the View menu that can be helpful when moving multiple objects into position). Let go of the mouse before letting go of the Control key.

If you clicked with the Crop tool and simply want to start over, the Escape key on the keypad will return you to standard editing mode.

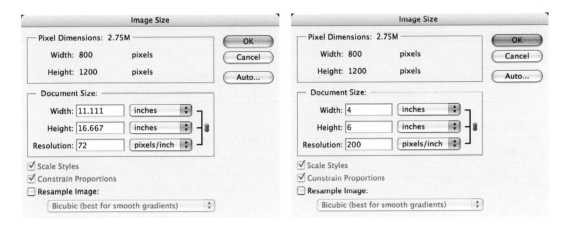

FIG 8.3 Notice the button for Resample Image is not checked in the Image Size dialog box on the left. In the Image Size dialog box on the right, where the resolution value was changed to 200 DPI, the width and height that the image will be when it is printed is reduced to 4 by 6 inches and the number of pixels (in the top part of the box) remains the same

4. At this point, it is not a bad idea to check the Image Size dialog box (Image > Image Size) to evaluate the resolution settings. (Fig 8.3) Ask yourself, at what size do I plan to print this image? If your image comes from a digital camera, there is a good chance the resolution is 72 DPI and the file's pixel dimensions are very large. To change this in the Image Size dialog box, be sure to uncheck Resample Image before adjusting the resolution to a higher number, such as 300 DPI. You should see that as the value of the resolution (measured in dots per inch) increases, the width and height of the file decreases and the amount of pixel information (in the top boxes, which should be grayed-out) remains the same. If all of this is not happening for you, and you are trying to increase the resolution of the file, something is not right!

EXERCISE
02 Understanding the histogram

rgb-trees_gray.psd @ 66.7% (Gray/8)

FIG 8.4 Image saved as grayscale.

Now we will take a look at the tonal range within the image. This can be done in any color mode, but to keep this process easy for the first time, we'll change the image to grayscale.

1. Choose Image > Mode > Grayscale to convert the image from RGB color mode to grayscale. (Fig 8.4)

2. Click OK through the Discard Color Information dialog box.

3. Choose File > Save as and add "_gray" to the end of the file name. Be sure to save it as a Photoshop native, or .psd file type.

4. Click on the Histogram tab within the Navigator and Info panel to the right side of the screen.

5. Observe the way the Histogram panel conveys information about the grayscale tones in the document. (Fig 8.5)

There are 255 levels of gray in any 8-bit image. Consumer scanners and digital cameras capture 8-bit images. The overall graph displays the amount information within the image (y-axis) at the various levels of gray from black (on the left side of the x-axis) to white (the right side of the x-axis).

> **Note:** Color images are rendered digitally by compositing separate color channels (red, green, and blue, for example), each with corresponding grayscale values. So, the histogram displays information about grayscale values, even if they correspond to color information.

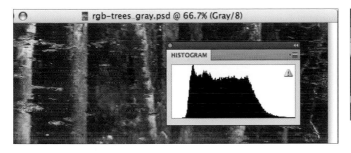

LEFT TO RIGHT:

FIG 8.5 The histogram for this image is clipped on the shadow side.

FIG 8.6 Clicking this icon will refresh the histogram.

Look at the histogram to make the following observations:

A. Does the histogram start at the beginning (dark values) and end (light values) of the x axis? This would mean that there actually exists image information in the darkest shadow areas and the lightest highlight areas. If the graph ends before the edge of the histogram's frame, it means there is no information at that end of the spectrum. There is probably a noticeable lack of detail in the image where the graph is clipped.

B. On the x-axis of the graph, where is most of the image information stored? In other words, where are the spikes in the graph? This should give you a sense of how dark or light overall the image appears. Imagine in the histogram above that the midway point is where 50 percent gray occurs in the image. In this image, the highest spike appears somewhere between the blackest shadow and 50 percent gray.

C. Does the histogram have any gaps where information does not exist? This means that there is no image information in those areas, where gray values between black and white are expected. This is usually a result of over-tweaking an image with tonal adjustments. Small gaps are not noticeable and are a reasonable result of increasing contrast in an image, especially when certain areas have bright highlights. In this image, the histogram has no gaps. In the next exercise, we will be making changes to the histogram and you will see gaps as a result.

Watch Out: The triangle-in-the-excla-mation-point icon is an alert. In Photoshop, it usually means that there are colors in the image that are out of that color space's gamut, but in the histogram it is meant to alert you that the panel is showing cached information. Clicking the icon will refresh the histogram information. In this exercise we are not changing anything, so it is not important. (Fig 8.6)

Note: There are professional scanners and cameras that capture 16-bit images, yielding more options for adjusting the tonal range; but 8-bit images are more common and easier to work with, so we will remain focused on them.

03 Adjusting the image with Levels

For this exercise we will complete the first step (Levels) on the grayscale image that was used in Exercise 2. Then we will use the color version of the file again.

1. Choose Image > Adjustments > Levels, which we will use to adjust the tonal range of our image. (Fig 8.7) The Levels dialog box displays the histogram that we just viewed in the previous exercise. Shadows are represented on the left side, midtones in the middle, and highlights on the right.

2. Move the left input level sliders (the small triangles just beneath the graph) to the beginning of the shadow information. This sets the darkest tonal range in the original image at 100 percent black.

3. Move the right input level slider to the beginning of the highlight information. This sets the lightest tonal range in the original image to 100 percent white.

4. To adjust the contrast, move the contrast slider (the triangle below the middle of the graph) to the left.

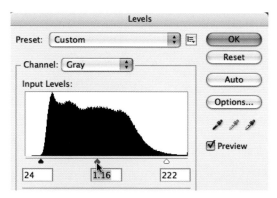

FIG 8.7 Levels dialog box.

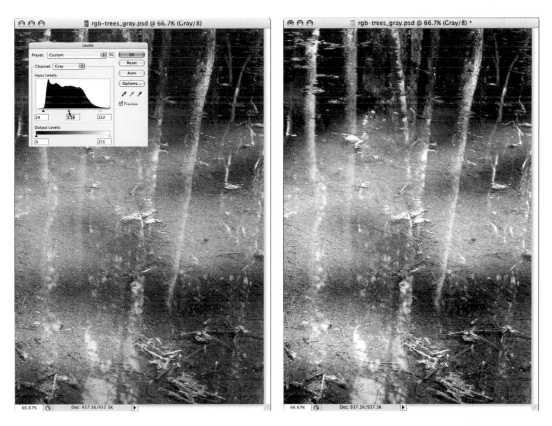

FIG 8.8 The image on the left with the Levels dialog box on top of it is the "before" version of the file. The image on the right is the "after" version. Notice that the shadows are considerably darker and it appears there is more contrast between the dark and light areas of image information.

EXERCISE
04 Adjusting the image with Curves

1. Download *rgb-trees.psd* from the wiki and open it in Photoshop. Look at the Histogram panel to see information about the grayscale values in the image.

2. From the upper right pull-down menu in the Histogram panel, choose All Channels View to see the histogram for the composite RGB channel as well as the single red, green, and blue channels that comprise the image. Even though the image is seen in color, the overall scale of gray values should be evaluated. Notice the graphs in the Histogram panel for each of the three separate channels (ask the same questions as we posed when evaluating a grayscale image in Exercise 2). (Fig 8.9)

3. Choose Image > Adjustments > Curves. Once again, the histogram is presented in the Curves dialog box. Curves, like Levels, can be used to adjust the tonal scale within the image.

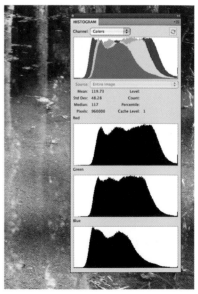

FIG 8.9 Look at the individual histograms for the red, green, and blue channels. Notice that there is more highlight information in the red channel, while all three channels peak around the same point in the shadow areas. Also notice that the red channel has the most color information across the x-axis, while the other two channels have steeper slopes towards the start and ending points of the curves.

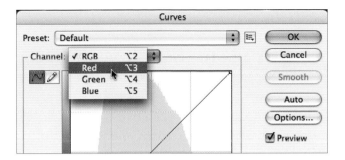

FIG 8.10 Channel pull-down panel menu in Curves dialog box.

BELOW, LEFT TO RIGHT:

FIG 8.11 Red Curves.

FIG 8.12 Green Curves.

FIG 8.13 Blue Curves.

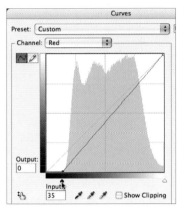
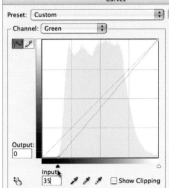
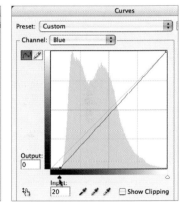

4. This time, don't touch the RGB composite curves. Instead, adjust each of the red, green, and blue graphs so that there is image information where the deepest shadows and lightest highlights appear. To do this, start by using the Channel pull-down menu in the Curves dialog box (Fig 8.10) to select Red (Command+1). Use the input sliders on the left and right sides to readjust the tonal scale so that the shadows and highlights begin with image information. (Fig 8.11)

5. Use the Channel pull-down menu to select Green (Command+2). Use the input sliders on the left and right sides to move the edges of the endpoints of the line graph to the point where image information exists. (Fig 8.12)

6. Use the Channel pull-down menu to select Blue (Command+3). Use the input sliders on the left and right sides to move the edges of the endpoints of the line graph to the point where image information exists. Click OK. (Fig 8.13)

Tip: Manually adjusting the Curves (or Levels, either panel could have been used for this last exercise) for each color channel produces a better result than making one adjustment in the composite channel.

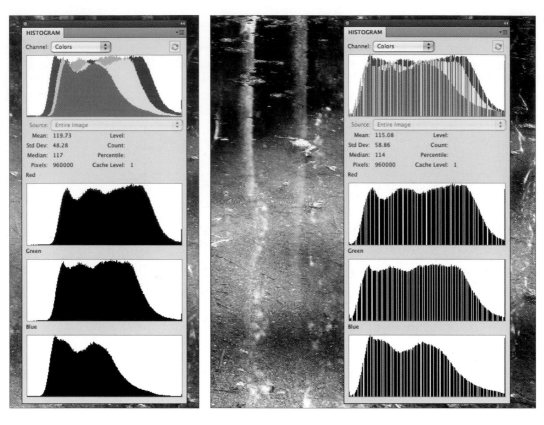

FIG 8.14 Look again at the histogram. It should show a graph with information that spans from the left side of the x-axis (shadows) to the right side (highlights). The image on the left includes our first set of graphs, the image on the right includes our modified histograms.

FIG 8.15 The image on the left is before the curves were altered, and the image on the right is after they have been modified. Information spans the entire x-axis on the histogram. Notice that the contrast is slightly modified, but the overall change to the image is slight. Be careful about pushing the sliders too far. The modifications should be minimal.

05 Targeting saturation levels

Image > Adjustments > Hue/Saturation can be used to increase or decrease the saturation of specific hues within the image. This panel is often used to make a dominant color appear more vibrant in an image, but it is hard to notice if the image is not being viewed at 100 percent. Even then, sometimes it is easier to see the results of this image adjustment in the final print. If you are using the file included on the wiki, the following details are the adjustments that we made to demonstrate this concept.

1. Choose > Adjustments > Hue/Saturation. Use the pull-down menu on the word "Master" to choose Green. You will work specifically on the green areas of the image. (Fig 8.16)

2. Use the Saturation and Lightness sliders to modify the image. The image on the facing page demonstrates our settings, but remember that our monitors may be calibrated differently. (Fig 8.17) It is best to eyeball these numbers, rather than follow our specific settings. Remember to be sure the image is showing at 100 percent (use the Zoom tool to zoom in or out) before making any adjustments.

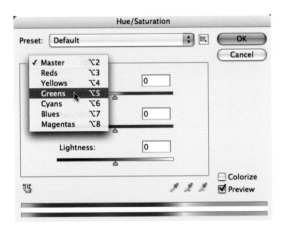

FIG 8.16 Green selected from Hue/Saturation drop-down menu.

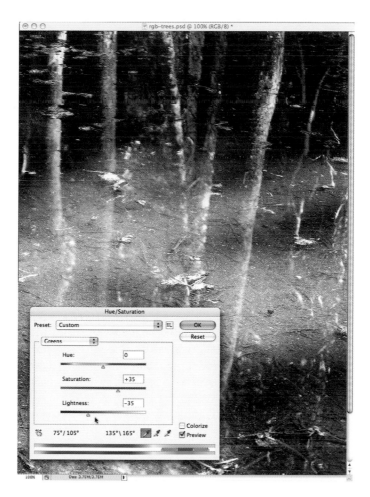

FIG 8.17 The preview results of changes made in
Hue/Saturation dialog box can be seen in the image.

06 Sharpening the image

Whenever an image is scanned or captured digitally, the process of transforming the continuous tone of reality or analog photography into pixels on a grid results in a loss of crispness. Unsharp Mask is a filter that is commonly used to compensate for this loss. This filter finds edges by looking for contrast and increases the contrast of those pixels, while leaving the flat areas untouched. The resulting image looks sharper, without introducing noise into the image.

1. Choose Filters > Unsharp Mask.

2. Be sure that the Preview button in the Unsharp Mask dialog box is checked. Look at the image while clicking the Preview button. Unchecking it displays the "before state" and checking it shows what the image will look like after the filter is applied. (Fig 8.18)

3. There are no set rules, but the guiding relationship is between the settings in this dialog box and file size. The larger the file size, the larger you will set the threshold, radius, and amount. With smaller file sizes (anything less than 30 megabytes) you will probably leave the threshold at 0 and the radius lower than 1.0, and adjust the percentage by eye between 20 and 50 percent.

4. You will know when you've gone too far. Too much contrast will create visible haloes at every edge. Applying this filter should produce a minor modification. In general, if the change is obvious, your settings were probably too high.

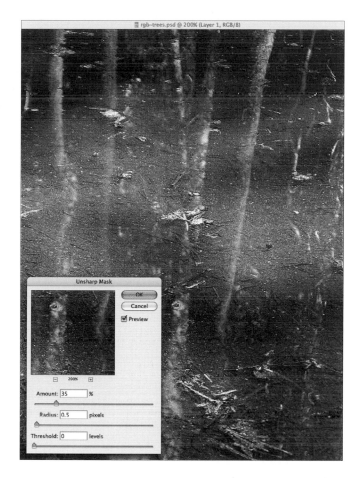

FIG 8.18 Clicking the Preview box will show results of filter adjustments.

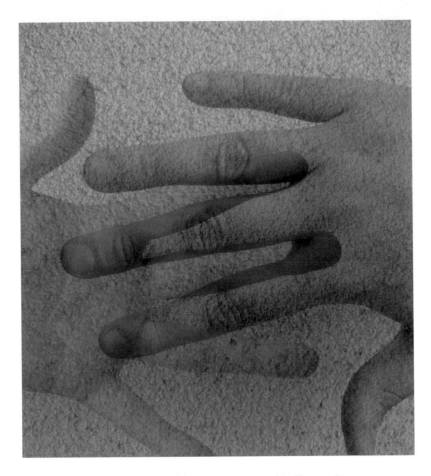

Double-exposure created in Chapter 9.

9 Layering and Collage

In the middle of the 1800s, Hippolyte Bayard created a photographic combination print in which two separate exposures were incorporated into a single photographic print. (Fig 9.1)

Following Bayard's experiments, combination prints and double exposures were made popular in the Victorian era as postcards.

Building on this tradition of combination prints, Cubists like Pablo Picasso and Georges Braque began adding found photographs, print materials, and other visual elements into their compositions. They called this technique *collage*, from the French word *coller*, or "to paste."

In the 1920s, Dada and Constructivist artists explored this collage technique in their work. They cut and pasted found photographs, their own imagery, and various printed elements together to form "anti-aesthetic" collages that challenged the viewer to decipher multiple messages within the final composition. El Lissitzky's *The Constructor* is an example of this type of work. Lissitzky's self portrait combines his own head with fragments of machinery, along with a hand that has been interpreted as the Hand of God passing over his face. (Fig 9.2)

The Lissitzky and Bayard prints employ different methods of artistic production. The combination print was made during the photographic printing process, while the photomontage combines various printed materials with adhesive. If Photoshop had been invented in the early 1900s, Dada and Constructivist artists would have been using it as their adhesive material.

FIG 9.1 *Self Portrait as a Drowned Man*, 1840, Hippolyte Bayard, combination print.

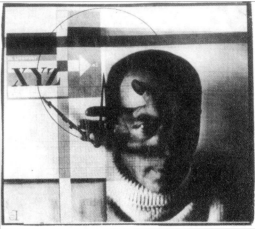

FIG 9.2 *The Constructor*, 1925, El Lissitzky, self portrait photomontage. The photomontage may have been re-photographed, so that the final print appears seamless.

EXERCISE
01 Using layers to create a double exposure

In the camera, a double exposure requires releasing the shutter to create one photograph, then releasing the shutter again to create another photograph on top of the first one. An example of this process can be seen in Henry Van der Weyde's image of the actor Richard Mansfield as Dr. Jekyll and Mr. Hyde. (Fig 9.3)

Note: Choose the Essentials work-space from the pull-down menu in the Application bar before working on the following exercises.

FIG 9.3 *Richard Mansfield as Dr. Jekyll and Mr. Hyde,* Henry Van der Weyde, between ca. 1885 and 1900. London, England.

⋆ **Finished exercise file available in the Download Materials area of the wiki.**

In Photoshop, we will create a double exposure by putting two images on separate layers and adjusting the blending mode of the top layer. We've provided two images on the wiki, but you might explore taking two images with a digital camera or scanning two photographs that address such subjects as time, dreams, paranoia, schizophrenia, otherworldliness, and duality. The double exposure is often used to express duality or the passing of time (also see the photographs of Duane Michals).

Tip: Working at 72 DPI, sometimes called screen resolution, is appropriate for any content that will appear only on a screen and that will not be printed.

1. Create a new document by choosing File > New. Set the width and height to 12 by 10 inches (be attentive to the units-of-measurement pull-down menus — 10 pixels results in a much smaller document than 10 inches). Set the resolution to 72 DPI and leave the color space in RGB mode. Name it *double-exposure*. (Fig 9.4)

2. Open *hand01.jpg*, downloaded from the wiki. The 12-by-10-inch blank file and the hand image are accessible through the tabs at the top of the document in Photoshop. There are many ways to copy the hand into the new document. We will copy a layer from the hand document and paste it into the new document using the Edit menu. In the *hand01.jpg* file choose Select > Select All then Edit > Copy. (Fig 9.5) The contents of the active layer (*Background*) were selected and copied. Click on the tab of the new document before choosing Edit > Paste. (Fig 9.6)

The hand is very large when it is placed into the new document. The hand file contains more pixels than the double exposure file. We did this on purpose to demonstrate that the number of pixels in a document has a noticeable effect on the way that the file is previewed in Photoshop.

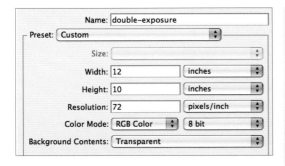

FIG 9.4 Create new document.

Note:

The Move tool can be used to drag a layer into a new document from the document window or from the Layers panel. First click on the tab at the top of one of the documents and undock the tab so that you can see both documents on the screen at once. Then use the Move tool to drag the layer to the center of the other document. Holding Shift while dragging a layer into another document will center the layer in the new document.

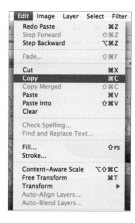

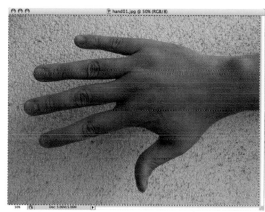

FIG 9.5 Select All then Edit > Copy.

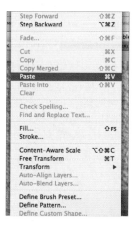

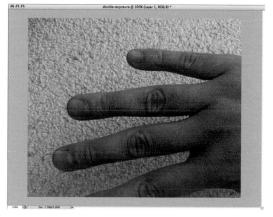

FIG 9.6 Edit > Paste.

FIG 9.7 Edit > Free Transform.

Note:

You can always create a new file with a higher resolution value, but for exercises that will not be printed, it is faster to work in a file with resolution no greater than the screen. The larger the resolution, the larger the file size; and larger file sizes require greater computer processing power and slow down your work.

3. In the Layers panel, double-click on the name Layer 1 to rename it *hand01*. To scale the hand so that it fits into the document, click Edit > Free Transform. (Fig 9.7)

4. When the image to be transformed does not run off the edges of the file document — as this one does — it is easy to transform it by using the arrows at one of the four corners of the transformation box to click and drag towards the center of the image. This type of transformation is similar to transforming objects in Illustrator.

In this situation, however, we cannot see all edges of the transformation box, so it is easier to use the transform tools in the Options bar at the top of the document. First, click the chain-like Link icon between the width and height percentage boxes to maintain the aspect ratios (or proportions). Now enter 65% into either the width or height box and notice that the other box also takes on the same value. Press the Return or Enter key on your keypad to finalize the transformation.

5. Open *hand02.jpg* and use the Move tool or another method to bring the image of the second hand into the *double-exposure* document. Notice that it has already been scaled for you. While the second hand is still active in the Layers panel, click Edit > Transform > Flip Horizontal. (Fig 9.8) The Transform submenu will modify any layer, or

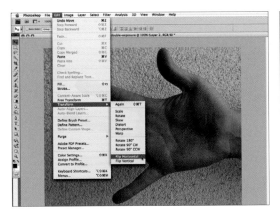 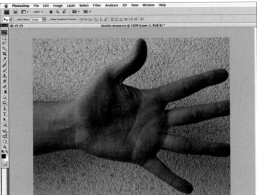

FIG 9.8 Edit > Transform > Flip Horizontal.

a selection on any layer. It does not modify the entire document. Notice that this transformation only occurred on the second hand and not on the *hand01* layer. In the Layers panel, double-click on the name of Layer 2 to rename it *hand02*.

6. Use the Move tool to move the separate layers into position. Clicking one time in the Layers panel activates a layer. Notice that the active layer can be moved with the Move tool. Once both layers are named and positioned, use the Layer Blending Modes pull-down panel menu in the top left area of the Layers panel to choose Multiply for the top layer, *hand02*. (Fig 9.9) Leave the *hand01* layer in Normal mode. Blending modes define how layers interact. We will continue to explore these in the third exercise.

The double exposure happens in the area where the two images overlap. Multiply Blending mode allows us to see the two images together, as if they were photographed on the same piece of film. In the next exercise, we will crop the image so that only the double-exposure remains.

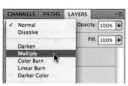

FIG 9.9 Multiply in Layers blending mode pull-down panel menu.

02 Cropping and adjusting the hue

FIG 9.10 Final image for Exercise 2.

The above illustration demonstrates the results of Exercises 1 and 2. (Fig 9.10)

1. Click on the Crop tool in the Tools panel and notice the options for this tool in the Options bar. Enter "6 in" into the Width box, "9 in" into the Height box, and "72" into the Resolution box. Drag a crop box around the area of the document where the two layers overlap.

Notice that the Crop tool will only create a rectangular shape in the aspect ratio of 6:9 as you are dragging. Finalize the crop by pressing Return or Enter on your keypad or by clicking the Commit icon in the top right area of the Options bar. (Fig 9.11)

2. Click on the Add Adjustment Layer pull-down panel menu at the bottom of the Layers panel and scroll to Hue/Saturation.

3. In the Hue/Saturation dialog box, check the Colorize box and then use the Hue slider to create a cyan wash over the image. (Fig 9.12) Click OK when you are satisfied with the colorization. Remember that you can always double-click the thumbnail icon of the adjustment layer in the Layers panel to access this dialog box and modify the settings.

Tip: While dragging the Crop tool, if you hold down the Spacebar you can reposition the crop area without changing its shape. Let go of the Spacebar before letting go of the mouse. Once you let go of the mouse, click and drag inside the crop area to reposition it.

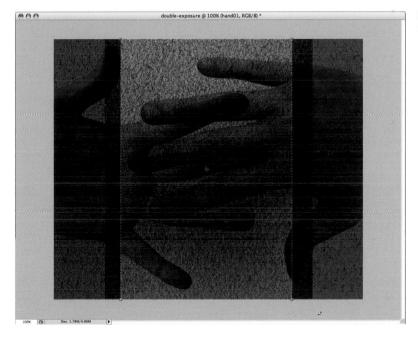

FIG 9.11 Crop tool and its option bar.

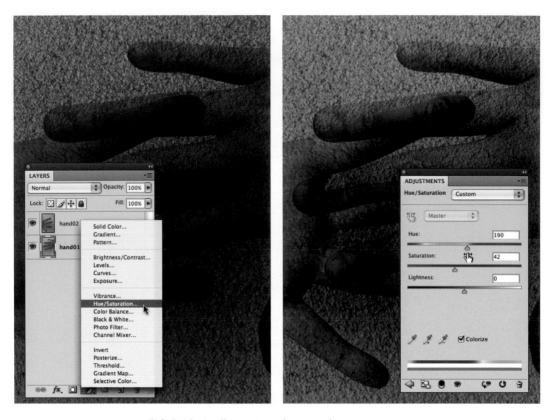

FIG 9.12 Hue/Saturation adjustment layer.

Exquisite Corpse (in two parts)

Exquisite Corpse is a parlor game that the Surrealists developed in 1925. In this game, each player submits images (drawings, paintings, photographs) of heads, torsos, and legs, and they are combined to produce surprising new bodies. We have played this game with students using images of each other that we captured in class on a digital camera, as well as by using images from pop culture, found on the web. Collaging celebrity and politician body parts can provoke thoughtful discussion. Images of students are on the wiki, but it's more fun to try this with pictures of your friends or family!

03 Creating and manipulating layers

1. We'll work on top of the double exposure file that we just created, so save the file as *exquisite-corpse.psd*. Your file should look like our illustration. (Fig 9.13)

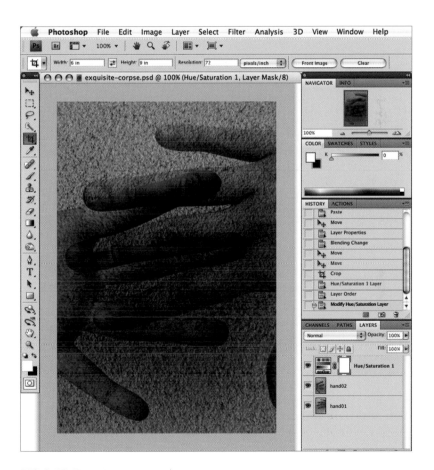

FIG 9.13 *Exquisite-corpse.psd.*

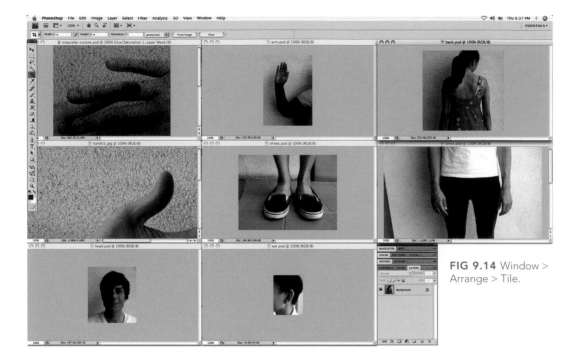

FIG 9.14 Window >
Arrange > Tile.

FIG 9.15 Organized
Layers panel.

2. Keep *exquisite-corpse.psd* open and choose File > Open in Photoshop to open all of the documents used in this exercise. (On the wiki, the files are: *arm.psd, back.psd, ear.psd, head.psd, shoes.psd, and torso.psd.*) You can view all of the documents by clicking through tabs. We wanted to see all files at once in a neat arrangement. To view your images as we did, choose Window > Arrange > Float All in Windows, followed by Window > Arrange > Tile. (Fig 9.14)

3. Move all of the body parts into the *exquisite-corpse* document, just as we moved the hands into the *double exposure* document in Exercise 1. Once all of the parts are on separate layers in the *exquisite-corpse* document, rename each layer to indicate which body part it contains. Use the Eyeball icon in the Layers panel to hide and show the layer. This will help you to quickly assess which image is on the layer.

4. Click on a layer and drag it above or below another layer. The order of the layers in the Layers panel is referred to as the stacking order. This determines which image appears in the foreground and which images go behind it. Organize the layers so that they appear like the stacking order in the illustration. (Fig 9.15) Notice that our layer stack has a left and right arm! We created both from the same image. Name your first arm *right arm*, then choose the Layer menu > Duplicate Layer… and name the duplicate layer *left arm*. Choose Edit > Transform > Flip Vertical to flip each arm (be sure to activate the layer first) and then Edit > Transform > Flip Horizontal to distinguish one from the other. (Fig 9.16)

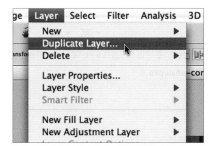
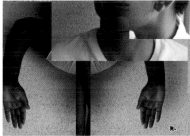

FIG 9.16 Layer > Duplicate Layer…

Note:

Bitmap images can be thought of as maps of pixels on a grid. When bitmap images are scaled, the pixels are remapped. Scaling a bitmap image down remaps the pixels to existing locations on the grid. Scaling a bitmap up requires new pixels in order to fill the larger grid. Photoshop can only interpolate, or guess what the new pixels should look like, based on what their neighbors look like. Scale up too much, and an image looks mushy and horrible.

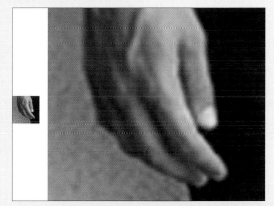

FIG 9.17

5. Click on each layer to activate it, then use the Move tool to reposition the layer and choose Edit > Free Transform in order to scale it. Some of the layers will need to be scaled if you want your exquisite corpse to look just like ours. Remember to hold the Shift key while dragging on one of the four anchor corners in the Free Transform box or to link the width and height if you are using the Options bar to make the transformation. Also, keep in mind that it is always safe to scale an image down in Photoshop, but it is never a good idea to scale an image up, as this will add random pixel information and degrade the quality of the image.

6. Once each layer is renamed, repositioned, and scaled, click on the top layer once to activate it, then hold Shift and click on the last layer in the stacking order above the adjustment layer from Exercise 2. We clicked the *ear* layer and Shift-clicked on the *torso* layer. Click on the Layers panel pull-down menu in the top right corner of the panel and choose Create Group From Layers... In the dialog box, name the new group *corpse*. This will make a new folder in the Layers panel for the group of body parts. (Fig 9.18)

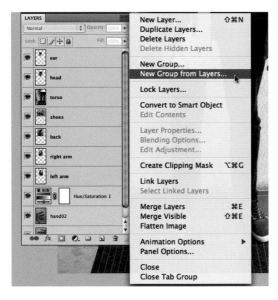

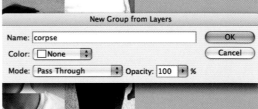

FIG 9.18 New Group from Layers... in Layers panel pull-down menu, and New Group from Layers dialog box.

EXERCISE 04 Adding an adjustment to some layers

FIG 9.19 Final image for Exercise 4.

The above illustration demonstrates the results of Exercises 3 and 4. (Fig 9.19)

In this exercise, we want to add an adjustment layer to the top of the Layers panel, except there is one major problem: doing so would cancel out the adjustment layer in use towards the bottom of the panel! One way to make an adjustment layer act on only some layers is to merge the parts of the image that should respond to the adjustment, add the adjustment on top of that layer, and then use a clipping mask between the adjustment and the merged layer.

1. Expand the *corpse* group (click the sideways arrow on the left side of the name) so that you can see all of the layers within the group. Click once on the top-most layer to activate it, then Shift-click on the last body layer in the group (ours is *torso*) so that all of the body parts are highlighted.

2. There is one trick here: we never merge layers without keeping our individual layers intact underneath. Hold the Option key on your keypad before you click on the Layers panel pull-down menu (top right of the Layers panel) and choose Merge Layers.

Adding the Option key results in a new layer above those that were activated, which merges all of the activated layers together. (Fig 9.20) Notice that the layer called *ear* was at the top of the list, so the name of the new layer is *ear (merged)*. Use the Eyeball icon to turn this layer on and off, and notice that while you have a layer that has merged all of the body parts, you also have each body part on a separate layer. This will give you flexibility if you need to make revisions after merging the layers.

FIG 9.20 Option > Merge Layers.   **FIG 9.21** The merged result.

3. Drag the merged layer outside of the group so that it is on top of the stacking order in the Layers panel. Close the *corpse* group folder and turn off its Eyeball icon. (Fig 9.21)

4. Click on the merged layer to activate it, then add an adjustment layer for Hue/Saturation. Use the Colorize button again and add a wash of orange. Notice that this will colorize the entire document. (Fig 9.23)

Clipping masks

Masks are used in conjunction with layers in Photoshop to hide part of a composition. There are three masking techniques in Photoshop. We will review other methods of masking in Chapters 10 and 11.

The easiest mask to create is a clipping mask. A clipping mask works between two layers. It uses a base layer to define the mask area. The layers clipped to the base act only on the base layer. We will use a clipping mask here to limit the effects of the adjustment layer strictly to the merged layer.

5. To apply the clipping mask, press the Option key while clicking on the line between the adjustment layer and the merged layer. You will see the cursor change to an icon that looks like a figure eight. (Fig 9.22) When you see this cursor change, click the mouse. This will create a clipping mask between the adjustment layer and the merged layer. Now the adjustment layer will only affect the merged layer. The background images should appear cyan again.

6. Use the Blending Mode pull-down menu in the Layers panel to set the mode to Linear Light and enter "50%" for the layer opacity (to the right of the Blending Mode pull-down menu). A decreased opacity enables the viewer to see through the image on this layer and helps to blend the two layers. (Fig 9.24)

> **Note:** Sometimes layer blending modes can create a murky image where the foreground and background are hard to decipher. Experiment, and remember that every image communicates a message.

> **Tip:** Don't forget that you can use the History panel if you need to undo multiple steps. Even if you saved over a layered file with a flattened file, you can use History to recover the layered file as long as the document is still open. Once you close the document, the history states are lost.

> **Tip:** A clipping mask can also be used to fit a photographic image into a text area. It is easy to experiment with this idea. Create a large, bold word that nearly fills the document. To use the word as the base layer, place it beneath a photograph that is as large as the document. Option-click between the photograph and type layer to create a clipping mask. The photograph will be clipped to the type layer.

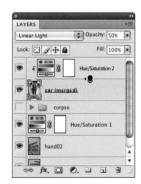

FIG 9.22 The merged result.

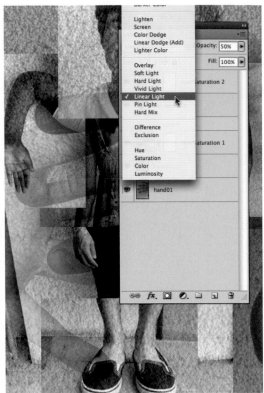

FIG 9.23 Hue/Saturation adjustment layer.

FIG 9.24 Linear Light in the Blending Mode pull-down panel menu.

The final digital image created using exercises in Chapter 10.

10 Repetition and Cloning

Digital tools empower creators to transform visual imagery with ease. Media-makers have the ability to change the appearance of virtually anything with techniques such as copy, paste, mask, and clone. Given the opportunity to change any image, message, or text, where would you begin?

Your answer depends upon your goals. Some creators use the tools for fun to make graphics such as LOLcats. Others create professional graphics such as advertisements, news, or entertainment content. In this chapter we review the Billboard Liberation Front and the Anti-Advertising Agency, which have created parodies of pre-existing advertisements. These artists reclaim media messages by altering the images themselves. The messages might appear in museums, on city streets, or in cyberspace. The aesthetics of the altered media rely upon the viewer's visual and intellectual understanding of the original, pre-altered visual references.

Not too surprisingly, this counter cultural, playful method of protest has already been co-opted by the advertising industry. In her book *No Logo*, Naomi Klein illustrates how advertisers, like contemporary artists, exploit the audience's familiarity with cultural references to create brand awareness.

From the Billboard Liberation Front manifesto:
> *And so we see, the Ad defines our world, creating both the focus on 'image' and the culture of consumption that ultimately attract and inspire all individuals desirous of communicating to their fellow man in a profound fashion. It is clear that He who controls the Ad speaks with the voice of our Age.*

FIG 10.1 *Marlebore*, The Billboard Liberation Front, used by permission of the artists. The Billboard Liberation Front is a group of San Franciscan message-makers who aim to repurpose and "improve" billboard messages by painting or pasting on top of pre-existing billboards. The group began its mission in 1977 and has grown into a worldwide phenomenon by collecting images on the web.

FIG 10.2 *People Products 123*, The Anti-Advertising Agency, CC-BY.

Note:

Read the entire Billboard Liberation Front manifesto at www.billboardliberation.com/manifesto.html

The Anti-Advertising Agency creates subversive media that opposes the role of advertising in contemporary society. Many of their projects are participatory, which means that viewers become doers or art-makers. In *People Products 123*, participants download package designs that feature images and information about the workers responsible for producing the consumable product. The participant prints the package designs and shop-drops the re-covered product in the store, where an unassuming shopper will purchase the product contained in the newly informative packaging. (Fig 10.2)

EXERCISE
01 Replace part of one image using the Clone tool

In this exercise, we will use two U.S. government images from the public domain. We begin with a group photograph of the first all-female crew of an Air Force C-130 Hercules on a combat mission, photographed and made public by the Air Force. (Fig 10.3) The second image is a cropped photograph of Amelia Earhart from NASA. (Fig 10.4) In the final image, Amelia Earhart's head replaces the head on the center figure of the Air Force crew and the image is rendered in black-and-white.

Note: Choose the Essentials work-space from the pull-down menu in the Application bar before working on the following exercises.

1. Download materials for this chapter from the wiki. Open the group image of the crew in Photoshop. Zoom in on the central figure of the crew. We will start by replacing her head with a sample of the flag.

LEFT: FIG 10.3 The first all-female crew of an Air Force C-130 Hercule.

ABOVE: FIG 10.4 Amellia Earhart.

★ Finished exercise file available in the Download Materials area of the wiki.

FIG 10.5 Rectangular selection with the Marquee tool.

FIG 10.6 Marquee selection of flag.

FIG 10.7 Flag selection on new layer.

2. Create a rectangular selection around her head with the Rectangular Marquee tool. (Fig 10.5) As long as any selection tool (aside from the Move tool) is active, when you place the cursor inside the selected area, the tool changes into a white arrow with a small rectangular selection icon. Drag the selection marquee straight above the figure's head so that part of the flag is selected and the head is no longer in the selection boundary. (Fig 10.6) You are only moving the selection — no part of the image is moving.

3. Copy the flag from the background layer and paste it. Choosing Edit > Copy followed by Edit > Paste will create a new layer. Name the new layer *flag*. Use the Move tool to position the flag on top of the head. (Fig 10.7) The head has been replaced by a sample of the flag on a new layer.

Key Command: Command+J is the hot key to float, or copy and paste, part of a layer onto a new layer directly on top of the selection.

FIG 10.8 Clone tool.

4. Choose the Clone tool from the Tools panel. (Fig 10.8) Set the brush to about 20 pixels. Check the Align button and make sure that Sample All Layers is selected from the pull-down menu in the Options bar.

Create a new layer called *clone*.

The Clone tool is used to replace small areas of a layer with a sample of an image. The Clone tool is applied with a brush. Using a soft brush will make the cloned sample appear to blend into the original image, even though we will do all of our cloning on a new layer. Be careful with your application of the Clone tool. The soft brush creates a little bit of a blur on the image. A small amount of blur is necessary in order for the sample to blend in, but clicking with the soft brush repeatedly will result in a blurry area in your image. The purpose of cloning is to create an unidentifiable image hoax. Creating a blurry area on the image will draw attention to that area. In order to achieve the hoax, the clone must be made in such a way that the viewer is deceived!

5. Now for the most important part of this exercise — sample parts of the flag in order to blend the areas around the edges where the pasted image is an obvious manipulation. The Clone tool requires that part of an image is sampled before it is applied to another part of the document. Sample part of the flag near the edge between white and red by Option-clicking in that area. Then position the mouse on top of the corner where the pasted flag needs to be blended, and click once to cover it with a soft, brushed sample. Pay close attention to the brush work. Determine if the first click is blended by looking at the surrounding values. Decide if your new sample is blending in. If it is,

Key Command:

The open and close bracket keys on the keypad — "[" and "]" — are the hot keys used to increase and decrease the brush size.

Tip: Click on the down arrow next to the brush in the Options bar to modify the brush settings, such as the hardness or softness and the brush size.

FIG 10.9 Before the Cloning tool.

FIG 10.10 After the Cloning tool.

move on to the next area. Always Option-click to create a new sample before brushing. If the first click did not blend perfectly (it probably did not — this takes some getting used to), use Command+Z to undo the last step and try it again.

Work around all the edges by creating a new Option-click to sample the flag and then clicking with the brush to apply the clone. Command+Z will be used often in this process! We finished the clone in about 30 mouse clicks. (Fig 10.9-10)

6. View the clone layer by turning the Eyeball icons off for all the other layers. When viewed alone, our clone layer looks like random, abstract shapes. (Fig 10.11) When viewed with the original layer, the clone layer helps create the illusion of a seamless background for the next exercise: replacing the head.

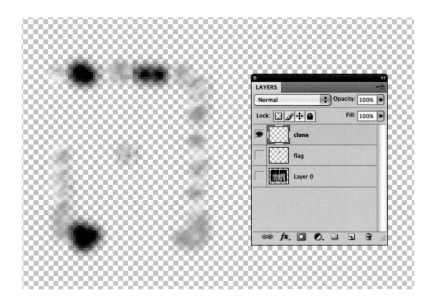

FIG 10.11 The clone layer viewed alone.

02 Add Amelia Earhart to the image of the crew

1. Since the image of Amelia Earhart was originally a black-and-white photograph, we should change the image of the Air Force crew into grayscale. Use a black-and-white adjustment layer on top of the clone layer. Apply the adjustment in the Layers panel. (Fig 10.12) Save your work in Photoshop format. The file should have the .psd extension.

2. Open the image of Amelia Earhart, select her head and neck with the Rectangular Marquee tool, and choose Edit > Copy. (Fig 10.13) Toggle back to the Photoshop document and choose Edit > Paste. Use Edit > Free Transform (Command+T) and hold Shift while scaling Amelia Earhart's head down so it is in proportion with the body. Name the new layer *Amelia*. (Fig 10.14)

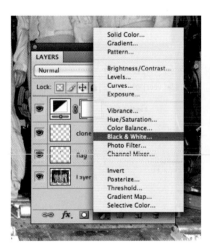

FIG 10.13 Rectangular Marquee selection.

FIG 10.12 Black-and-white adjustment layer.

EXERCISE
03 Add a layer mask

Add a mask over an image to hide part of it. Masks do not delete or alter image data, they simply hide or show parts of images. Masks operate in black (hidden), white (revealed), and shades of gray (transparent, partially hidden). We will use a layer mask on the *Amelia* layer to blend her into the new background.

Watch Out: Do not delete image data. Do not use the eraser. Using the eraser is destructive editing. Now that you are learning to use masks, you can practice making non-destructive edits. This is so important that it is the dominant topic in Chapter 11.

> **Note:**
>
> Other types of masks include clipping masks (see Exercise 4 in Chapter 9) and vector masks, where vector data instead of bitmap data determines what is black and what is white. We will work with layer masks in this chapter and in Chapter 11.

1. Create a layer mask on the *Amelia* layer with the "Add layer mask" button at the bottom of the Layers panel. This mask will hide the background around Amelia's head. Notice that the layer now has an icon for the image and an icon for the mask. The mask is currently active — there is a frame around the mask icon. (Fig 10.15)

FIG 10.14 Paste the copied image of Amelia onto the new layer of the Air Force image.

2. Click the Brush tool and make sure that the default colors are loaded into the foreground/background color chips (black as foreground, white as the background color) by clicking the small Black/white Color Chip icon to the top left of the actual color chips in the Tools panel.

3. Notice that the icon for the mask is white in the Layers panel. Since everything on the layer is revealed, the entire mask is white. Use the Brush tool with black paint on the mask in order to hide the background. If you make a mistake, switch to white paint to retrieve hidden parts of the image. Practice painting with black-and-white paint. Paint with different sized brushes and notice what happens with a soft or hard brush, or with the brush set at different opacities.

We used a soft brush for the background area and kept it far away from Amelia's head. As we brushed closer to her hair, we reduced the opacity of the brush in the Options bar to about 40 percent. At a reduced opacity, clicking a few times near her head with black paint removes the background while keeping her hair from being cut to an unnatural shape.

Key Command:

Press the letter *d* on the keypad to load black-and-white as the default colors in the foreground and background color chips. Press the *x* key to switch the foreground and background colors.

FIG 10.15 Create a layer mask on the *Amelia* layer.

EXERCISE
04 Burning and dodging

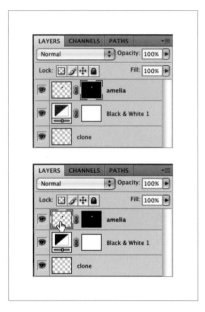

FIG 10.16 Deactivate mask layer.

The last step is to correct Amelia's skin tones. Before you can do that, you will have to click back on the content portion — leaving the mask — of the *Amelia* layer. Photoshop indicates which part of the layer you are working on by bracketing the corners of its icon in the Layers panel. The title bar in the document also reflects the area that is currently active. If the mask is active, the Burn tool used in the next step will affect only the mask, so make sure *Amelia* layer's content is active! (Fig 10.16)

1. Notice that Amelia's photograph was taken outdoors, while the Air Force crew was indoors. The harsh light on Amelia's face is noticeably different from the light on the crew's faces. We will make a quick adjustment to Amelia's skin tone in order to create a more realistic collage with the Burn tool. Burning and dodging are photographic manipulations native to the traditional darkroom. In the darkroom, additional exposure time increases the amount of light hitting the paper. This can be done selectively, resulting in a "burned" area of the image. Burning darkens the value of that portion of the print. Light can also be blocked during the exposure by "dodging" over image areas where the tonal values are too dark with a small tool, resulting in a lightened area of the print.

Use the Burn tool (Fig 10.17) with a soft brush set at an exposure of about 10 percent. Quickly brush over Amelia's face with the Burn tool. Each time you click the mouse, the tones will darken.

2. Repeat Step 1 with the tool options set at both midtones and highlights.

FIG 10.17 Burn tool.

Finished composite photograph created
in Chapter 11. Original image of Salvador
Dali with ocelot friend at St Regis, World
Telegram & Sun, by Roger Higgins, from
the US Library of Congress [LC-USZ62-
114985].

11 Non-Destructive Editing

In Chapter 9 we referred to Hippolyte Bayard's *Self Portrait as a Drowned Man* from 1840 as the first combination print. The history of photographic manipulation reaches almost as far back as the first photographic images. Digital tools extend this history of image manipulations from the subtlety of the slightest tonal range adjustment to the creation of completely fictional imagery.

As the digital artist becomes capable of creating fantastical visions and manipulating images of the world, she must be aware of the ethics behind her craft. These rules shift depending on the context; Photoshopping a photojournalistic image carries different ethical considerations than Photoshopping an art image.

The National Press Photographers Association maintains a code of ethics for journalism students and professionals to abide by. Photojournalists seek to document moments that existed in actuality, and any alteration, big or little, important or unimportant, is in that context a visual lie. A *National Geographic* 1982 cover image was manipulated to move two pyramids closer together so they would fit into the frame. This seemingly harmless alteration has nevertheless been added to the history of ethics violations in documentary journalism, because the magazine's short-term gain was far outweighed by the damage done to the credibility of their profession.

See this link for a group exhibit in 2000 at the Laurence Miller Gallery titled Alternative Realities. http://www.laurencemillergallery.com/alternativerealities.htm

Time magazine made an infamous photo-manipulation for their June 27, 1994, cover featuring O.J. Simpson's mug shot. *Time* illustrator Matt Mahurin adjusted the photo of Simpson, resulting in an image much darker than it actually was. Mahurin said he "wanted to make it more artful, more compelling." But readers and media critics immediately objected to what they saw as racism and visual bias when they saw the magazine side-by-side with *Newsweek*'s photograph of Simpson. *Time* took the unprecedented action of pulling the cover from the market to issue a new cover with a different image.

For art-making, editorial illustration, or opinion commentary, manipulation can be used to challenge the viewer's expectations. An image can be reinterpreted as it relates to other images in a composition through the modification of scale or proximity. Philippe Halsman's *Dali Atomicus* uses image manipulation to create an illusion. (Fig 11.1) The viewers' expectations about floating chairs or flying cats are challenged. This image was captured with a 4-by-5 camera in his studio after "six hours and twenty-eight throws," wrote Halsman in *Halsman on the Creation of Photographic Ideas* (1963).

http://en.wikipedia.org/wiki/Image:OJ_Simpson_Newsweek_TIME.png

http://bztv.typepad.com/.shared/image.html?/photos/uncategorized/oj_arrested.JPG

http://www.time.com/time/covers/0,16641,19940627,00.html

http://www.nppa.org/professional_development/self-training_resources/eadp_report/digital_manipulation.html

Dada artist Kurt Schwitters' *Dada Soirée* demonstrates that typography can also be manipulated in the construction of a collage. (Fig 11.2) While both of these works were made before the advent of digital tools, alternate realities and manipulations are often created with computer software.

Within the exercises of this chapter, we will focus not only on manipulating an image, but also on practicing non-destructive work habits. To edit the digital file non-destructively is to work in such a way that the original image is preserved. Any edits or modifications to the original file are placed on separate layers or in masks, which we will explore further in Exercise 2.

FIG 11.2 *Dada Soirée*, Kurt Schwitters, 1922.

FIG 11.1 *Dali Atomicus*, Philippe Halsman, 1948. This version of the photograph shows an element missing in the final print: the hands holding the chair. Also, the final print contains one of Dali's paintings (*Leda Atomica*) in the frame on the easel.

EXERCISE 01 Using quick masks and alpha channels

Note: Choose the Essentials workspace from the pull-down menu in the Application bar before working on the following exercises.

1. In Photoshop, choose File > Open to open the downloaded file from the wiki of Salvador Dali holding a cat.

2. Use the Lasso tool from the Tools panel to make a selection around the left part of Dali's mustache. (Fig 11.3) The Lasso tool can be used to make freehand selections. Click+drag with the Lasso tool all the way around the mustache. The selection is completed when you bring the mouse back to the point where you first pressed the mouse button. Your selection will not be a perfect tracing of the mustache. The Lasso tool serves to make a fast draft of a selection that can be used as a starting point for masks. We will modify the selection in the next step.

3. Enter Quick Mask mode by pressing the *Q* key on the keypad or clicking on the Quick Mask icon at the bottom of the Tools panel, just beneath the Foreground/Background Color Chip icons. Quick Mask will turn all of the image areas that are not selected bright red, leaving the selected areas easily visible. (Fig 11.4)

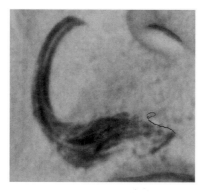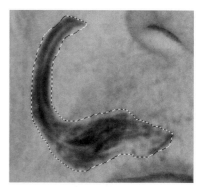

FIG 11.3 Selection of Dali's mustache with the Lasso tool.

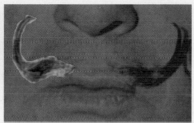

FIG 11.4 Quick Mask mode

Note: Quick Mask is a temporary mask that can help modify a selection. It stores your hidden/revealed states in a temporary alpha channel. When you leave Quick Mask mode, it uses the black, white, and gray of the alpha channel to construct a marquee selection, and throws that alpha channel away.

4. The Quick Mask is used to modify the selection area. On any mask, the color black will hide part of the image and the color white will reveal part of the image. (Fig 11.5) The red overlay in the Quick Mask is used as a guide, so you can easily see where you have painted with black or white to hide or reveal parts of the mask. A red transparent overlay shows where the mask areas, painted with black, are located. Painting with white paint on the Quick Mask will take away red, masked parts. (Fig 11.6) Painting with black paint on the Quick Mask will add red parts. The image that is not covered by the red mask becomes part of the selection when you leave Quick Mask mode.

As you are painting, press the letter *Q* to exit Quick Mask mode. You will see the resulting selection. Press *Q* again to re-enter Quick Mask mode and continue painting to modify the mask.

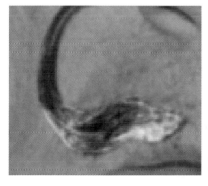
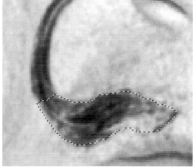

FIG 11.5 Black paint added to the red area of the Quick Mask on top of Dali's mustache results in a smaller selection area.

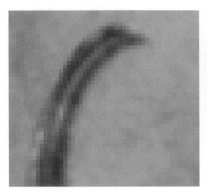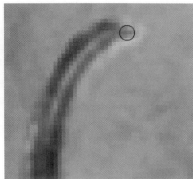

FIG 11.6 Painting with white paint on top of the Quick Mask adds part of the mustache to the selection.

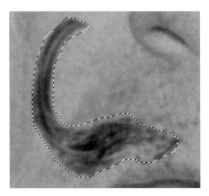

FIG 11.7 Here is an image of our Lasso tool selection before Quick Mask and the final selection after making modifications with the Paintbrush in Quick Mask.

5. Exit Quick Mask and return to standard editing mode when you are finished modifying the selection. Your selection should more closely fit the contour of the mustache. (Fig 11.7)

6. Choose Select > Save Selection and name the new selection *left mustache*. Click OK. (Fig 11.8)

FIG 11.8 Save Selection dialog box.

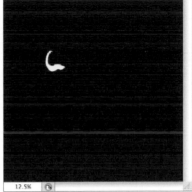

FIG 11.9 Mustache alpha channel.

7. When a selection is saved, it becomes an alpha channel. An alpha channel is a grayscale channel that defines which parts of an image are visible. All the types of channels Photoshop creates can be viewed separately by clicking on their names in the Channels panel. Click on the Channels tab in the Layers panel, then click on the name *left mustache*. The file now shows the left mustache alpha channel. (Fig 11.9) Everything that is not included in the mask is black, and the once-selected shape of the left side of the mustache is white.

8. Click back on the gray channel to return to standard editing mode. Deselect the left side of the mustache by choosing Select > Deselect or use Command+D. Then reselect the left side of the mustache by loading it from the Channels panel by Command-clicking the icon of the *left mustache* alpha channel. Practice deselecting and then loading the alpha channel, or reselecting by using Command+D then Command-click on the alpha channel.

9. Use File > Save as to save the Photoshop file. We named ours daliwithcat.psd.

Building an image with layers, masks, and transformation

Watch Out: If the *left mustache* layer was not active (highlighted) you may have moved the layer containing the original file. Make sure the layer that you want to edit is active before editing.

1. Start with the selection of the left side of the mustache loaded.

2. Copy and paste the half-mustache to a new layer by either using the Edit menu or Command+J.

3. Rename your layers. We renamed the Background layer *original file* and the copied layer *left mustache*. (Fig 11.10)

4. Use the Move tool to position the mustache on the left side of the cat's face. Then use Edit > Free Transform to rotate the mustache to the left. (Fig 11.11)

We will add a final adjustment for contrast at the end of this exercise, but you can add an adjustment with Levels now to make the mustache darker.

FIG 11.10 Layers panel.

FIG 11.11 Mustache placed.

5. To further control how the layer blends with the original image, add a layer mask by clicking the "Add layer mask" button in the bottom of the Layers panel. (Fig 11.12)

6. Zoom in to at least 100 percent before editing the mask.

Now we will blend the edges of the mustache using the Paintbrush tool on the layer mask. This will make the mustache appear more realistic on the cat's face. Black will be used on the mask to hide parts of the layer content. Use the Options panel to set the brush opacity to a number between 50 and 80 percent. We used 70 percent but you may be happier with a different value as our monitors are different. Use a big, soft brush. We set our brush at 30 pixels and 0 percent hardness. Trace just around the edges of the mustache, with the edge of the Brush tool brushing against the edge of the mustache. (Fig 11.13)

FIG 11.12 *"Add layer mask"* button.

Tip: Click the icon of the layer content or the layer mask to activate either layer component.

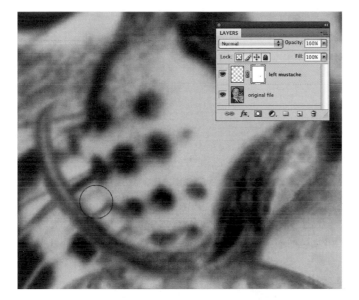

FIG 11.13 Blending edge of mustache.

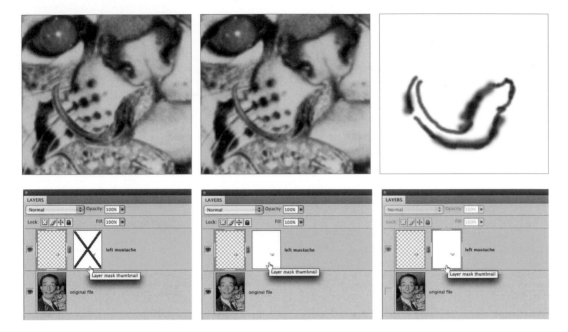

FIG 11.14 Layer mask disabled.   **FIG 11.15** Layer mask enabled.   **FIG 11.16** Option-click layer mask.

7. Zoom out to Fit on Screen viewing mode by using Command+0, and then view the image with and without the layer mask. Shift-click on the Mask icon to disable it. (Fig 11.14) Then Shift-click again on the mask icon to enable it. (Fig 11.15)

8. To view the mask by itself in the document window, Option-click on the Mask icon. (Fig 11.16) It is possible to edit the mask with black or white paint in this mode, too, although you cannot see the layer content or how it is affected by the mask. Option-click the icon of the layer mask to return to standard mask editing mode.

9. Now for the true test: repeat all of the steps in both exercises with the other half of the mustache!

10. Once again, repeat these steps for the eyes. Use the Ellipse Selection tool to select one of Dali's eyes. (Fig 11.17) Then hold Shift while selecting the other eye with the same tool. Make the *original file* layer active by clicking on it. Press Command+J to float the selected eyes to a new layer. Rename the layer *eyes*.

11. Use the Move tool to position the eyes onto the cat's face. (Fig 11.18) Since the eyes are far apart on their layer, selecting each eye is easy to do with the Ellipse Selection tool. Select one eye, then move it into place and use Edit > Free Transform to rotate it. Deselect the eye and repeat the transformation on the other eye. Once both eyes are in place, add a layer mask and use black paint on the mask to hide their edges. (Fig 11.19)

Watch Out: If you see this warning, "Could not make a new layer from the selection because the selected area is empty," you probably did not make the correct layer active before pasting or floating.

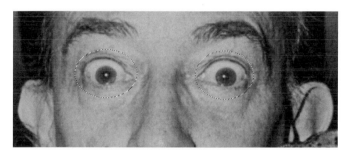

FIG 11.17 Dali's eyes selected.

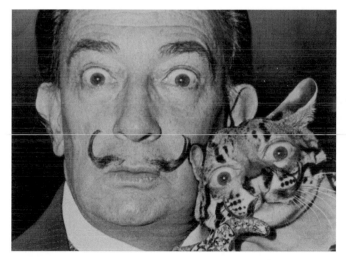

FIG 11.18 Eyes positioned on cat's face.

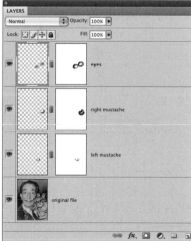

FIG 11.19 Layer mask.

Adding an adjustment layer and organizing layers with groups

1. Add a Levels adjustment layer on top of the *eyes* layer. We used the button in the bottom of the Layers panel. (Fig 11.20)

2. Push the Input Levels sliders beneath the shadow and highlight areas towards each other in the Levels Adjustments panel to create more contrast in the image. (Fig 11.21)

3. Now we will organize all of our manipulations into one folder. Click once on the *left mustache* layer then Shift-click on the layer *Levels 1* to select all layers above *original file*. Use the Layers panel pull-down menu to choose New Group from Layers... and name the group *manipulations*. (Fig 11.22) Now the non-destructive layers are grouped into one folder. The folder can be collapsed or expanded using the small triangle on the left side of the Folder icon in the Layers panel.

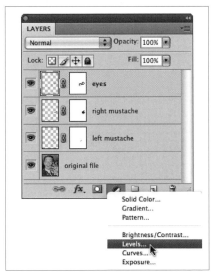

FIG 11.20 Levels adjustment layer.

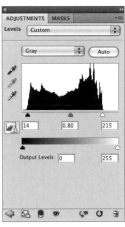

FIG 11.21 Levels Adjustment panel.

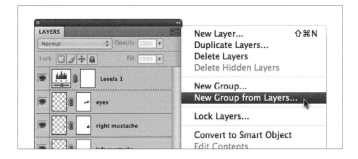

FIG 11.22 New Group from Layers...

04 Adding a shape layer

1. Choose the Rounded Rectangle tool from the Tools panel. This tool hides behind the Rectangle tool. (Fig 11.23) All of the tools grouped beneath the Rectangle tool are called Shape tools. In Photoshop, Shape tools and typography created with the Type tool are vector layers.

2. Look in the Options bar to verify that you are using the Rounded Rectangle tool to make a shape layer (Fig 11.24), instead of a path (which creates a path like the Pen tool) or a pixel layer (which creates a selection).

3. Draw a rounded rectangle in the image near Dali's fingers. Notice that you will have a new layer named *Shape Layer 1* in the Layers panel. Shape layers appear in the Layers panel as an overall color masked by the vector that was drawn. (Fig 11.25)

FIG 11.23 Rounded Rectangle tool.

FIG 11.24 Shape Layers.

4. It's easy to change the color of a Shape layer as long as the document is in a mode that supports color! Try to load a red hue into the foreground color chip. It's gray! Use Image > Mode > RGB color to convert this grayscale image to RGB color mode. At the "Merge layers before mode change?" warning, choose Don't Merge.

Now put a red hue into the foreground color chip using the Color Picker or the Color panel. As long as the vector layer is active, use the key command Option+Delete to fill the *Shape 1* layer with the color you loaded into the foreground color chip.

5. Use the Type tool to type "Dali and his cat" on top of the rectangular box. We used News Gothic Italic in 62 points with 40-point letter spacing. (Fig 11.26) You can fill your type with black however you like, but try the key command on this layer, too. We had black loaded in the background color chip. Command+Delete will fill with the background color.

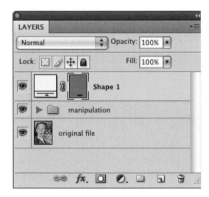

FIG 11.25 Shape layer.

FIG 11.26 Type tool on top of rectangular box.

ANTIADVERTISINGAGENCY

Orbitz Ad: Distinct Lack of Imagination

"Michael Kraus saw the alert about the long taxi line. So he called his brother who lives nearby and got a ride home. Now he owes him a turkey sandwich."

So advertising is about imagining potential futures. It is about hope, and aspirations and dreams. Is getting a ride home from the airport all those ad people could imagine using their service for? How about finding the subway station so they could take public transport. Now that would be something for the "community."

Written by Michael Mandiberg, on August 17, 2008, filed under News and tagged billboard, branding, justfollowingorders, not creative, self-loathing, you don't need it. Follow any comments here with the RSS feed for this post. Post a comment or leave a trackback: Trackback URL. Edit

Search

[   ] (Find)

Contact

Contact Us

Join the mailing list

RSS Feeds

RSS POSTS

RSS COMMENTS

Recent Posts

The Great 2008 Political Ads That Weren't Political Ads

Hey guess what?

Drunk Depressed Penguins

We are not an advertising agency

Quick Links

Tags

AAAFFF **ad creep** add-art ads everywhere **art** billboard **branding** brands chicago china consumer resistance **free** graffiti greenwashing grl hack **haha** history **how to illegal advertising** justfollowingorders **marketing** media music **nyc** online **outdoor** politics poster prank

A published blog post complete with digital image.
Orbitz Ad, Michael Mandiberg, CC-BY.

12 Graphics on the Web

The Internet emerged from a Cold War project initiated by the United States Department of Defense. The Advanced Research Projects Agency (ARPA) wanted to create a way to communicate and share information between networked computers. The objective of ARPANET was to maintain communication even if one part of the network was damaged due to disaster or nuclear war. As with many *firsts*, there are conflicting points of entry to this technology. For instance, before ARPANET came online in 1969, researchers in France and England separately developed packet switching, an essential component of routing data over a network.

Through the 1980s the number of hosts, users, and technological advancements expanded. Desktop computers and dial-up modems brought the Internet into the home. President Bill Clinton adopted the e-mail address president@whitehouse.gov when the U.S. White House created a web site (www.whitehouse.gov) in 1993. In that same year, the National Center for Supercomputing Applications (NCSA) released Mosaic, the first web browser to display images inline. In 1994 you could shop online and order pizza from Pizza Hut's web site. (Fig 12.1-4)

Despite its short history, the Internet has seen rises and falls in techno-utopianism, a made-for-technology depression known as the dot-com bubble burst, and a resurgence of interactivity on user-generated content sites such as MySpace, Facebook, LinkedIn, YouTube, and Flickr.

Now that web *surfers* have become user-generated content *creators*, every Internet user's education should include the basics of image optimization, uploading, and publishing. In the following exercises, we will optimize an image for the web using Photoshop, upload the image to flickr.com, and publish that image on a blog.

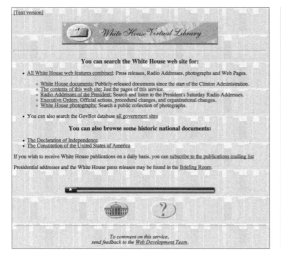

FIG 12.1 Whitehouse.gov on October 23, 1997.

FIG 12.2 Whitehouse.gov on November 12, 2008.

The Wayback Machine is an archive of web pages dating back to the early 1990s. We used the Wayback Machine to view web sites from the 1990s to compare them with the same sites in 2008. Notice how the aesthetics of web graphics has changed in the past two decades. These new aesthetics are possible due to increased network speed, changes in programming techniques, and the evolution of information design. Greater connection speeds result in the ability to upload and download larger files. Graphics are larger, more frequent, and more colorful on current web sites than the graphics made for the web in the 1990s.

FIG 12.3 Pizzahut.com on February 14, 1997.

FIG 12.4 Pizzahut.com on November 12, 2008.

Note: The Wayback Machine contains an archive of over 85 billion web pages. You can use this search engine at http://www.archive.org.

01 From digital input to web ready

FIG 12.5 *orbitzad1.jpg* open in Photoshop.

Note: Choose the Essentials workspace from the pull-down menu in the Application bar before working on the following exercises.

1. Download and open *orbitzad1.jpg* from the wiki, or get any image from your digital camera or scanner. (Fig 12.5)

2. If you followed the exercises in Chapters 8 and 9, you should be comfortable changing the tonal range and color of this image. Adjust the tonal range and color to your liking by creating adjustment layers. (Fig 12.6-8)

3. Save this file as a master copy by choosing Save As from the file menu, adding "_master" to the file name, and then choosing PSD as the file format. We saved ours as *orbitz_master.psd*.

⁎ Finished exercise file available in the Download Materials area of the wiki.

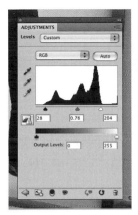

FIG 12.6 Levels.   **FIG 12.7** Blue Curves.   **FIG 12.8** Green Curves.

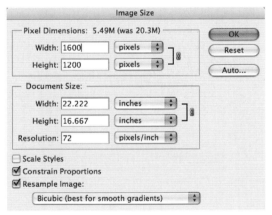

FIG 12.9 Image Size set to 72 pixels per inch.

Tip: Monitors generally have display settings such as 1280 by 800 or 1024 by 768 pixels. A file whose longest side is 1600 pixels is likely more than big enough to fill a web browser window on any monitor. The only measurement unit relevant to us in this exercise is pixels, as the image will be shown on a platform that also uses pixels.

4. The image from the wiki is straight off a 7-megapixel digital camera, and is much larger than can be displayed on a web site. Choose Image > Image Size and notice the size of your image in pixels. Check the boxes next to Resample Image and Constrain Proportions, then change the pixel dimensions at the top of the box so the largest dimension is no larger than 1600 pixels. If your image is less than 1600 pixels on its long side, you can use the Cancel button to close this dialog box without making any changes. (Fig 12.9)

5. Add an unsharp mask (Filter > Sharpen > Unsharp Mask). Make sure you have the image layer selected, and not one of the adjustment layers. We used the following settings for the Orbitz ad photo: Amount, 25 percent; Radius, .6 pixels; Threshold, 0 levels. Your image may require different settings. (Fig 12.10-11)

6. Choose File > Save for Web & Devices. Photoshop and Illustrator share this Save for Web interface. It allows you to compress your images, flatten layers, and prepare an image for the web. (Fig 12.12)

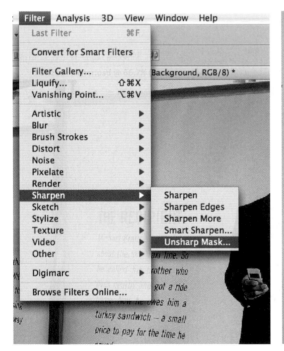

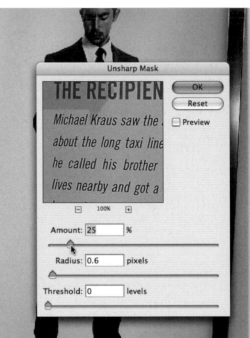

FIG 12.10 Filter > Sharpen > Unsharp Mask...

FIG 12.11 Unsharp Mask dialog box with preview.

7. The Save for Web & Devices dialog box has several important parameters to set. The most important parameter is the Optimized file format. As a general rule, photographic images and other images with more than 256 colors are saved as JPEGs. Graphic images — images with few colors such as logos and line art — are saved as GIFs or PNGs. Since this image is a photograph, select JPEG from the Format pull-down menu. (Fig 12.13)

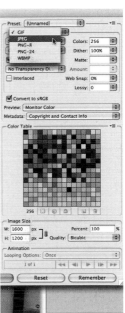

FIG 12.12 File > Save for Web & Devices.

FIG 12.13 Select JPEG.

8. Select the default quality of High, or 60. Saving a file for the web compresses the saved image into a smaller file size by removing color information and pixel detail. This is called *lossy compression*.

9. Click on the 2-Up tab to show the original image in its native format next to the compressed image. Notice that the original image has a file size of 5.49 MB, and the file size of the optimized image is 368 KB. The compressed image is 15 percent of the original file size. This is important because the smaller the file size is, the faster the image will download as part of a web page. (Fig 12.14-15)

Tip: The Zoom and Hand tools allow you to get a closer look at the image and move to important details.

10. Reduce the quality to Low, or 10. Notice how much detail is lost. Visible compression artifacts are introduced into the image. Our file size is much smaller at 85 KB, but we have compromised too much image quality for the sake of the smaller file size. (Fig 12.16-17)

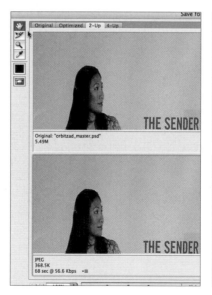

FIG 12.14 2-Up view.

FIG 12.15 Compare the file sizes. Above, the source image is 5.49 MB. Below, the JPEG is 368.5 KB.

Note:

The human eye cannot detect image compression artifacts if used with a light touch and when the image is viewed on a computer screen. Compression runs from Low to Maximum, and corresponds to a numerical range from 0 to 100. Zero is a very low quality, where you will definitely be able to notice the loss of quality in the image, while the maximum 100 level, although still having had image data thrown away, shows no visible decline in quality. The trade off is that more compression creates a smaller file. Weigh your needs for file size against your perception of image quality to decide what level of compression to use.

Tip: If your settings disappear, click on the lower preview window.

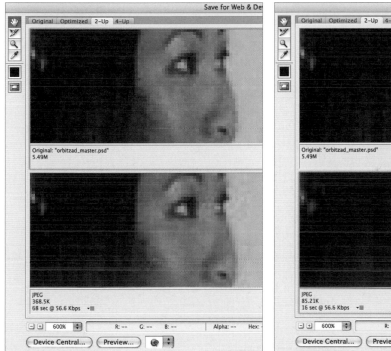

FIG 12.16 The High quality JPEG.

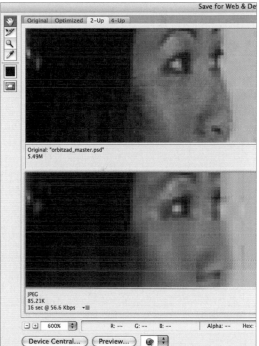

FIG 12.17 The Low quality JPEG.

Watch Out: When you open a file and resize it, it is no longer the master file. This may seem confusing, but it is a situation you will commonly experience when maintaining master files and resized web ready files. There's nothing stopping you from using Save As to save your scaled-down master file as well, but it's probably overkill and could mislead you later into believing it's the largest version you have.

11. Return the Compression Quality setting to High, and click the Save button.

12. Name your file with an underscore and the word "web," like we did when we named ours *orbitzad_web.jpg*, and save it to the Desktop. Remember web standards when naming files: only use lowercase alphanumerics, underscores, and dashes.

13. Close and *do not* save the *orbitz_master.psd* file that is currently open. (We saved the master file in Step 3 before scaling the image and we don't want to save this smaller version over it.)

14. In Photoshop open the JPEG you just saved for web (ours is *orbitzad_web.jpg*) in Photoshop, and notice that there are no adjustment layers. By saving for the web, we flattened the image.

EXERCISE
02 GIF vs. JPEG

As stated in Exercise 1, photographic images with many colors are saved as JPEG files, and graphic images with few colors are saved as GIFs. Following these rules will produce better images and smaller file sizes. (Fig 12.18)

EXERCISE
03 Uploading to Flickr

Since we will be using both Flickr.com and a blog, we are referencing the wiki for the remaining exercises in this chapter. These exercises are available at http://wiki.digital-foundations.net/index.php?title=Chapter_12.

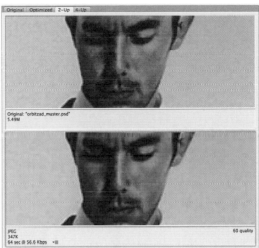

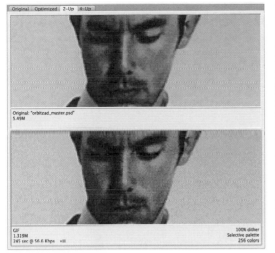

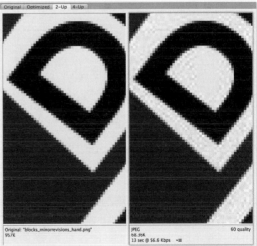

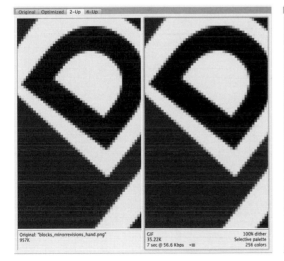

FIG 12.18 Notice in the above images that the photograph optimized as a GIF file is larger and of lower visual quality than the photograph optimized as a JPEG file. Likewise, the graphic optimized as a JPEG has a larger file size with a lower image quality than the graphic optimized as a GIF.

"All the News We Hope to Print"

The New York Times

Special Edition
Today, clouds part, more sunshine, recent gloom passes. **Tonight**, strong leftward winds. **Tomorrow**, a new day. Weather map throughout.

VOL. CLVIV . . No. 54,631   NEW YORK, SATURDAY, JULY 4, 2009   FREE

Nation Sets Its Sights on Building Sane Economy

True Cost Tax, Salary Caps, Trust-Busting Top List

By T. VEBLEN

The President has called for swift passage of the Safeguards for a New Economy (S.A.N.E.) bill. The omnibus economic package includes a federal maximum wage, mandatory "True Cost Accounting," a phased withdrawal from complex financial instruments, and other measures intended to improve life for ordinary Americans. (See highlights box on Page A10.) He also repeated earlier calls for passage of the "Ban on Lobbying" bill currently making its way through Congress.

Treasury Secretary Paul Krugman stressed the importance of the bill. "Markets make great servants, terrible leaders, and absurd religions," said Krugman, quoting Paul Hawken, an advocate of corporate responsibility and author of "Blessed Unrest, How the Largest Movement in the World Came into Being and Why No One Saw It Coming."

"At this point, the market is our

leader and our religion. No wonder the median standard of living has been declining so much for so long."

Krugman said that the new Treasury bill seeks to ensure the prosperity of all citizens, rather than simply supporting large corporations and the wealthy. "The market is supposed to serve us. Unfortunately, we have ended up serving the market. That's very bad."

Much as Roosevelt, after the Great Depression, put the brakes on C.E.O. wages and irresponsible banking practices, administration officials claim that today we need to rein in the industry that has caused such chaos and misery.

"The building blocks of post-World War II American middle-class prosperity have all been swept away," said House Speaker Nancy Pelosi, who initially op-

Continued on Page A10

IRAQ WAR ENDS

U.S. Army helicopters begin moving troops and equipment from Saddam Hussein's former Baghdad palace.
COURTESY ARMY.MIL

Troops to Return Immediately

By JUDE SHINBIN

WASHINGTON — Operation Iraqi Freedom and Operation Enduring Freedom were brought to a close today with a quiet announcement by the Department of Defense that troops would be home within weeks.

"This is the best face we can put on the most unfortunate adventure in modern American history," Defense spokesman Kevin Sites said at a special joint session of Congress. "Today, we can finally enjoy peace — not the peace of the brave, perhaps, but at least peace."

As U.S. and coalition troops withdraw from Iraq and Afghanistan, the United Nations will move in to perform peacekeeping duties and aid in rebuilding. The U.N. will be responsible for keeping the two countries stable; coordinating the rebuilding of hospitals, schools, highways, and other infrastructure; and overseeing upcoming elections.

The Department of the Treasury confirmed that all U.N. dues owed by the U.S. were paid as of this morning, and that moneys previously earmarked for the war would be sent directly to the U.N.'s Iraq Oversight Body.

The president noted that the Iraq War had resulted in the burning of many bridges. "Yet our history with our allies runs deep," he said, "and we all know that friends forgive friends for anything. Or nearly." A spokesperson for the French Ministry of Defense confirmed that France would assist the U.S. withdrawal. "The U.S. helped the Soviet Union defeat Hitler. We do recognize that."

In conflict zones worldwide, leaders and rebels pledged peace. (See "In Conflict Zones Worldwide, Peace Moves," on Page A4.)

On Wall Street, reactions were mixed, with the Dow Jones Industrial Average up 84 points, to close at 4,212. While KBR stock was quickly downgraded to a "junk" rating of BBB-, defense contractors such as Lockheed Martin and Northrop Grumman started up.

Continued on Page A5

Maximum Wage Law Succeeds

Salary Caps Will Help Stabilize Economy

By J.K. MALONE

WASHINGTON — After long and often bitter debate, Congress has passed legislation, fiercely fought for by labor and progressive groups, that will limit top salaries to fifteen times the minimum wage. Tying the bill to a plan of overall reform of the U.S. economy, the bill echoes a similar effort enacted by President Franklin Roosevelt in 1942, which was followed by the longest period of growth for the middle class in U.S. history.

"When C.E.O. salaries remain stable thanks to high taxation of high salaries, there's little incentive to take big risks with shareholders' money, and the economy remains in a steady growth mode," said Senator Barney Frank, one of the bill's co-sponsors. "But when C.E.O. salaries can fly through the roof, there's a very strong incentive for C.E.O.s

Continued on Page A10

TREASURY ANNOUNCES "TRUE COST" TAX PLAN

By MARCUS S. DRIGGS

The long-awaited "True Cost" plan, which requires product prices to reflect their cost to society, has been signed into law.

Beginning next month, throw-away items like plastic water bottles and other items which are wasteful or damaging to the environment will be heavily taxed, as in many developed countries. Steep taxes will also apply to large cars and gasoline.

The new plan calls for a 200 percent tax on gasoline, comparable to the one long in effect in most European countries. Companies and consumers are already switching in droves from inefficient gas vehicles to new electric cars. "We suddenly have a waiting list 200 names long for the EV1," said Jake Cluber, the owner of Cluber Chevrolet in

Continued on Page A10

Recruiters Train for New Life

As a ban is imposed on recruiting minors, ex-recruiters nationwide look for new work. The Times follows one on his job-hunt odyssey through Manhattan and surrounding areas.

BY BARRY GLOAD, PAGE A12

Last to Die

Two proportional monuments — one to the Iraqi dead, 300 feet high, and one to the American dead, 15 feet high — are unveiled in Baghdad, and a five-year-old boy whose lifespan coincided with that of the Iraq War is remembered.

BY J. FINISTERRA, PAGE A5

USA Patriot Act Repealed

Eight years later, a shamefaced Congress quietly repeals the much-maligned USA Patriot Act, unanimously... or almost.

BY SYBIL LUDINGTON, PAGE A8

Evangelicals Open Homes to Refugees

Up to a million Iraqi exiles — nearly half of them women — will find sanctuary in Christian homes across the U.S., vows the National Association of Evangelicals. Other denominations are expected to follow.

BY W. WILBERFORCE, PAGE A7

Public Relations Industry Starts to Shut Down

The public relations industry has been criticized for misleading the American people, corrupting politicians, and even helping to start wars. Now, it's beginning the process of shutting down for good.

BY LOUIS BECK, PAGE A9

Ex-Secretary Apologizes for W.M.D. Scare

300,000 Troops Never Faced Risk of Instant Obliteration

By FRANK LARIMORE

Ex-Secretary of State Condoleezza Rice reassured soldiers that the Bush Administration had known well before the invasion that Saddam Hussein lacked weapons of mass destruction.

"Now that all of you brave servicemen and women are returning, it's important to us to reassure you, and the American people, that we were certain Hussein had no W.M.D.s and that he would never launch a first strike against the U.S.," Ms. Rice told a group of wounded soldiers at a Veterans' Administration hospital yesterday.

"I want you to know that if we had had the slightest suspicion that Saddam could use W.M.D.s against you, we never would have sent hundreds of thousands of you to be sitting ducks on the Iraqi border for several months."

Mr. Rice was referring to the fact that by August 2002, eight months before the ground invasion, the US had over 100,000 troops stationed in countries throughout the Gulf, a number that grew to over 300,000 shortly before the 2003 attack on Baghdad. Most of these were within range of the Scud missiles used by Mr. Hussein in the 1991 Gulf War, that could easily have been fitted with chemical or biological weapons if they had existed.

Rice noted that in the 1991 Gulf War, Hussein had used missiles to launch attacks on Israel, which made him popular with Arab citizens throughout the Middle East.

"Do you really think we would have given Saddam a major public relations coup by allowing him to annihilate tens of thousands of you right there on holy territory?" asked Ms. Rice.

Former Secretary of State Henry

Popular Pressure Ushers Recent Progressive Tilt

Study Cites Movements for Massive Shift in DC

By SAMUEL FIELDEN

The spate of reform initiatives undertaken by the Administration and both houses of Congress can be attributed directly to grassroots advocacy, according to a comprehensive study due out this month.

"In education and health care, most notably, but also in housing, banking, and the environment, we have documented unprecedented responsiveness on the part of political leaders," said Dr. Joyce Wellmon, director of the Plains Institute for Policy Analysis, a New York-based think tank. "Our data show a direct correlation between the level of activity of particular coalitions, on the one hand, and specific legislative action, on the

The report includes extensive interviews with House and Senate staff, who speak of "unimaginable change," a "dramatic policy shift," and "a new era of accountability" since the elections.

"Not since the Great Depression has the interaction between popular movements and public leaders been so robust," said Jorge Lazaro, head of the U.S. Government Accountability Office. Lazaro cited, in particular, the Wagner Act, also known as the National Labor Relations Act of 1935, which recognized the right of workers to organize and bargain collectively with their employers.

"Roosevelt showed no interest in the Wagner Act until it became

Protests organized by Witness Against Torture helped pave the way
KC IVEY/THE NEW YORK TIMES

Nationalized Oil To Fund Climate Change Efforts

By MARION K. HUBBERT

Congress has voted to place ExxonMobil, ChevronTexaco, and other major oil companies under public stewardship, with the bulk of the companies' profits put in a public trust administered by the United Nations, and used for alternative energy research and development in order to solve the global climate crisis.

While unusual, this is not the first time the government has chosen to take control of large corporations. From 1942 to 1944, U.S. car factories were retooled in order to produce tanks for the war effort. And Fannie Mae and Freddie Mac were both created as "government sponsored enterprises" with a significant amount of government

---

The Special Edition, The Yes Men, The Anti Advertising Agency, CODE PINK, Not An Alternative, and hundreds of volunteers, 2008

13 Multiples — Creating Unity

The grid is the principal way of organizing page elements in multi-page documents. A grid divides a page into columns to follow strictly, or to use as a rough guide. The *Gutenberg Bible* follows a very rigid grid structure: the two columns of text have the same line length, which is a measurement of how long a line of text is before it breaks to a new line. (Fig 13.1) The two columns of text also have the same vertical length. When two pages are viewed together in an open book such as this, the pages read together as a *spread*. The pages in this spread follow the grid in exactly the same manner.

The grid can also adapt to flexible layouts. In the visual reference example of the *New York Times* layout from 1918, the grid is more complex and versatile. (Fig 13.2) This grid divides the page into eight columns.

Note:

Counting the columns on the page is easy: find the smallest column and measure its width. Then divide the width of the page with the width of the smallest column.

With eight columns, the designer has options. Instead of eight even columns of text flowing down the front page of the newspaper, some larger graphic elements like the headline at the top of the page expand across all eight columns. Other text blocks are given visual emphasis, or create visual hierarchy on the page, by spanning multiple columns. Also notice the distribution of negative space on the page. Since there is a lot of text on this front page, contrast is created by increasing the leading in some areas of the page and by allowing some of the text blocks to expand beyond one column.

FIG 13.1 A copy of the *Gutenberg Bible* owned by the U.S. Library of Congress. In the fifteenth century, 180 copies of the Bible were printed in Mainz, Germany, by Johannes Gutenberg. Photograph taken by Mark Pellegrini on August 12, 2002.

FIG 13.2 The front page of the *New York Times*, 1918.

Unity through repetition — master pages

1. Open InDesign and create a new document by choosing File > New > Document. Notice that a document can have many pages. We will work on just two pages. For this lesson, specify the letter page size, no facing pages, two pages, one column, and leave the margins at their default settings. (Fig 13.3)

2. Click on the Pages panel. (Fig 13.4) In this panel, each rectangular icon represents a page in the document. Double-click the Page 2 icon to jump to that page and then double-click the Page 1 icon to go back. Another way to navigate through the pages in a document is to click the Next Page or Previous Page arrows at the bottom of the document window. You can also use the Hand tool to drag the pages around within the document window.

Tip: A workspace can also be selected from Window > Workspace.

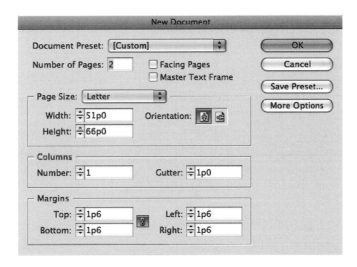

FIG 13.3 Create a new document that is two pages.

⁕ Finished exercise file available in the Download Materials area of the wiki.

Notice that pages 1 and 2 are labeled with the letter *A*. The letter *A* signifies that these pages are based on the master page called A-Master. You can create multiple master pages, which can be applied to any page within the document. Master pages commonly contain a grid and any recurring design elements. They allow you to create a consistent layout throughout the pages in a publication, and they make it possible to automate layout changes, because any modification you make to a master page is automatically reflected on all the pages to which it is applied.

By default, a new document's pages are all based on A-Master, even though A-Master is empty. We will work on the A-Master page next.

3. Double-click the A-Master page icon in the Pages panel. (Fig 13.5) You are now on the master page. Anything you place on this page will be stored on A-Master and will automatically appear on all the pages based on it. You can also see that A-Master is the page you are currently working on by looking at the page box at the bottom of the document window.

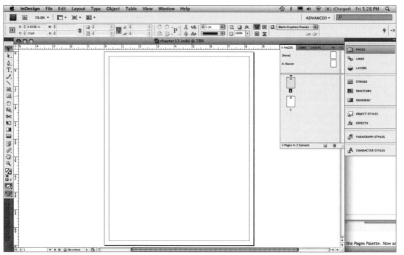

FIG 13.4 The Pages panel.

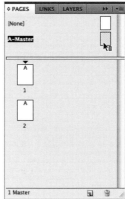

FIG 13.5 Double-click the A-Master page icon..

4. We will now set up guides on the master page similarly to the Illustrator exercises in Chapter 4. Guides are created by dragging them from the horizontal and vertical rulers in all Adobe programs. If your rulers were not displaying in inches, you can Control-click (or right-click) each ruler and choose Inches before adding guides to the page. (Fig 13.6)

5. Click and drag to create guides. Starting with the horizontal ruler at the top of the document window, click into the ruler and drag a guide to 3 inches, using the vertical ruler at the left of the document window as a reference. Then drag a guide from the vertical ruler to 5 inches, using the horizontal ruler as a reference. (Fig 13.7)

> **Key Command:** Show or hide rulers from the View menu in any Adobe program, or press Command+R.

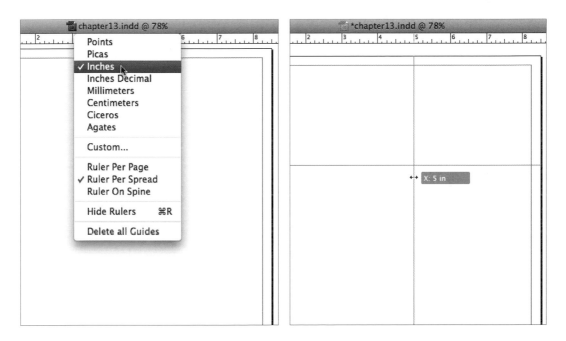

FIG 13.6 Control-click to change ruler units.

FIG 13.7 Guide dragged to 5 inches.

FIG 13.8
Line tool.

6. Now we will use the Line tool (Fig 13.8) to draw a heavy line along the horizontal guide. Click the Line tool in the Tool panel to select it. Starting at the right edge of the page, Shift-click and drag toward the left edge of the page to draw a straight line along the horizontal guide. (Fig 13.9) Notice that we didn't draw the line all of the way to the left edge, so the negative space remains active as it did in Chapter 4. When you release the mouse button, you'll notice that the line almost disappears into the guide. We will hide the non-printing guides to make it easier to see the line.

7. To hide the guides, press Command+Semicolon. This will enable you to see the thin line you just made. (Fig 13.10) Next, we will make the line thicker.

8. Use the Selection tool to select the line if it isn't already selected, and then choose a line weight from the Stroke pull-down panel menu in the Control panel at the top of the work area (we used 20 points). (Fig 13.11)

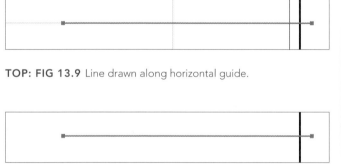

TOP: FIG 13.9 Line drawn along horizontal guide.

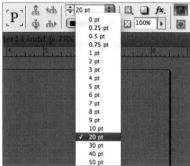

FIG 13.10 Hide Guides.

FIG 13.11 Stroke pull-down panel menu.

9. Open the Swatches panel. Click the Stroke icon to bring it to the front, and then click on the red color swatch (C=15, M=100, Y=100, K=0). (Fig 13.12) Notice that all the swatches are defined with CMYK values. Since InDesign is the main application to use for creating documents that are output to a commercial printer, the default colors in the Swatches panel are using the CMYK color space.

Watch Out: Make sure the Stroke icon is on top of the Fill icon so that the color red is applied to the line.

10. Turn on the guides again by pressing Command+Semicolon or choosing View Menu > Guides & Grids > Show Guides.

11. Double-click the Page 1 icon in the Pages panel to view the first page of the document. Notice that the guides and thick, red line are in place on Page 1. Double-click the Page 2 icon in the Pages panel and notice that the guides and red line are also in place on the second page of the document. (Fig 13.13) Objects on a master page automatically show up on any pages based on that master. It's important to understand that the items on a master page can only be modified or deleted from the master page they belong to (unless they are overridden first, which we will do in Exercise 2). Try to select the red line or move the guides on Pages 1 or 2, and you will see that they are not selectable.

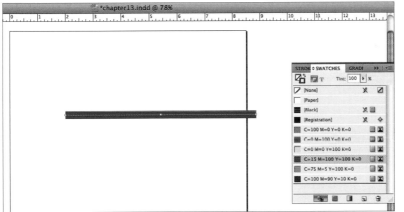

FIG 13.12 Red stroke chosen in Swatches panel.

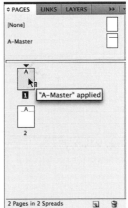

FIG 13.13 Page 1 in Pages panel.

EXERCISE

02 Creating B-Master

The document we are creating contains only two pages, so only one master page is needed. However, in larger documents that have several layout variations, it is often helpful to use multiple master pages. We will make a second master page in this document in order to demonstrate the process.

1. Click on the pull-down panel menu at the top right corner of the Pages panel, and choose New Master. (Fig 13.4)

2. In the New Master dialog box, set B-Master to be based on A-Master using the pull-down panel menu. (Fig 13.15) Click OK to create the new master page.

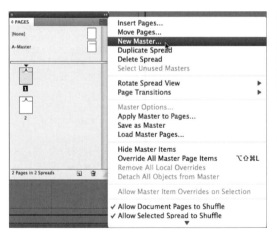

FIG 13.15 B-Master is based on A-master.

FIG 13.14 Create New Master...

3. In this document, B-Master will be similar to A-Master, but we will modify the color of the line so that it is cyan instead of red. Try selecting the red line with the Selection tool, and you will notice that it cannot be edited. Override the red line (and not the guides) by Shift+Command-clicking on the line with the Selection tool.

Tip: To view all the master pages without having to scroll to find them, drag the horizontal divider line in the Pages panel downward.

Note:

You can right-click or Control-click on any page icon in the Pages panel and choose Override All Master Page Items. This would make master page items editable on the entire page.

4. Use the Swatches panel to change the color of the line to cyan (C=100, M=0, Y=0, K=0). (Fig 13.16)

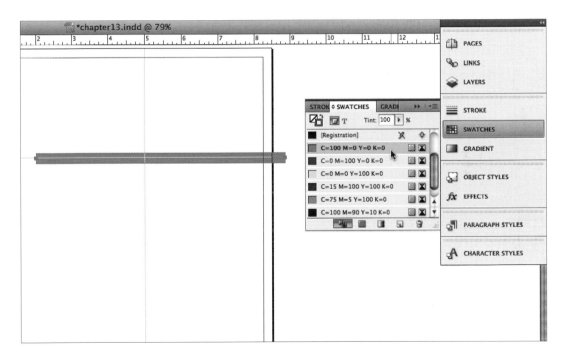

FIG 13.16 Cyan stroke chosen in Sawatches panel.

5. Apply the B-Master page to Page 2 by right-clicking or Control-clicking the Page 2 icon in the Pages panel and choosing Apply Master to Pages from the contextual menu. (Fig 13.17) In the Apply Master dialog box, choose B-Master from the pull-down panel menu.

6. Double-click the Page 2 icon in the Pages panel to view the second page. We will now create a typographic headline that will be copied to page 1. (This is something that would normally be done on the A-Master page, but we want to demonstrate a useful paste function that is not available in every Adobe program.)

Click and drag with the Type tool to draw a text frame, which is like a text box in Illustrator. Type the words "Unity on the Grid" into the frame.

7. Now format the headline by selecting all the text with the Type tool and then specifying a font and type size. In the following example, we are using Futura Condensed Extra Bold at 48 points. Pay attention to the kerning, making sure that the spaces between the characters in the headline are visually equal. If necessary, use the same manual kerning techniques we learned in Chapter 4 to improve the kerning.

FIG 13.18 Headline aligned with cyan line.

FIG 13.19 Headline copied to page 1 with Paste in Place.

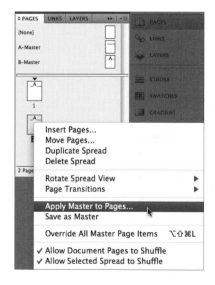

FIG 13.17 Apply Master to Pages...

8. Next, use the Selection tool to select the text frame and then reposition it so that the left edge of the frame aligns with the left edge of the cyan line and the baseline of the text aligns with the top of the line. (Fig 13.18)

9. Now we will copy the headline to Page 1. With the text frame still selected, choose Edit > Copy. Double-click the page 1 icon in the Pages panel, and then choose Edit > Paste in Place. The headline appears in the same position on this page as it is on Page 2. (Fig 13.19)

Tip: InDesign's Copy command copies both the type and its location on the page.

EXERCISE

03 Linking text frames

InDesign is often used to create multi-page documents for commercial printing or for viewing as a PDF file on a screen. In either case, long documents can contain a lot of text. InDesign allows you to place as much text as you want into one single text frame and then use the Threading function to link multiple text frames together so that the text can flow from one frame to another. In this exercise, we will link two text frames on Pages 1 and 2 with about five paragraphs of Lorem Ipsum dummy text. In Chapter 4 we used Lipsum.com to generate five paragraphs of dummy text. InDesign has Lorem Ipsum placeholder text available inside the application, so you can easily fill a text frame with placeholder text without pasting it from someplace else.

1. On page 1, use the Type tool to click and drag a large text frame on the Page area. We need to load more placeholder text into the frame than we intend to use in order to illustrate the Threading feature.

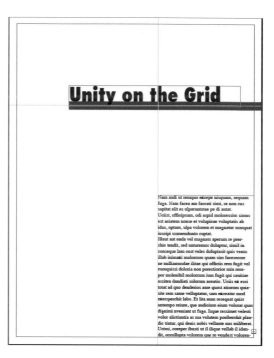

FIG 13.20 Dummy text.

FIG 13.21 Dummy text placed in layout.

FIG 13.22 Text stored.

FIG 13.23 Text-loaded cursor.

2. Choose Type > Fill with Placeholder Text to fill the frame with dummy text. (Fig 13.20)

3. Use the Selection tool to move and resize the text frame so that the left edge of the text frame is aligned with the vertical guide. Pull the top edge of the frame down so it starts at 6 inches. The right and bottom edges of the text frame align with the right and bottom margins on the page. (Fig 13.21)

4. Look at the bottom right corner of the text frame and notice the red square that surrounds a plus sign. (Fig 13.22) This icon means that there is more text stored (but not visible) in the text frame. Using the Selection tool, click the plus sign. Notice that your cursor has changed to a loaded cursor. InDesign knows that you are ready to link this first text frame to another text frame in the document. (Fig 13.23)

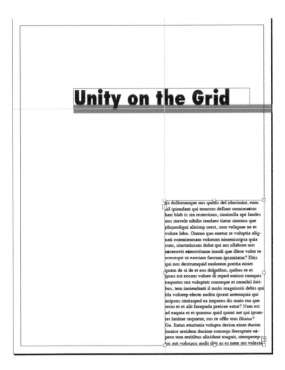

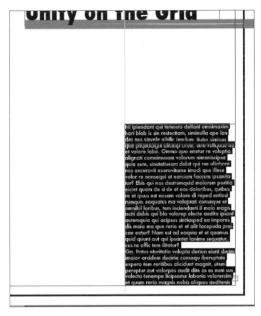

FIG 13.25 Command+A.

FIG 13.24 Page 2, text linked to frame on Page 1.

5. Now navigate to page 2. With the loaded cursor, click and drag a text frame in the same location as the frame you created on page 1. The overflow of text from the first frame will flow into the second text frame, since the frame on page 1 is now linked to the frame on page 2. (Fig 13.24)

6. Using the Type tool, click inside either of the two text frames and press Command+A to select all of the text. Make a change to the typeface using the Font Family menu in the Control panel or the Character panel (Window > Type & Tables > Character). Our type is set with Futura Medium in 11 points with the leading (the space between the lines) set at 13.2 points. Notice that the typeface changes in both text frames because Command+A (or Edit > Select All) selects the text in all of the linked frames. (Fig 13.25)

Tip: Choose View > Show Text Threads to see a visible line that indicates which frames are linked together.

04 Creating shapes

In Chapter 4 we created unity on the page through the repetition of shape and color. We will create unity in this chapter with the same technique, but this time we will place the colored square in the same location on sequential pages.

1. Use the Rectangle tool and hold the Shift key to draw a square on page 1 and then go to the Swatches panel to assign the red color to it. Note: Use the Curved Arrow icon above the Fill and Stroke icons at the bottom of the Toolbox or at the top of the Swatches panel to swap the fill and stroke colors. The white square with the diagonal red stripe is used to assign no color.

2. With the Selection tool, drag the red square to align its left side with the vertical guide, and position the bottom of the square against the top of the body copy. If necessary, use the arrow keys on your keypad to nudge the square into place. Once the square is just touching the text, press Shift+Up Arrow one time to move the square 10 points higher than the text. (Fig 13.26)

3. While the square is still selected, choose Edit > Copy then navigate to page 2 and choose Edit > Paste In Place to create a second square in the same location as the one on page 1. Use the Swatches panel to change the color of this square to cyan. (Fig 13.27)

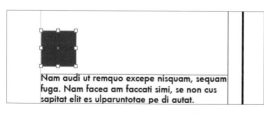

FIG 13.26 Red square aligned with vertical guide.

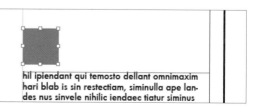

FIG 13.27 Square Pasted in Place on page 2 and color changed to cyan.

EXERCISE
05 Exporting a PDF

It is important to continually save a file as you are working on it. The InDesign file, designated by the file extension .indd, is the native file. A PDF file is most commonly used for sharing a document to view or proof, and it can also be used for printing. When an INDD file is exported as a PDF file, the graphics and fonts are embedded in the document, making it a portable package that is easy to share with others.

While printers and copy centers can print INDD files, we often suggest sending a PDF file as well to avoid common problems such as different application versions or absence of fonts or linked files. Sending an INDD file to print requires sending the native file, fonts, and images. InDesign can make a package of the required files, but in some cases it's simpler and just as effective to send a high-quality PDF.

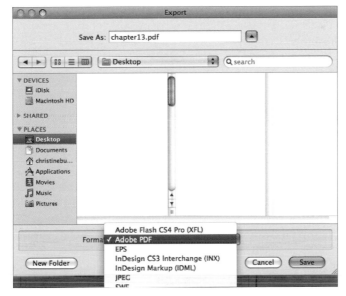

FIG 13.28 Export menu. Choose Adobe PDF.

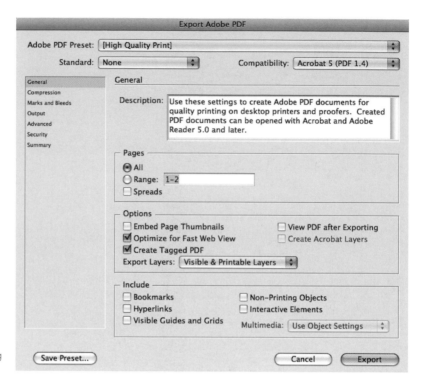

FIG 13.29 Export dialog box.

1. Save the InDesign file by choosing File > Save As. Notice that the file extension is .indd. Specify a name and location for the file and then click the Save button.

2. Now we'll export a PDF file for sharing, viewing, or printing. Choose File > Export. In the Export dialog box, choose Adobe PDF as the format. (Fig 13.28) Specify a name and location for the file and click the Save button.

3. In the Export Adobe PDF dialog box there are many options, which change depending on which category at the left side is active. In the General category, notice the Pages area – it contains three choices: All, Range, and Spreads. For this exercise, leave the All option selected so that all the pages are exported. Leave the Spreads option deselected since we did not design the layout as spreads (or facing pages). (Fig 13.29) Notice the Compatibility pull-down menu at the top right corner. If you know that the person you are sharing this PDF with has an older version of Acrobat, or if you need to comply with specifications from

FIG 13.30 Overset text warning.

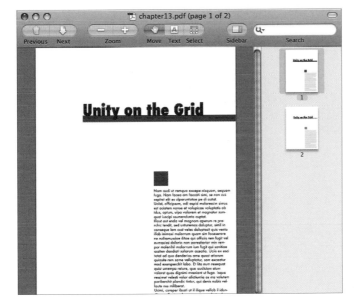

FIG 13.31 Layout viewed in PDF reader.

a commercial printer, choose an option from this pull-down menu to format the PDF document for a particular Acrobat version.

4. Click the Export button. You may see a warning about overset text. If there is more dummy text in the second text frame than what is visible on the page, the Export to PDF function prompts you with a warning message. (Fig13.30) We are aware of the abundance of text in this exercise, so you can click OK through the dialog box. During another project, you could modify the text frame so that all of the text is visible within the frame.

5. Open the PDF file in Adobe Acrobat Professional, Adobe Reader, or Preview. Notice that the layout or design of the file can be viewed but not easily edited. (Fig 13.31) To edit the design, open the native .indd file in InDesign.

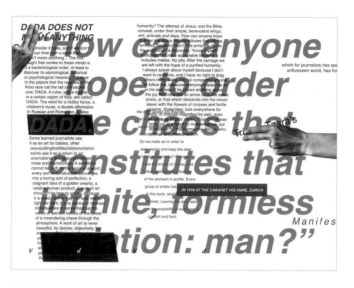

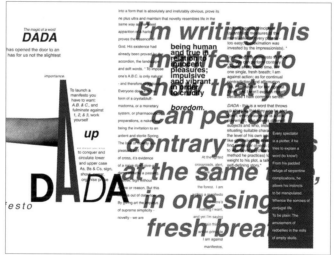

When Exercises 1 and 2 from this chapter are complete, the InDesign file contains two pages. Print page 1 on a sheet of paper and page 2 on the back of the same sheet, then fold the single sheet in thirds to create a tri-fold.

14 Multiples – Creating Tension

The tri-fold brochure is a common exercise in print design. In a tri-fold layout one piece of paper is printed on both sides of the page and folded into three panels. A very typical tri-fold size is created from a letter-size sheet of paper in landscape orientation (11 by 8.5 inches). Straddling each fold is a small empty space, called a *gutter*, where you would generally not place text or important detail. Large images or headlines can run across the gutters and folds.

Creating a sense of chaos with tension among type and images was part of the Futurist, Constructivist, and Dadaist anti-art aesthetic in the early 20th century. For these exercises, we will use the tri-fold brochure as the platform for an approach to graphic design that resists the rules of the grid. The urge to stray from the rigidity of the grid resurfaced in the latter part of the 20th century when designers became interested in a more subjective interpretation of the content that they were communicating. Although the aesthetics in Neville Brody's work on *Fuse* magazine and David Carson's *Ray Gun* magazine feel as chaotic as a montage by Hannah Höch or Raoul Hausmann, the Dadaists were motivated by passionate opposition to World War I and to the alienation wrought by modernity since the Industrial Revolution, while the designers in the late 20th century were incorporating post-modern theory into their work, and responding to an overall stagnation in graphic design.

FIG 14.1 Researchstudios.com, screen shot taken on November 13, 2008; David-carsondesign.com, screen shot taken on November 13, 2008.

Carson's work is often referred to as deconstruction in graphic design. In Hillman Curtis' documentary short film about David Carson, Carson says, "When I started doing magazines I just did what made sense to me. I read an article and tried to interpret it.... So as we get more computerized, I think it becomes more important than ever that the work become more subjective, more personal... so that you pull from who you are as a person and put that into the work."

Deconstruction is also a philosophical movement developed by Jacques Derrida in the 1960s, in which the structure of a linguistic system is revealed through a critical analysis of how it is used. Carson's interpretation of the essays he designed in *Ray Gun* attempted to expose the underlying meaning of the copy with graphic design, an approach which bears a resemblance to Derrida's notion of deconstruction.

While the tri-fold is often considered anything but experimental, we will approach it with deconstruction in mind. We will use part of the text from Tristan Tzara's Dada Manifesto. The first exercise is the back side of a single sheet. The second exercise is the front of the sheet.

FIG 14.2 Paper telescope for locating your future home in outer space from the LET'S MOVE! campaign, the League of Imaginary Scientists, year of completion: 2020, used by permission of the artist The step-by-step directions are legible along the edge of this poster, while the overlapping text and images create a sense of chaos and disarray.

When you finish the exercises you can print out page 1, turn the paper over, and print page 2. Fold the paper in thirds and you will create a tri-fold. In keeping with a design approach that is chaotic, tense, and full of disarray, we will cover some of the text by other portions of the type. We may overlap images with words, set type in narrow columns, and establish hierarchy through contrast, scale, and value.

Note: We saw Hillman Curtis' videos here at the time of writing this book: http://www.hillmancurtis.com/index.php?/film/watch/david_carson/

01 Placing text and using frame breaks

1. Create a new document with two pages. (Fig 14.3) Do not check the facing pages or master text frame options. Use letter size set in landscape orientation. Since the printer we use cannot print borderless, we need to account for margin space. Set the margins at a quarter of an inch. Notice that when you type ".25 in" in the margin area, InDesign will change the units of measurements to inches from whatever units of measurement were last used. The default units are picas.

2. Since we will mainly be editing the typography in these exercises, use the typography workspace. Choose Window > Workspace > Typography.

Note:

Picas are measurement units for graphic production that originated before the process became digital. A paragraph set with 12-point leading has 1 pica from baseline to baseline. Six picas are equivalent to 1 inch. A letter-size sheet measures 66 picas wide on its longest side.

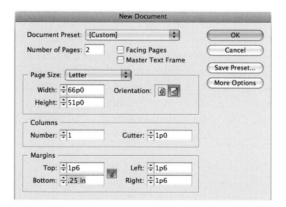

FIG 14.3 New Document.

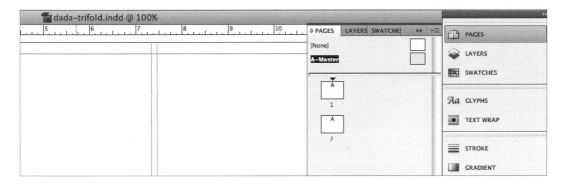

FIG 14.4 Pages panel.

FIG 14.5 "Manifesto" rests on the baseline.

3. Double-click on the A-Master page in the Pages panel. (Fig 14.4) On A-Master, pull two guides from the left ruler with the Selection tool to divide the page into thirds. Add two more guides .125 inches to the right of the first two guides — these will be used to establish a small gutter between the fold and some of the text. Add a horizontal guide at 7 inches by pulling from the top ruler.

4. Double-click on page 1 in the Pages panel. Click File > Place to import the graphic named *dada-title.ai*. Remember that the Place command creates a loaded cursor, so you have to click the mouse to drop the image onto the page. On page 1, the baseline of the word "Manifesto" should rest on the guide at 7 inches. The *e* in *Manifesto* will barely touch the edge of the left margin. (Fig 14.5)

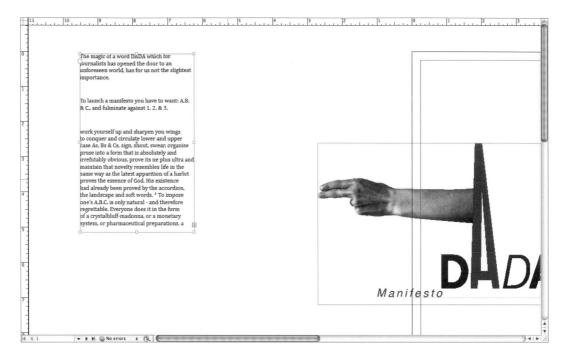

FIG 14.6 Place text.

5. Choose File > Place and browse to the document *dada-manifesto. doc* to load the cursor with all of the copy for the brochure. When the cursor is loaded with the text, click and draw a box on the pasteboard. (Fig 14.6) The Place command can be used to load the cursor with text or images.

6. For this tri-fold, we will work in separate text boxes, also called frames. We will link the text frames just as we did in Chapter 13, but this time we will set breaks in the frames so the amount of text in the frame does not change when the shape of the frame is modified. A frame break is like a page break in Microsoft Word. At the break, any text that follows is pushed into the next frame.

Put the cursor at the end of the word "importance" and from the Type menu choose Insert Break Character > Frame Break. The frame ends at the end of this word. Use the Selection tool to click on the red plus sign at the right edge of the frame. The cursor is loaded with the rest of the body copy. Draw a new text box. (Fig 14.7)

7. In the new frame, delete any paragraph breaks towards the top of the frame. Then place the cursor at the end of the word "prose" and set a frame break. Repeat this process between the word pairs "the/same," "are/being," "boredom./At," "manifestos,/as," "story/Every," and "skulls./DADA."

There will be nine text frames. (Fig 14.8) Placing text and keeping it in linked frames is a much better method than copying and pasting from the Word document to separate text boxes in InDesign for two reasons: with linked frames, it is less likely text will be missing or excluded, and you can select all the text at once for formatting.

8. Place the last frame beginning with "DADA DOES NOT MEAN ANYTHING" on page 2. Return to page 1.

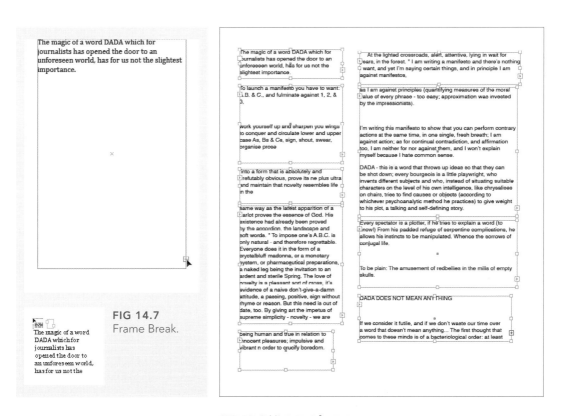

FIG 14.7 Frame Break.

FIG 14.8 Nine text frames.

EXERCISE
02 Working with styles

1. Insert the Type tool in any text frame, and press Command+A to select all of the text. The entire copy is selected in all of the linked text frames. Modify the font in the Control panel or Character panel to the typeface Helvetica Regular at 10 points with 12 points of leading.

> **Note:** For the rest of this chapter we will refer to the typeface, style, point size, and leading like this: Typeface style size/leading. For example, in this step we used Helvetica Regular 10/12.

Tip: Command+A selects the text in all linked frames. Clicking with the Type tool four times on a paragraph will select all of the text in that paragraph. Clicking with the Type tool five times in a text frame will select all of the text in 1 frame.

2. You can save text formatting to apply to other paragraphs and words by creating styles. Styles are collections of attributes that can be applied to selected text, saving time and assuring accuracy in formatting. InDesign has both Paragraph and Character Styles panels. Paragraph styles affect all the text between paragraph breaks and include both character-level and paragraph-level formatting. Character styles are useful for styling short runs of text without altering paragraph-level formatting (for instance for emphasizing the first words of a list or making book titles italic).

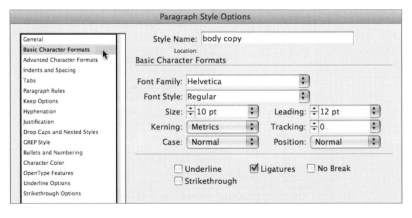

FIG 14.10 Style named *body copy.*

FIG 14.9 Paragraph Style Options dialog box.

While the text is still selected, click on the Paragraph Style panel then click the Create New Style icon at the bottom of the panel. A new style is created with the attributes of your selected text or frame. Now it is easy to apply this style to other paragraphs just by selecting text or a text frame and applying the style by pressing its name in the Paragraph Styles panel. (Fig 14.9)

3. Double-click the new paragraph style to see the Paragraph Style Options dialog box. Change the name of the style to *body copy*. (Fig 14.10) If you change some of the formatting characteristics of that style, all text subscribing to that style immediately updates to the new formatting.

The Style Options display the formatting settings that are saved in this paragraph style. Use the menu on the left to make changes to the style.

4. Modify the text in the first text frame. We'll use Helvetica as the font face for most of the copy. Select all of the text in this paragraph by clicking four times with the mouse. Press the Align Right button in the Control panel or the Paragraph panel. Deselect the text and press the Return key to set the paragraph breaks for the typographic treatment. Set "DADA" in Helvetica Bold Oblique 30. Set "The magic and importance" in Helvetica Oblique 9. Increase the leading for the gap between "slightest" and "importance." With the Direct Selection tool, click on the lower right anchor point and drag it to the right to create the slanted right margin edge. You may have to use the Selection tool to increase the height of the text box as in the illustration (Fig 14.11).

5. Position the text frame so the word "importance" is just over the top of the letter *A*. Also notice that the *s* in "has" (on the second line) is just barely inside the left margin. (Fig 14.12)

6. Since this type hangs off the page, it also needs to be precisely positioned on page 2. Shift-click the title graphic and the type treatment in the first text frame. With both elements selected, use Command+G to group them

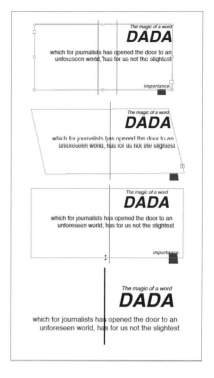

FIG **14.11** New Document.

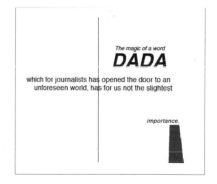

FIG **14.12** Positioning the word "importance".

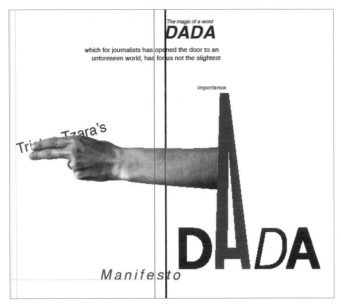

LEFT: FIG 14.13
Text sent to back.

RIGHT: FIG 14.14
Lean text.

together. Then use Command+C to copy the group and double-click on page 2 in the Pages panel. Press Command+V to paste the group on page 2. Position the baseline of the title on the guide at 7 inches and watch for the position of the *e* in *Manifesto* as you did in Step 4 of Exercise 1.

7. Create a text box and type in it, "Tristan Tzara's." We used the typeface Helvetica Regular 24/28.8.

Send the text box to the back using Object > Arrange > Send to Back. Place the text just beneath the fingers as in the illustration (Fig14.13). Choose the Rotate tool from the Toolbox and click and drag to the left on the type box.

The rotated text is the only element on this folded part of the page that is not on a horizontal or vertical grid. The rotation breaks out of the grid and creates contrast. Even though the letters are partially hidden beneath the fingers, the viewer is directed to the typography.

8. Return to page 1 and format the typography in the next text frame. Send it behind the title graphic using Object > Arrange > Send to Back. Set the word "up" in Helvetica Bold Oblique 30. Format the phrase "and sharpen your wings" at a barely legible 4 points, and increase the kerning by selecting the words and using the key command Option+Right Arrow.

9. Use the Direct Selection tool again to make the text box lean into the pink letter *A* in the Dada title graphic. Shift-click on the bottom two anchor points to make both active and move them to the right. (Fig 14.14)

10. Set the next text frame in Helvetica Regular 9/18. Create a new character style called *loose copy* based on this setting. (Fig 14.15) Use the same method to create a character style from the Character Styles panel as we did in Step 3 when we made a paragraph style in the Paragraph Styles panel.

11. Apply the character style to the fourth text box and use the Selection tool to modify the width of the box on the page. Send this text box behind the title graphic. (Fig 14.16)

Tension, like stress, occurs whenever the viewer is confronted with an unexpected variation or instability. When reading or legibility becomes difficult, the typography is stressed. When the typography is its focus, a composition will take on the attributes of the type treatment. Because tension is being created in the typography through leading, scale, and contrast, the entire tri-fold feels chaotic and tense.

12. Set the type in the text frame from "being human…" to "crucify" in Helvetica Regular 18/14, which tightens the leading and creates tension in the typography. The letters overlap because the space between the rows of letters is smaller than the size of the letters. This type treatment could be difficult to read. However, at a larger font size than the typical 9- to 11-point body copy, a small section of text with tight leading remains legible.

Open the leading a lot for the word "boredom" at the bottom of the text frame. In the illustration (Fig 14.17) you can see the type settings we used, but try seeing this with your eyes and intuition. Use the cursor to highlight the

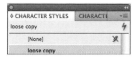

FIG 14.15 *Loose copy* character style.

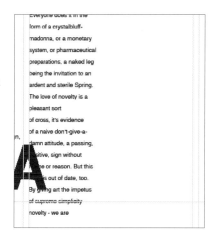

FIG 14.16 Fourth text box.

FIG 14.17 Type set in text frame.

word "boredom" then use the key command Option+Down Arrow to open the leading.

13. Format the type in the next text frame with the *loose copy* character style.

14. Highlight the text through the word "things," then use the Swatches panel to change the Tint value of the black swatch to 75 percent.

15. Now we will create a pink color swatch to match the color used in the vector title graphic. Click on the pull-down menu from the top right corner of the Swatches panel. Choose New Color Swatch... and choose CMYK as the color mode. (Fig 14.18) Enter the values C = 20, M = 90, Y = 50, K = 5. Uncheck the Name with Color Value button and type "pink" into the Name field. (Fig 14.19) Click OK to exit the dialog box. Select the remaining text in this frame with the Type tool and apply the new color swatch by clicking on it from the Swatches panel. (Fig 14.20)

16. Set the seventh frame on the page at the start of the third column. Use the *body copy* paragraph style to format the frame. (Fig 14.21)

17. The next frame is placed slightly on top of the last one, so some of the words will be hidden. Select the text frame with the Selection tool and use the *loose copy* character style to format the type. While the

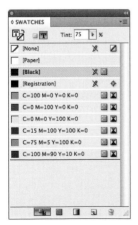

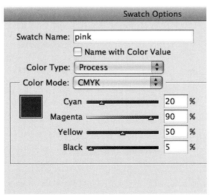

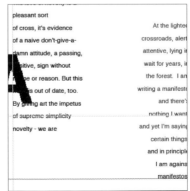

FIG 14.18 New Swatch.   **FIG 14.19** Name Swatch.   **FIG 14.20** Pink text.

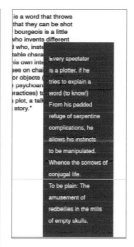

text frame is selected, click on the pink color swatch we made in Step 13. This will put pink into the background color of the frame. Select all of the text in the frame and click on the white, or paper, swatch. (Fig 14.22)

LEFT: FIG 14.21 Set the third column.

RIGHT: FIG 14.22 Pink text frame.

18. Text frames can have inner margins, or padding. Control-click on the text frame and choose Text Frame Options from the contextual menu. In the Insert Spacing section, click the Link icon so you can enter the padding value once. The same value will be automatically entered in each side of the text frame — we used .125 inches. Also, in the Vertical Justification section, use the Align pull-down panel menu to vertically center the copy in the text frame.

The line created by the left horizontal justification creates unity between the type and the edge of the pink box, yet the box hinders the reader from accessing the black copy and simultaneously draws the reader's attention to the text inside itself. Creating confusion for the reader through chaotic design treatment is a communications strategy that may be used when the subject matter speaks to topics like radical change or rejection of the status quo, as does Tzara's manifesto. The goal is to heighten the audience's emotions. Learning how to create tension intentionally can also help you avoid creating it unintentionally when your communications task involves topics related to stability and permanence.

Watch Out: At the bottom of the Toolbox, make sure that the Fill icon is on top when loading the text frame background color. If the Stroke icon is on top, the text frame will be outlined instead of filled.

19. Create a new text box that will be placed across the two-thirds of the page from the first guide to the right margin. Since this typography is going to sit on top of text that is already in position on the page, we would create and format this typography on the pasteboard and then position it on top of the other page elements. Type "I'm writing this manifesto to show that you can perform contrary actions at the same time, in one single, fresh breath;" into a new text box. This is a pull-quote from Tzara's manifesto, which you can copy and paste if you can find it in the text. (Sometimes it is faster to type, but if you type anything new, always use the spelling check available from the Edit menu.) Highlight the text and use the pink swatch to modify the text color. Use the Swatches panel to decrease the value by setting the Tint value to 75 percent. Use the Character or Control panel to set the type to Helvetica Bold Oblique 60/68 and center the type. Position the text box into the tri-fold (see Fig 14.23). Press Command+B to access the frame options and vertically center the text. Finally, send the text frame to the back using Object > Arrange > Send to Back.

Press *w* on the keypad to change the screen mode. Now you see the page design without guides and frame edges in the way. The following image illustrates what the first page should look like. (Fig 14.23)

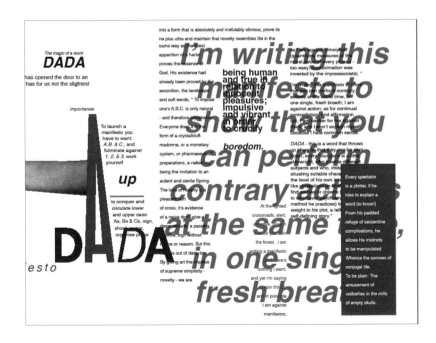

FIG 14.23 First page.

EXERCISE 03 Using text frame options, hue, and saturation to create contrast

DADA DOES NOT MEAN ANYTHING

If we consider it futile, and if we don't waste our time over a word that doesn't mean anything... The first thought that comes to these minds is of a bacteriological order: at least to discover its etymological, historical or psychological meaning. We read in the papers that the negroes of the Kroo race call the tail of a sacred cow: DADA. A cube, and a mother, in a certain region of Italy, are called: DADA The word for a hobby horse, a children's nurse, a double affirmative in Russian and Romanian, is also: DADA. Some learned journalists see it as an art for babies, other Jesuscallingthelittlechildrenuntohim saints see it as a return to an unemotional and noisy primitivism - noise and monotonous. A sensitivity cannot be built on the basis of a word; every sort of construction converges into a boring sort of perfection, a stagnant idea of a golden swamp, a relative human product. A work of art shouldn't be beauty per se, because it is dead; neither gay nor sad, neither light nor dark; it is to rejoice or maltreat individualities to serve them up the cakes of sainted haloes or the sweat of a meandering chase through the atmosphere. A work of art is never beautiful, by decree, objectively, for everyone. Criticism is, therefore, useless; it only exists subjectively, for every individual, and without the slightest general characteristic. Do people imagine they have found the psychic basis common to all humanity? The attempt of Jesus, and the Bible, conceal, under their ample, benevolent wings: shit, animals and days. How can anyone hope to order the chaos that constitutes that infinite, formless variation: man? The principle: "Love thy neighbour" is hypocrisy. "Know thyself" is utopian, but more acceptable because it includes malice. No pity. After the carnage we are left with the hope of a purified humanity. I always speak about myself because I don't want to convince, and I have no right to drag others in my wake, I'm not compelling anyone to follow me, because everyone makes his art in his own way, if he knows anything about the joy that rises like an arrow up to the astral strata, or that which descends into the mines strewn with the flowers of corpses and fertile spasms. Stalactites: look everywhere for them, in creches magnified by pain, eyes as white as angels' hares.

Thus DADA was born* , out of a need for independence, out of mistrust for the community. People who join us keep their freedom. We don't accept any theories. We've had enough of the cubist and futurist academies: laboratories of formal ideas. Do we make art in order to earn money and keep the dear bourgeoisie happy? Rhymes have the smack of money, and inflexion slides along the line of the stomach in profile. Every group of artists has ended up at this bank, straddling various comets. Leaving the door open to the possibility of wallowing in comfort and food.

1916 AT THE CABARET VOLTAIRE, ZURICH

Watch Out: The Direct Selection tool is picky. If you pull on the edge of a frame with the Direct Selection tool and the whole box moves, you didn't click right on the edge of the box. You need to click exactly on the edge of the box in order to move two anchor points together. If it doesn't seem to work for you, Shift-click on the two anchor points on either side of the line and move those instead.

FIG 14.24 Text box on page 2.

1. Start by repositioning the text box on page 2 into the first column and linking the remaining text into a frame in the second column. (Fig 14.24) Select all of the text and apply the *body copy* paragraph style.

2. Select the headline "DADA DOES NOT MEAN ANYTHING" with the Type tool and change the typeface to Helvetica Bold Oblique 21/25.2. Change the color of the headline to pink using the Swatches panel. Use the Selection tool to resize the text box until the word "MEAN" drops to the second line. Click File > Place and

FIG 14.25 Position the image over text.

FIG 14.26 Dynamic line.

browse to the file downloaded from the wiki named *hand.ai*. Use the Selection tool to position the hand over the text. (Fig 14.25)

3. Create a dynamic line on the page by moving the bottom two anchor points of the text frame in the first column to the right with the Direct Selection tool. You can Shift-click on the bottom two anchor points and adjust them together, or you can pull on the edge of the box with the Direct Selection tool to modify it. Adjust the bottom left anchor of the text frame in the second column to create a similar line. (Fig 14.26)

4. Move the text box edge with the Selection tool to make the column narrow while watching the sentence fragment, "a double affirmative in Russian and Romanian, is also: DADA." Skew the text box until the word "DADA" drops to the beginning of a new line. (Fig 14.27)

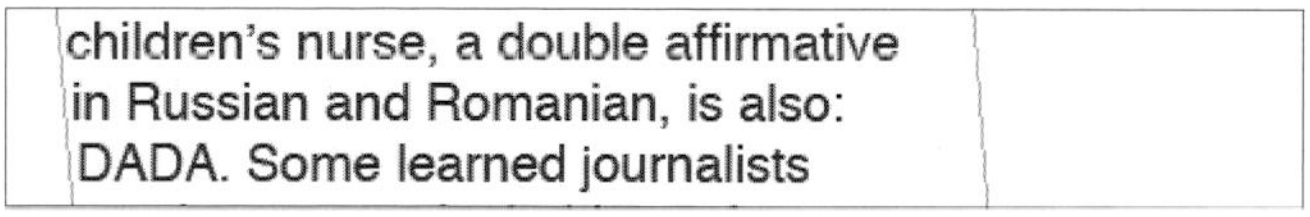

children's nurse, a double affirmative
in Russian and Romanian, is also:
DADA. Some learned journalists

FIG 14.27 Skew a text box.

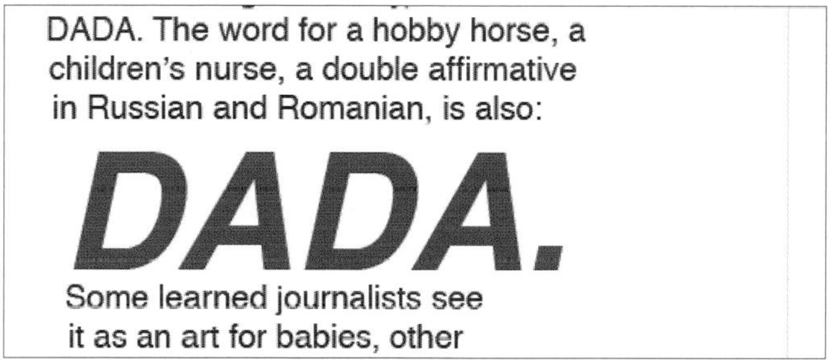

DADA. The word for a hobby horse, a
children's nurse, a double affirmative
in Russian and Romanian, is also:

DADA.

Some learned journalists see
it as an art for babies, other

FIG 14.28 "DADA" adjusted.

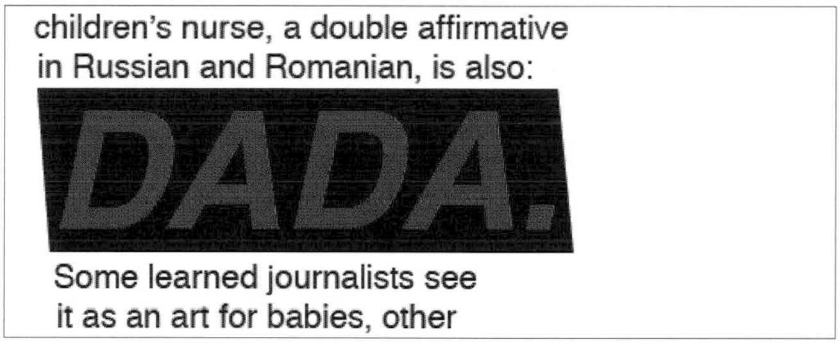

children's nurse, a double affirmative
in Russian and Romanian, is also:

DADA.

Some learned journalists see
it as an art for babies, other

FIG 14.29 Draw a rectangle.

5. Adjust the typographic treatment of the word "DADA." We used Helvetica Bold Oblique 50/46. Change the type color from black to pink. Look closely at the kerning. We made two adjustments. (Fig 14.28)

6. Draw a rectangle with the Rectangle tool on top of the word "DADA." Fill it with black from the Swatches panel. Use the Direct Selection tool to modify the shape of the box so it is unified with the shape of the text frame. Click Object > Arrange > Send to Back. Adjust the leading for the next line of type. (Fig 14.29)

7. Create a frame break (Type > Insert Break Character > Frame Break) after the words "We don't accept any theories" towards the end of the second column.

Tip: Chapter 4 has details and images related to adjusting kerning and leading in Adobe Illustrator. In Chapter 13 we modified kerning in InDesign. Kerning and leading can be adjusted in the same way in all Adobe programs.

stewn with the flowers of corpses and fertile
spasms. Stalactites: look everywhere for
them, in creches magnified by pain, eyes
We don't accept any theories
We've as white as angels' hares. Thus DADA was
born, out of a need for independence, out
cubist and figurist academies
of mistrust for the community. People who
laboratories join us keep their freedom.

Do we make art in order to

earn money and keep the dear

bourgeoisie happy? Rhymes

have the smack of money, and

inflexion slides along the line

of the stomach in profile. Every

group of artists has ended up

at this bank, straddling various

comets. Leaving the door open

to the possibility of wallowing in

comfort and food.

FIG 14.30 Overlapping text.

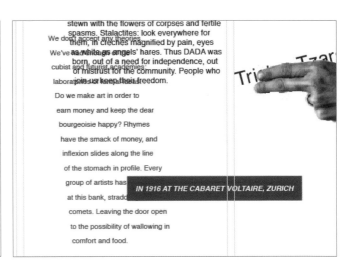

FIG 14.31 Pink text box.

8. Click the red plus sign to load the rest of the text into the Selection tool and draw the new text box beneath the first one in the second column. Use the *loose copy* character style and change the color of the text to pink. Drag the bottom two anchor points of the text frame to the right with the Direct Selection tool. Modify the width of the frame with the Selection tool. Position the text frame so that it overlaps the frame above it. Again, tension and chaos are created by the difficulty in legibility. (Fig 14.30)

Tip: Hold the Shift key while dragging the Rotate tool to constrain the rotation to 45-degree increments.

9. Cut (Command+X) the last line, "IN 1916 AT THE CABARET VOLTAIRE, ZURICH," and paste it in a new text box. Place the box so that it covers some of the text in the last text frame, and be sure that "CABARET" is after the fold on the title page. Load the pink color from the Swatches panel into the background of the text frame. Vertically center the type using Text Frame Options via Command+B. (Fig 14.31)

10. Create the four letters *d A d A* in separate text frames using an italic serif font. We used Adobe Garamond Pro Bold Italic 16/19.2. Use the Rotate tool to turn both *A*'s upside down. Create a black rectangle and use the Direct Selection tool to modify its anchor points. The shape repeats the angle of the text box above it. Select the letter *d* on top of the box and use the Swatches panel to make it white. (Fig 14.32)

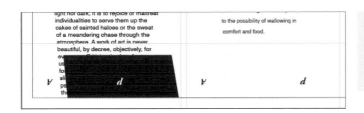

Note:

Adobe Garamond Pro is one of the fonts installed with Adobe Creative Suite.

FIG 14.32 Four letters in separate text boxes.

12. Create a new text box on the pasteboard. Type "How can anyone hope to order the chaos that constitutes that infinite, formless variation: man?" Select the type and change its formatting to Helvetica Bold Oblique 84/94.8. While the type is still selected, use the Swatches panel to apply the pink color and reduce the Tint to 60 percent. Position the text box on top of page 2, then send it behind all other elements with Object > Arrange > Send to Back. Press *w* on the keyboard to preview the page as it would be when printed and trimmed. (Fig 14.33)

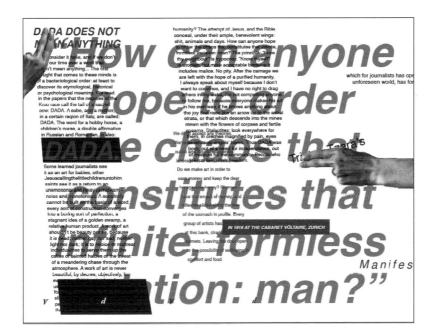

FIG 14.33 Preview of page 2.

Hello World is the first exercise you learn in any code or mark-up language. Photo credit: Windell H. Oskay, www.evilmadscientist.com.

15 Hello World

Every web page is code made visual by the web browser. Open any page in a web browser and use the View menu to see the page source. There you will see the code used to create that page. This code tells the browser how to render the layout, images, links, and interactivity of the page. Whereas in the previous applications, we have clicked and dragged our way to good design, with web pages we design interface elements and then write the code that describes what we want our interface to look like in the browser.

While web sites are usually programmed to hide the presence of code in a seamless graphic façade, experimental artists often revel in exposing it. The artist group JODI (Joan Heemskerk and Dirk Paesmans) works extensively with the materiality of code. In the early moments of the dot-com boom, when corporations began to stake out an aesthetic and functional claim online (1995–96), JODI hosted a series of confrontational pages. Theirs responded to the corporate attempt to professionalize the aesthetics of online media and conceal the presence of code. The site wwwwwwwww.jodi. org looks like disorganized text in the browser and viewing the source reveals a rough diagram of a nuclear bomb made with the letters of the source code. (Fig 15.1)

Note:

Code is language. Think of it as material that hides its own materiality

Jodi.org reversed the order of the medium. Where design elements are organized to create visual messages in the browser, Jodi.org appears random and frantic. In the source code Jodi.org reveals the message of the work in a simple illustration. JODI throws a bomb at clean design. Web pages are written in Hypertext Markup Language (HTML), which ignores extra spacebar characters. Ignoring this basic principle allowed Jodi to make a brilliant visual and conceptual argument for breaking the rules of web design.

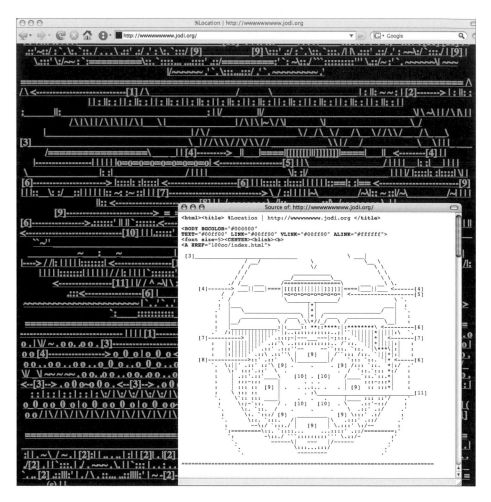

FIG 15.1 *wwwwwwwww.jodi.org*, JODI (Joan Heemskerk and Dirk Paesmans), 1995, website and HTML source code, used by permission of the artists.

In the early years of the World Wide Web, bandwidth was small. A large amount of communication took place on text-only listservs, chat rooms, multi-user dungeons (MUDs), and bulletin board servers (BBS). Pages were designed with few images because they took too long to download. In the absence of high-resolution images, people found creative ways of drawing with text.

Loosely defined, ASCII art is art made by arranging the 128 glyphs that are part of the American Standard Code for Information Interchange, usually in the form of figurative drawings. The shapes and densities of the characters are treated purely as formal elements to construct line, form, and shading.

As an example, Heath Bunting's 1998 portrait of Natalie Bookchin, an early net artist, can be seen here: http://www.irational.org/heath/imaging_natalie/. (Fig 15.2)

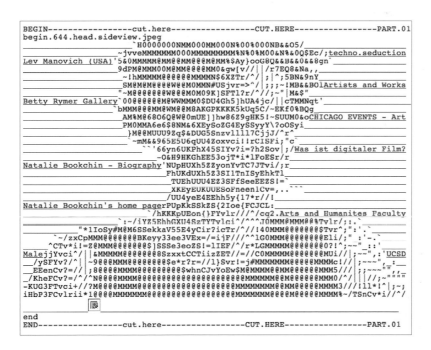

FIG 15.2 *Portrait of Natalie Bookchin*, Heath Bunting, 1998, http://www.irational.org/heath/imaging_natalie/, used by permission of the artist

EXERCISE
01 Hello World!

Choose the Designer workspace from the pull-down menu in the Application bar before working on the following exercises.

With the materiality of code in mind, we will construct our first web page.

For this chapter, create a folder on your desktop or hard drive and commit to saving everything that you make from or related to this chapter into that one folder. Do not make sub-folders. Do not make more than one folder. Our folder is named *chapter15*.

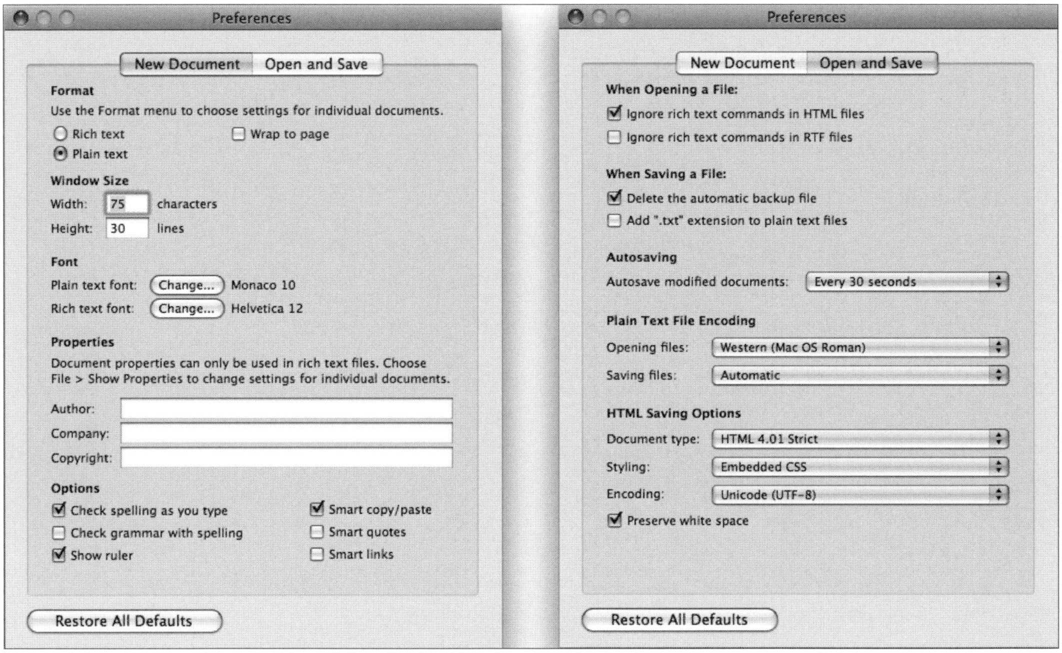

FIG 15.2 Preferences New Document dialog box.

1. Open a text editing application such as TextEdit, Text Wrangler, TextMate, Smultron, or BBEdit. On a PC, use Notepad or WordPad. Since we often teach this in labs with TextEdit installed, the screenshots will be from that interface. The first, very important step when writing HTML in any text editing application is to make sure that it is working in plain text format.

Watch Out: It is absolutely essential that you are aware of where your files are saved when you are working with code.

2. From the TextEdit menu, choose Preferences. In the Preferences New Document dialog box, click the Plain Text radio button. In the Open and Save dialog box, check "Ignore rich text commands in HTML files", check "Delete the automatic backup file", and uncheck "Add '.txt' extension to plain text files." These preferences will be in effect on new documents. (Fig 15.2)

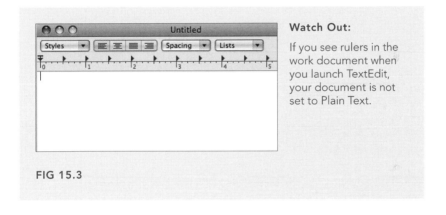

Watch Out:

If you see rulers in the work document when you launch TextEdit, your document is not set to Plain Text.

FIG 15.3

FIG 15.4 Opening and closing HTML tags.

FIG 15.5 Opening and closing body tags.

FIG 15.6 "Hello World!" typed inside the body tags.

3. Close any open documents in TextEdit and click File > New to start on a new document.

4. Type the opening and closing HTML tags. (Fig 15.4)

The <html> opening tag tells the browser that we are writing in Hypertext Markup Language, and the same tag with a slash, as shown, tells the browser to stop rendering HTML. All tags within HTML follow the same scheme. Other markup languages that a browser understands will have similar rules with some variation.

5. Position your cursor after the opening HTML tag. Press Enter and press the Tab key. Tabbing is used to add visible structure to the code so that it is easier to read. Tabs and other extra white space are ignored by the browser and do not affect the display or functionality of the code.

Add the opening and closing body tags. (Fig 15.5) All media placed inside the body tags is displayed on the web page.

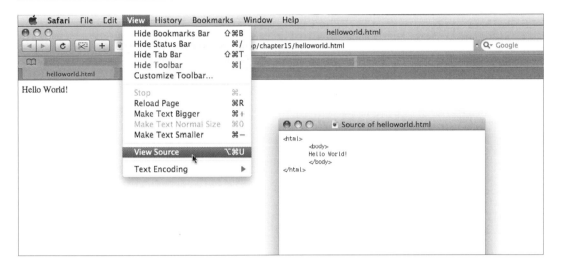

FIG 15.7 Save file.

FIG 15.8 View > View Source.

6. Inside the body tags type "Hello World!" (Fig 15.6)

7. Save the file as *helloworld.html*. (Fig 15.7) Make sure that you add the .html extension to the end of the file name. The file extension is important. It communicates to the browser that this is an HTML file.

8. Open a web browser, click File > Open and find the *helloworld. html* file. We opened Safari, clicked File > Open File... and browsed to Desktop > *chapter15* > *helloworld.html*. Notice that the message "Hello World!" is the only part of the code that is displayed. In the Browser, choose View > View Source to see all of the code. (Fig 15.8)

In Exercise 2 we will be returning to this file in the web browser, so leave it open if you are going to work on that exercise next.

Watch Out: When saving files for the web, do not use capital letters, spaces, or reserved characters. Only use *a-z, 1-9, -,* and *_*. Stay away from reserved characters like:
( ) ! + @ & = ?

Watch Out: Double-clicking on the HTML file in your folder may not open the file in a web browser. If your intent is to view the file in a web browser, be sure to launch the browser and choose File > Open File or drag the HTML file to the browser icon in the Dock.

EXERCISE

02 Hello Dreamweaver

In the previous exercise, we wrote the Hello World! code using a text editing program. A text editor is the most basic application required for writing code, but it can be a lot of work when hand-typing lots of code. Most artists and designers prefer to use a WYSIWYG (what you see is what you get) application such as Dreamweaver to develop code. Dreamweaver actually writes the code for you, which makes creating the HTML file much easier.

In this exercise, we will modify the file we just made. We will make changes to the existing file and save on top of it, meaning we will not use Save As. At the end of this exercise you should have only one file in your folder.

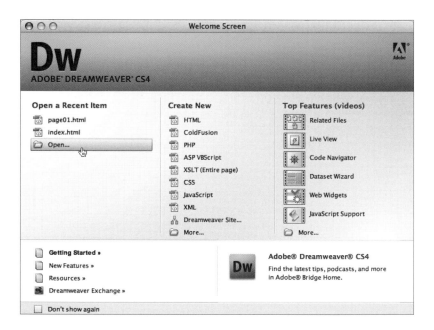

FIG 15.9 Dreamweaver Open File..

1. Open Dreamweaver from the Dock or Applications folder. In Dreamweaver choose File > Open and open the *helloworld.html* file. (Fig 15.9) We will click File > Open then Desktop > *chapter15* > *helloworld.html*.

2. In the upper left corner of the document, click the Split button. (Fig 15.10) Split view displays both the code and the result of the code in a browser. Another way to think about this is that the code view is the set of instructions to the browser and the design view is what the browser should do with those instructions.

> **Note:**
>
> Dreamweaver is a WYSIWYG editor because you can change the code by using Dreamweaver pull down menus and buttons in Design view. It should be called a WYSIWYGMOTT, or What You See Is What You Get Most Of The Time. The Design view is going to be about 95 percent accurate. When designing for the web, always preview your work in the browser.

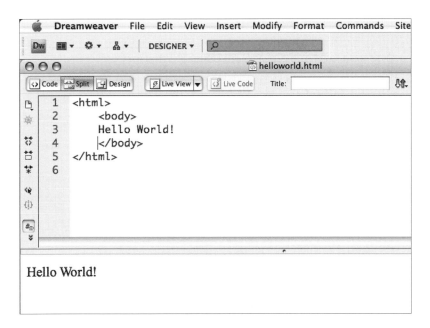

FIG 15.10 Split view.

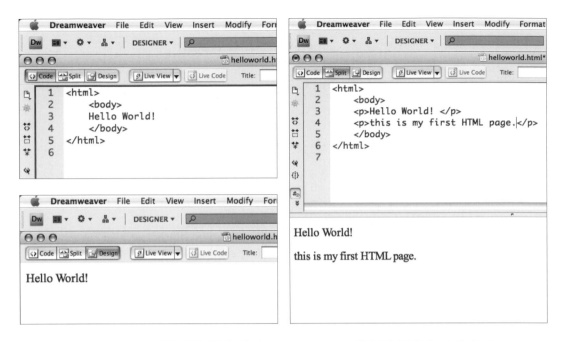

TOP: **FIG 15.11** Code.
BOTTOM: **FIG 15.12** Design.

FIG 15.13 Typing in Split view.

3. In the upper left corner click Code. (Fig 15.11) Only the code is displayed. Note that your markup language is color-coded. Tags are blue, and text is black.

4. Click Design. (Fig 15.12) Now we can only see the result of the code, or what will be displayed in the browser.

5. Switch back to Split view. In the Design view half, place your cursor at the end of "Hello World!" Press the Return key and type "This is my first HTML page." (Fig 15.13) Save the document using File > Save. Note how Dreamweaver changes the code for you. A paragraph tag has been added to the code to format the new paragraph we requested when we pressed the Return key in Design view.

The paragraph tag is opened and closed around the new line of text. This is an example of nesting. Nesting is when a set of open and closed tags are placed inside of another open and closed tag. The relationship between where each set opens and closes is important. One is structured around the other so that they never overlap. (Fig 15.14)

6. Return to the browser where you viewed *helloworld.html* in Exercise 1. (Fig 15.15) Refresh the browser page and observe the changes we made to the file in Dreamweaver. If the file was closed, use File > Open and open the *helloworld.html* file. In this exercise we modified the *helloworld.html* file. We did not save a new file, we saved on top of the existing file. The browser displays changes to the file when changes have been made to the original file (File > Save) in Dreamweaver and the page is reloaded in the browser (Command+R in most browsers).

7. Go back to Dreamweaver and type a new paragraph in Design view: "Hello World is the first exercise you learn in any code or markup language." (Fig 15.16) Save the file and refresh the browser to see the new text display on the web page.

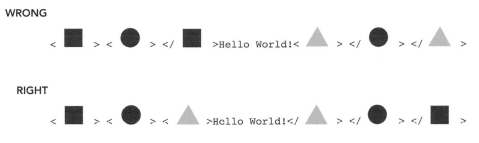

FIG 15.14 Example of nesting.

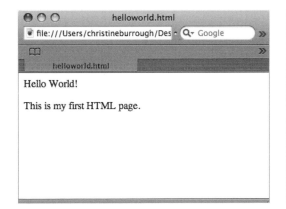

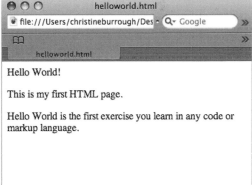

FIG 15.15 *helloworld.html.*

FIG 15.16 Type in *helloworld.html.*

03 Hyperlink

Hyperlinks, or links as they are commonly called, are a one-click route from one HTML file to another. Links are the simplest form of interactivity on the web.

Tip: If the Properties inspector is missing, select Window > Properties or reload the Designer workspace in the Application bar.

1. Open a new web browser tab or window and search for the phrase "Hello World! Collection." Click on the Hello World Collection, which was at the following URL at the time of this writing: http://www.roesler-ac.de/wolfram/hello.htm. This collection of Hello World! examples started in 1994, although "Hello World!" first appeared in a programming book in 1978. Copy the site's URL from the browser's address bar and return to the file we modified in Exercise 2 in Dreamweaver.

Watch Out: If you do not press the Return key, the link will not be created.

2. In Design view, select the text "the first exercise you learn in any code or markup language" by highlighting it with your mouse. If it isn't already active, click the HTML button on the left edge of the Properties inspector. Paste the URL you just copied into the field labeled Link.

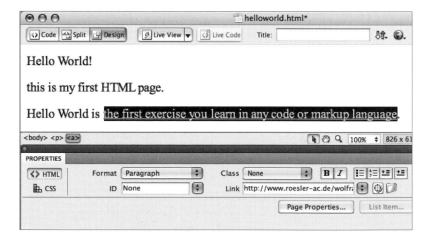

FIG 15.17 Text selected becomes a hyperlink.

3. Press the Return key and it will change the selected text from body copy to a hyperlink. (Fig 15.17) This is important: save the file. If the file is not saved, the updated work will not load in the browser.

4. Go to the browser and refresh the *helloworld.html* page. The link should function in the browser. Return to Dreamweaver and inspect the code that was created.

In the code, the "a" stands for anchor and "href" tells the browser that this is a hypertext reference, while the URL in the quote marks is the value that tells the browser where the hypertext reference points. The anchor tag is closed with </a>. Notice that the tag starts just before the word "the" and closes just before the period at the end of the sentence. This part of the sentence becomes the link. (Fig 15.18)

5. Move the closing anchor tag to just after the word "learn." The link will be shortened to include only the text that is between the opening and closing tags. (Fig 15.9)

FIG **15.18** The code for the hyperlink.

FIG **15.19** Moving the closing anchor tag.

EXERCISE
04 Images

To add an image to the HTML page, you need to have an image prepared for online viewing (see Chapter 12). For this exercise, we will search for an image on Flickr. In Chapter 2 we explained that Flickr is an online photo sharing website where viewers can search for images by tags. In this exercise we will use an image that has been placed in the public domain with a Creative Commons license.

1. Go to flickr.com. If you are not signed in, the Search field is vertically centered on the right half of the page. If you are signed in, use the Search field in the top left corner. Search for "Hello World." (Fig 15.20)

2. Click the Advanced Search button on the results page.

3. Scroll down and check the boxes next to "Only search within Creative Commons-licensed content." (Fig 15.21) Creative Commons is a licensing schema that presents an alternative to the standard U.S. copyright laws. All photographs uploaded to Flickr are automatically copyrighted, preventing other people from using or building upon them. Creative Commons allows you to post your work online and license it openly, allowing others to use it in their work. Online culture is a culture of sharing, remixing, and collaboration. Creative Commons licensing enables and empowers this culture. Reference Chapter 2 for a more detailed synopsis of copyright laws, fair use, and alternative licensing with Creative Commons.

FIG 15.20 flickr.com search for Hello World.

Note:

Web interface design changes often. It is possible that by the time you are reading this, these specific directions for Flickr will be out of date.

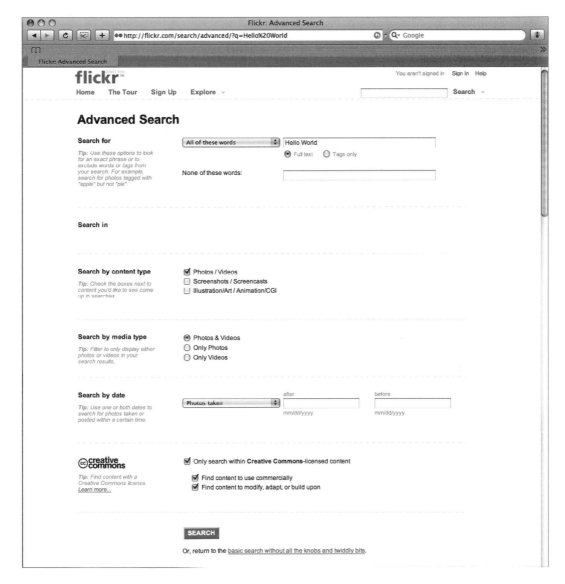

FIG 15.21 Advanced Search.

FIG 15.22 Click image.

FIG 15.23 Control-click.

4. Click on an image that you found in the Creative Commons "Hello World" Flickr search. (Fig 15.22) Now the image appears on the Flickr page maintained by its author.

Tip: URL stands for *Universal Resource Locator.* This is the web address that points to a file that is saved on an Internet server.

5. Contol-click or right-click on the image and choose Copy Image Address or Copy Image Location. (Fig 15.23) This copies the URL. The URL is the path to the location where the image file is saved on the server. The next time you use Edit > Paste in any text field, this address will be pasted. We will use this in Dreamweaver in the next step.

6. Go back to Dreamweaver and view the *helloworld.html* file in Code view. Type a new paragraph tag. Note that Dreamweaver automatically

FIG 15.24 After refreshing, the image appears on the page.

closes the tag. Now add an image tag like this, `<img src="url" />`. Replace the letters "url" with the URL that you copied from flickr.com by pasting it into that area. Leave the quote marks in the tag, and the space before the closing bracket.

The image tag closes itself. The combination of space, slash, and bracket at the end of the tag signifies a closing tag.

7. Save the file and refresh the page in your browser. The image appears on the page, with a paragraph break between it and the link we made in Exercise 3. (Fig 15.24)

05 Formatting type

If you have printed documents from Microsoft Word to a laser printer, you have used a markup language. The difference between working in Dreamweaver and printing from Word is that you are aware that you are creating the markup language in the HTML code. In essence, the **B** button in Word is a user interface component that marks up the selected type so it displays and prints as bold. The printer reads the file sent by the program and formats the typography. In Dreamweaver, you use the interface to add formatting, and you see the code that is being written for the browser. Thinking of the browser like a printer (and the web as the page) can be helpful for understanding markup language. You will discover that it is not always the perfect simile, as user interaction varies from the printed page to the web browser. The media environment always affects the audience.

FIG 15.25 A header tag transforms "Hello World!" into a headline.

1. The header tag will transform the words "Hello World!" into a headline. Insert the tag as demonstrated. (Fig15.25)

2. Formatting type in Dreamweaver is like formatting type in other Adobe programs. Bold and italic styles are one click away, but do notice the tags that are added to the HTML so that the styles are displayed properly in the browser. Click on Split view. Make the word "first" bold by selecting it and clicking the B button in the Properties inspector. (Fig 15.26) Dreamweaver will surround the word with the strong tag.

3. Select the word "any" and click the Italicize button in the Properties inspector. Dreamweaver uses the em tag to italicize the word. (Fig 15.27)

FIG 15.26 Make the word "first" bold.

FIG 15.27 Italicize the word "any."

A modern server room.

16 Files and Servers

A *web page* is an HTML file that is stored on a web server.

A *server* is a computer with software installed on it that allows it to send and receive requests for web pages.

A *client* is a computer running software, such as a web browser, that sends requests to the server. When you click a link on the web, your computer sends a request to the server through the web browser and the server returns the requested web page.

Each web page has its own unique address, called a Universal Resource Locator, or URL. A properly formed URL has a domain name, such as www.digital-foundations.net. URLs may include folders and file names. Folders are denoted by forward slashes, and HTML files end in .html. For example, www.digital-foundations.net/folder/file.html is a URL pointing to a file named *file.html* stored in a folder named *folder* on the server that hosts the domain digital-foundations.net. Files and folders on a server are like folders on your own computer. The difference is that anyone on the Internet can view them!

One way of thinking about URLs and servers is through the metaphor of the postal mail system. An address specifies the exact location of the addressee. To do this, it takes a name, street name and number, city, state, postal code, and country. Likewise, a URL is the exact location of the file you are requesting. The domain name is like the city, state, zip and sometimes the nation; the folder is like the street address; and the file name is the addressee's name. Everything has to be included, or the right file will not be requested.

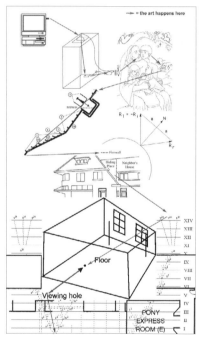

Simple Net Art Diagram

The art happens here

MTAA ca. 1997

FIG 16.1 *Simple Net Art Diagram*, MTAA-RR, 1997, http://www.mtaa.net/, CC-BY.

FIG 16.2 Detail of *Complex Net Art Diagram*, Abe Linkoln, 2003, http://www.linkoln.net/complex/

Artists experiment with their materials, whether they are paint, marble, photographic paper, or for Internet artists, the communication between clients and servers. In an attempt to describe their Internet artworks, MTAA (M. River & T. Whid Art Associates) created *The Simple Net Art Diagram* (1997). (Fig 16.1) The concept of the diagram is that Net Art is about communication. The art is not just the code on the server or the aesthetic results of the code when displayed in the browser. The art happens through communication.

The artist Abe Linkoln took MTAA's work one step further, with the *Complex Net Art Diagram* (http://www.linkoln.net/complex/). (Fig 16.2) For Linkoln, the web is a repository of found images and massive quantities of information. Notice the appropriation of Jodi's code bomb in this work.

A server is just a computer loaded with software that delivers files requested by web browsers. The artist duo Eva and Franco Mattes, who work as 0100101110101101.org, created a project called Life Sharing, where they turned their own computer into a web server, exposing their entire computer and all of its contents. (Fig 16.3)

EXERCISE
01 Defining a site in Dreamweaver

Defining a site tells Dreamweaver how to keep track of the site's files on your local machine and how to keep them synchronized on the remote web server. If you do not define your site, you can drive yourself crazy with broken links and missing images.

Note: Choose the Designer workspace from the pull-down menu in the Application bar before working on the following exercises.

1. Choose HTML from the Create New menu when Dreamweaver launches. (Fig 16.4) If the Welcome Screen is disabled, use File > New > Blank Page > HTML > <none>.

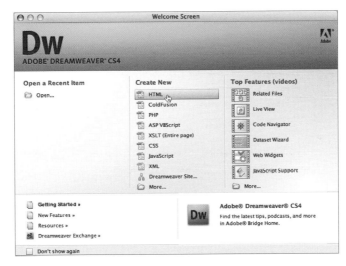

FIG 16.4 Create New > HTML

FIG 16.5 Site > New Site...

2. Choose Site > New Site... (Fig 16.5)

3. In the New Site dialog box, use the Basic tab at the top of the box. This will make the dialog box act like an installation wizard, guiding you through the process of defining your site. On the first screen, name your site and enter its URL. (Fig 16.6) The name of the site can be anything, but we tend to keep it simple. If you don't have a URL, you can leave this field blank. Click the Next button.

4. The next screen is for defining a server technology, such as PHP, that you would like to use. Don't worry about what this means, just leave the radio button for No selected, and click the Next button.

5. Check the radio button for "Edit local copies on my machine." When you edit locally, your pages are designed and coded on your hard drive before they are transmitted to the server. (It is rarely a good idea to edit directly on the server until you are more experienced.) Use the Folder icon to the right of the Text Entry field to browse to a folder location. It will launch a window similar to the Open or Save window where you can choose or create your root folder. (Fig 16.7-8)

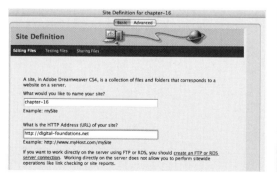

FIG 16.6 URL settings.

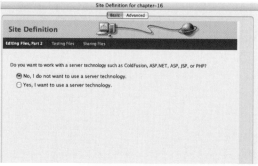

FIG 16.7 Server technology.

The root folder is the location where all of the web files are saved. This is important because when you are ready to upload your content to the server, you will re-create the same file structure at the root directory of the web site.

Here is where metaphor can be used to understand this digital idea. You have a home that is located at a particular address. The postal service delivers your mail to that address. If you are in the kitchen or the bedroom, you are positioned in some area of the house, contained within that address, so you will receive mail delivered to the address. The domain name is your address. The root folder is your home. All the files in your root folder are at home. Any folders you create inside the root folder are contained by the root and can be accessed like rooms in a house.

6. If you have a web domain and want to send files to the server, select FTP (File Transfer Protocol) from the pull-down menu that asks, "How do you connect to your remote server?" If you do not have a domain name, use the pull-down menu to select None.

Enter the FTP hostname and your assigned file directory, your FTP login (sometimes referred to as username), and the FTP password. (Fig 16.9)

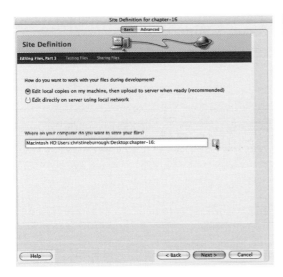

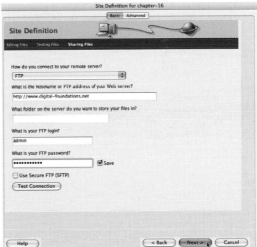

FIG 16.8 Root folder.

FIG 16.9 FTP information.

If you do not have a web server and want to set one up, we recommend our students use Lunarpages.com or Dreamhost.com because of their ease of use and customer service. Use the discount code DGTLFNDTNS for a $50 discount when you register for Dreamhost.com hosting. This book just paid for itself!

Click the Test Connection button to verify that Dreamweaver can successfully connect to your server. If you are using this in a computer lab at a school, there is a very good chance that the lab does not allow connections through this panel. If you are unable to connect in a public location, try it again at home. Click the Next button.

7. Do not enable check-in and check-out at this time, as you are the only person working on your own files. Click the Next button. (Fig 16.10)

8. Click the Done button. (Fig 16.11)

9. Look in the Files panel to view the root folder for the site you just defined. Click the button in the top right corner to expand the view in order to see both the local (files on your hard drive) and remote (files on the server) sites. (Fig 16.12-13)

10. If you have a domain name and entered the log-in information when you defined the site, clicking on the "Connect to remote host" button will access the server where your files are stored. If you do not have a domain name, this button will return an error message. Click the button to collapse the view so that you are only viewing the local

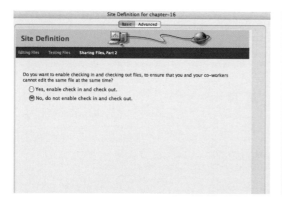

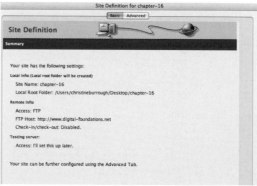

FIG 16.10 Check-in and -out.

FIG 16.11 Summary.

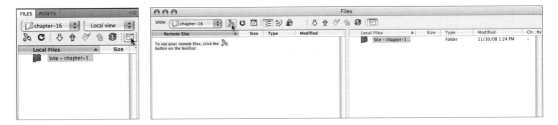

FIG 16.12 Root folder.   **FIG 16.13** Expanded view.

files. If you do have access to a server, uploading files to it so that they are published on the web is as easy as dragging the files from a folder on the local side of this panel to a folder (called a *directory*) on the remote side.

EXERCISE

02 File and folder management

1. View the HTML document in Split mode. Type "Hello World" into the Design view. Highlight the text and choose Heading 1 from the Format pull-down panel menu in the Properties inspector. Notice that the H1 tag is added in the code. (Fig 16.14)

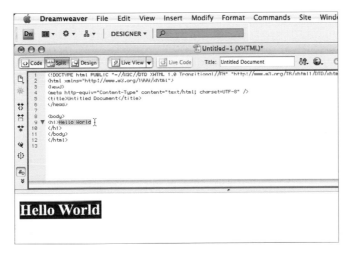

FIG 16.14 Hello World.

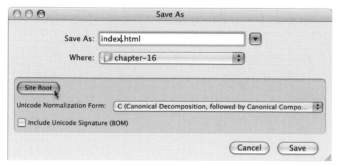

FIG 16.15 File > Save As.

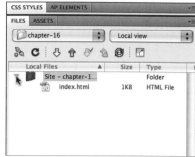

FIG 16.16 New HTML file: *index.html.*

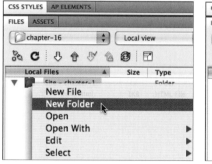

FIG 16.17 Contextual menu.

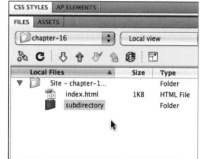

FIG 16.18 New folder: *subdirectory.*

2. Choose File > Save As to save the page with the name *index.html* in the root folder. You can save into the root folder in one click by using the Site Root button in the Save As dialog box. It is essential to have an index file with either an .html or .htm extension in your root directory because the browser automatically knows to load an HTML file with the index name from the root directory. Any other page that you intend to display in the browser will have to be accessed with a fully typed-out path or through a link from one of the other pages. (Fig 16.15)

3. Expand the Site folder in the Files panel to see the *index.html* file saved in the root folder. (Fig 16.16)

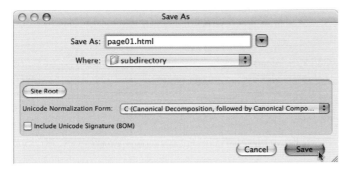

FIG 16.19 File > Save As.

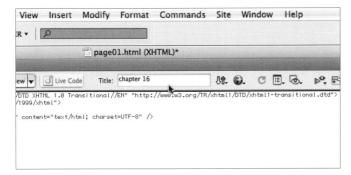

FIG 16.20 New title: *chapter 16*.

4. Control-click on the root folder to display the contextual menu and choose New Folder. Create a new folder called *subdirectory*. (Fig 16.17-18)

5. Make a new file by choosing File > New > HTML > <none>. Save it as *page01.html* inside the new folder named *subdirectory*. (Fig 16.19)

6. The new file already has code, even though we have only opened and saved the file. Look in the code portion of the Split view. At the top there is the Document Type Declaration. This tells the browser the version of HTML used to write the file. Next is the html tag followed by the head tag. Inside the head tag we will define the title of the page. The title appears at the top of the browser. Type "chapter 16" in the title field at the top of the document. Notice the title tag nested in the head area of the code has been modified to reflect the change. (Fig 16.20)

7. Type "Hello Subdirectory" on *page01* in Design view.

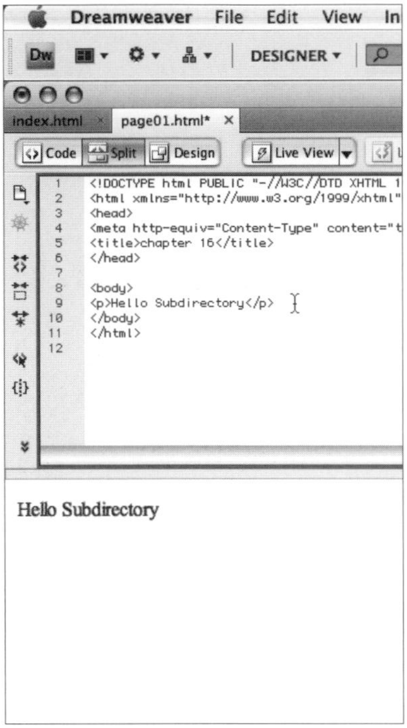

FIG 16.21 Hello Subdirectory.

FIG 16.22 Create a new link.

8. Go back to the first file, *index.html*. If it is still open, then it is one click away on a tab in the top left area of the document window. If you closed it, double-click the file *index.html* from the Files panel. Add the text "click to see page one" in the body of the page by typing in Design view. Now we will create a link to *page01.html* from the index page. Select the text "click to see page one" in Design view and mouse over the target button on the far right of the Properties inspector, beyond the Link field. Notice the Point to File tool tip that results from your mouse rolling over the target button. Click the Point to File button and drag the arrow to *page01.html* in the Files panel. When you release the mouse, the link will appear in the link field and in Code view as an href tag. Notice that "subdirectory/page01.html" is the path for the new link relative to the site home. *Subdirectory* is the name of the folder, and *page01.html* is the file inside the folder. The slash tells the browser to look inside a directory. (Fig 16.21-22)

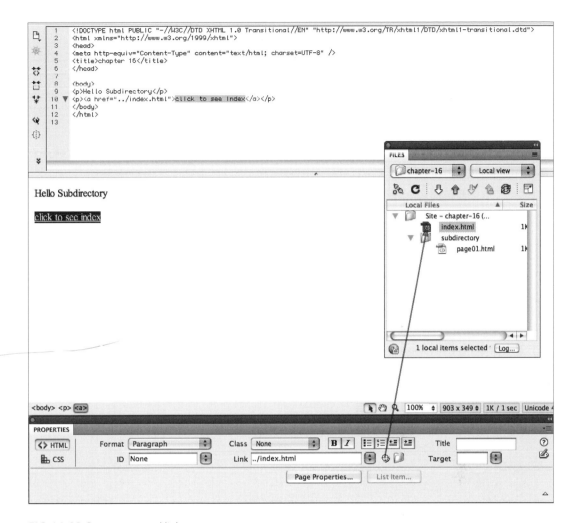

FIG 16.23 Create a second link.

9. Repeat the directions in the previous step on *page01* to create a link from *page01* back to *index*. Make the link read "click to see index" instead of "click to see page01." Notice that "../index.html" is the path for the new link. The dot-dot-slash syntax instructs the browser to move up one directory in order to find the file. On your hard drive, this means look inside the enclosing folder. (Fig 16.23)

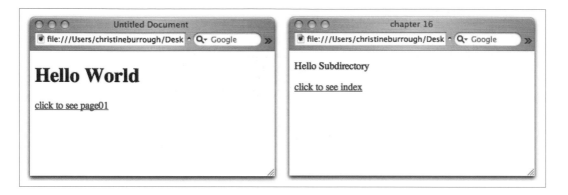

FIG 16.24 Notice that for each of the browser windows, that the two pages have many differences. *Index* is an untitled page, while *page01* has the title "Chapter 16." Also notice the difference in the leading on the web page as a result of the H1 tag applied to the words "Hello World" on the index page.

10. Remember to save all of your changes in Dreamweaver in order to see the links working in the browser. Links are not functional in Dreamweaver; clicking on a link in Dreamweaver will not open that HTML page. Either click to each page individually and use File > Save or use File > Save All to save all of the files that are open. Then test your work in a browser. Use File > Open File or drag the *index* file to the display area of a web browser. Notice that the location area of the navigation bar (where you type or read a URL) displays the name for each file as you click between the two pages. (Fig 16.24)

11. Finally, it is a good idea for beginning web developers to commit to the names applied to files and folders. However, if you have to rename a folder or a file, Dreamweaver will prompt you to update the files that are referencing it as a link. Dreamweaver can update the code in your files to reflect the name change. We'll demonstrate this by changing the name of the folder *subdirectory* to *subdirectory02*. As soon as the name is changed (click on the word "subdirectory," pause, type in the numbers at the end of the word, then hit the Return key), click the Update button in the Dreamweaver Update Files warning dialog box. (Fig 16.25)

12. Review the index page. Notice that "subdirectory" has now been changed to "subdirectory02" in the path to the link. (Fig 16.26)

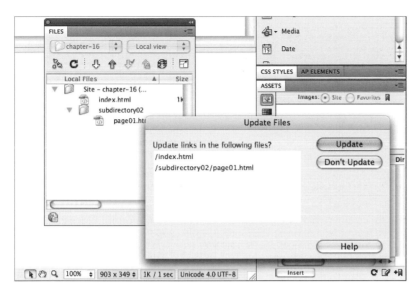

FIG 16.25 Update Files.

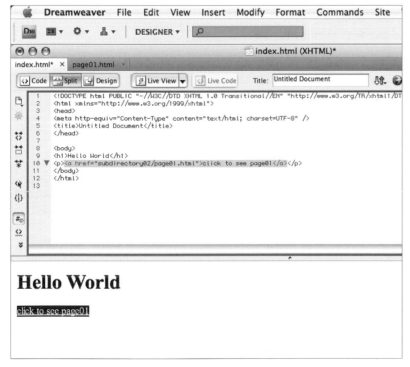

FIG 16.26 A refreshed link.

Louis Sullivan's Prudential Building, Buffalo, New York. Photo credit: Seth Tisue, http://flickr.com/people/tisue/, CC-BY.

17 Style Sheets — Separating Form and Content

In the last two chapters, we left many aesthetic design choices out of the exercises and focused on the tools for building code. However, aesthetics must not be left out of the conversation. As American architect Louis Sullivan (1856–1924) once said, "Form ever follows function." Sullivan's use of steel instead of masonry to create the structure of a building allowed it to be separate from the building's external elements of appearance. Sullivan is known for solving the problem architects faced when designing for these new buildings, which were no longer constrained by the technical limits of weight-bearing masonry. He embraced the changes that came with the steel frame and created a way to stylize the exterior appearance of the building. His call to allow form to derive from function has profoundly influenced design and art.

In constructing web pages, we too have a way to keep the structure separate from the *appearance* through the use of one or more style sheets. When you can make a web page look so many wildly different ways, you need to remember your site's function. Even the most experimental or conceptual art site has a function. In this chapter, we focus on relating to form and function: keeping the structural markup of the HTML document separate from the code that controls the aesthetics.

There are several reasons for keeping the content and form of a web page separated, including the following:

1. Web users display code on different browsers. Each browser follows different styling rules.
2. There are web standards that rely on the separation of content and form to make web content accessible for the greatest amount of users.
3. A web page can easily take on a whole new design, look, and feel with the switch of a style sheet.
4. It creates an efficient, productive workflow.

In the following exercises, we will write a new type of file called a Cascading Style Sheet (CSS) to contain our style information. This file will be attached to our HTML page. Our HTML page will contain all of our content, in structural <div> tags, and the CSS page will contain all of the style information for each of those labeled <div> tags.

The maxim form follows function dictates that the visual appearance of an object is derived from its use. Sometimes this visual appearance will necessarily be highly designed, and other times it will look like the bare-bones HTML in the previous chapter. Each function dictates a different form.

A List Apart Magazine (http://alistapart.com/about) "explores the design, development, and meaning of web content, with a special focus on web standards and best practices." A List Apart was one of the first web sites to advocate an exclusively CSS-centric design strategy. This web site is an excellent resource for developing web designers and information architects.

In addition to the wealth of articles, the site teaches by demonstration. It is written in well-crafted structural HTML code, fronted with easy-to-navigate typography written in CSS.

Notice the contrast in typographic hierarchies from the search area to the body content of the page, in the headers and links.

Compare AListApart.com with Craigslist.com, a popular web site that facilitates an exchange of information between people looking for buyers/sellers/traders and every other possible relationship to commodity, personals, or idea exchange. (Fig 17.1–2) When you are thinking about web design, Craigslist may not be the first web site on your mind. However, as a work of information design, it is successful: the type is easy to read and even easier to navigate. The hierarchy among the various types of exchanges and locations worldwide is intuitive.

FIG 17.1 Screen shot of http://www.alistapart.com taken on November 14, 2008.

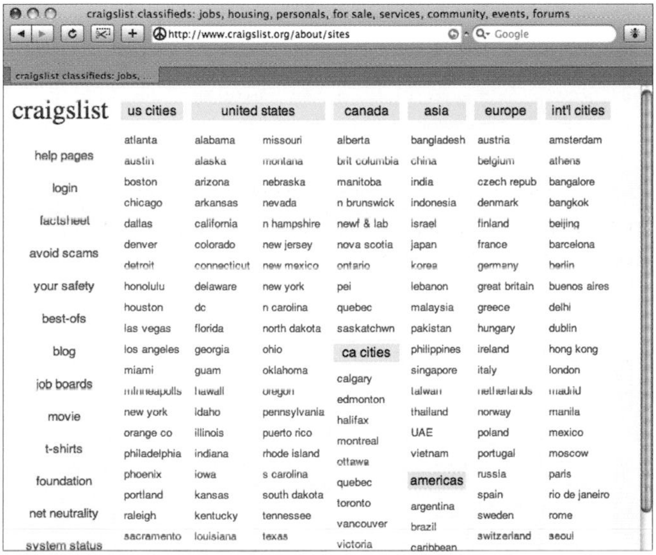

FIG 17.2 Screen shot of http://www.craigslist.org taken on November 14, 2008.

EXERCISE
01 Applying a style

Note: Choose the Designer workspace from the pull-down menu in the Application bar before working on the following exercises.

So far we have modified the HTML page properties and placed links and images on the web page using Dreamweaver. Until now, these page elements have all followed the default settings for font, font size, text color, and so on. By using CSS, we can control these and other design settings. We will separate the content of the page from its style properties, which will be stored in the CSS file.

1. Open Dreamweaver and choose HTML from the Create New area of the Welcome Screen. (Fig 17.3)

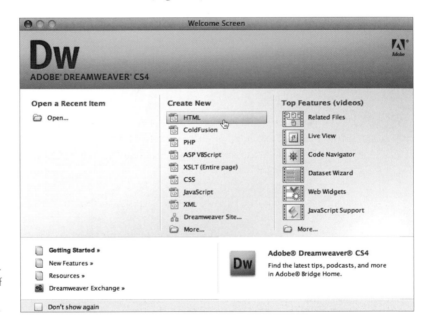

FIG 17.3 Choose File > New > HTML > [None] if you were not prompted by the Welcome Screen.

Note: Remember, certain aesthetic options are limited on the web. For instance, in order for a web page to load a specific font, the font must be installed on the user's computer. If the font is missing, the browser will load a different font. Therefore, most web pages are designed using "system" fonts (those installed on the computer at the time of purchase), including Helvetica, Arial, Times, Georgia, Verdana, Courier, and Geneva.

⋆ **Finished exercise file available in the Download Materials area of the wiki.**

FIG 17.4 HTML code displayed in Dreamweaver.

FIG 17.5 Modify > Page Properties.

2. Before adding content to the HTML file, choose File > Save As and save the file as *index.html* into a folder you will use for this chapter. We saved our file in a folder on the Desktop called *chapter17*.

3. Evaluate the code of the HTML file. (Fig 17.4) You can do this in Code view, or you can open the saved HTML file in a web browser and use the View menu to see the source code. So far, the code only contains HTML.

4. Open the Page Properties dialog box by choosing Modify > Page Properties and change the default font. We used the Page font pull-down menu to choose the default font: Verdana, Geneva, sans-serif. Click OK after choosing a font. (Fig 17.5)

5. Dreamweaver saves the default HTML page settings as a style. Choose File > Save. Look in Code view or reload the page in the browser so you can see the changes. We will evaluate this code in the next exercise. (Fig 17.6)

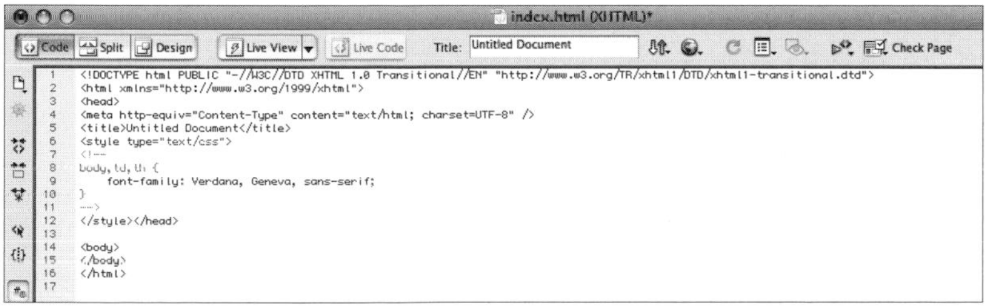

FIG 17.6 The changed Code view.

02 Evaluating the code

Dreamweaver adds the code for styles in style tags in the <head> section of the document. Styles are written in *declaration blocks*. Declaration blocks contain properties and values. Here we have a declaration block for the body of the HTML page. Inside the style tag, you will see:

```
body, td, th {
font-family: Verdana, Geneva, sans-serif;
}
```

In this code, "font-family" is the property. "Verdana, Geneva, sans-serif" is the value.

Note:

There are some very good, free resources available for helping evaluate code. When working with HTML, CSS, or any other code meant for the web for the first time, it's always a good idea to make use of the helpful web sites that exist. A Google search for whatever tag or concept you are struggling with will lead to a seemingly infinite supply of helpful lessons and tutorials. Some good places to start are:

World Wide Web Consortium

http://www.w3.org/

w3 Markup Validation Service

http://validator.w3.org/

EXERCISE

03 Creating a new rule

Styles can be created, modified, and deleted using the CSS Styles panel. To open it, choose Window > CSS Styles. You can redefine a default HTML tag (which we did in Exercise 1) or create a custom style called a *class*. We will work with classes throughout the remaining exercises. A class is a modifier that can be applied to an HTML tag in order to add a style.

1. Double-click the CSS Styles tab to expand the panel. The style for the font-family property that we just made is saved in this panel. Double-clicking the font-family property for the CSS Rule Definition dialog box would open the settings applied to that rule. (Fig 17.7) We use this panel to create or modify styles. Press cancel if you've opened the Rule Definition dialog box.

2. Create a new style using the New CSS Rule button in the lower right corner of the panel (it looks like a plus sign). Define a rule for the tag. A CSS rule is made of two parts, a *selector* and a *declaration*. The selector names the part of the HTML document that will be affected by the style. The declaration tells the HTML code how the selector is affected in the rule. (Fig 17.8)

FIG 17.7 CSS Rule Definition dialog box.

FIG 17.8 New CSS Rule button.

3. Leave the Selector Type pull-down panel menu set to Class. Our rule will format text that could be used as a headline. Name the selector *.headline*. Leave the Rules Definition pull-down menu on the selection "(This document only)." Click OK to exit the dialog box. (Fig 17.9)

Tip: Class names must begin with a period. If you forget to start the name with a period, Dreamweaver will add it for you.

4. Give the new rule values for the declaration using the CSS Rule definition that appears for the *.headline* dialog box. We formatted our headline type with the following: Font-family: Georgia, Times New Roman, Times, serif; Font Size: 36 pixels; Font-weight: bold; Font-style: italic; and Color: #F00. Click OK to exit the dialog box. (Fig 17.10)

5. Now we will apply the new rule. View the HTML document in Split View mode and type the phrase "CSS Separates Form from Content" in the design area of the HTML page.

Select the phrase in Design view and apply the new rule using the Class pull-down menu in the Properties inspector. (Fig 17.11) The phrase takes on the attributes that we defined in the *.headline* rule. Save the HTML file (Command+S).

FIG 17.10 Format the new rule.

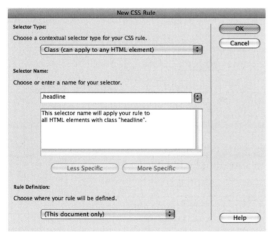

FIG 17.9 ".headline"

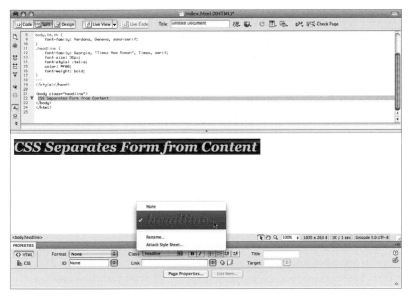

6. Evaluate the style in two places. First look in the CSS panel and notice that you can click on the All tab or the Current tab. Click on the All tab in order to see all of the styles that are defined for this HTML document. (Fig 17.12) You should see the rule *.headline* there. You can double-click it to modify the rule. Also look at the document code area. Notice that the phrase "CSS Separates Form from Content" is written in the body area of the HTML code. (Fig 17.13) This is the content on the page. The "form" of the content is applied by using CSS. In the head section of the page, the CSS code for the new rule, *.headline*, has been added. This rule has declarations for five different selectors: font-family, font-size, font-style, color, and font-weight. The style is actually being applied to the phrase within the body tag. Notice the additional code in the body tag, class="headline". Class modifies the body HTML tag so that the CSS rule *.headline* is applied to any content inside that tag.

LEFT: FIG 17.11 Select headline.

ABOVE: FIG 17.12 Properties for the style.

7. Since the *.headline* class is modifying the entire body tag, see what happens when you try to write some copy beneath the headline. In Design view, press the Return key at the end of the phrase and type in "Use the span tag to apply the class in specific areas." Notice that this text is also formatted in large, serif, red text. In the next step we will remove the formatting from this part of the text by adding the span tag.

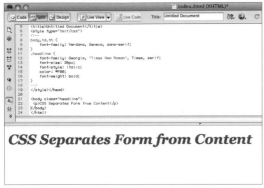

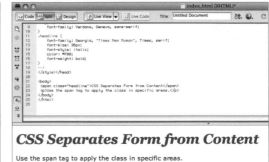

LEFT: FIG 17.13
The headline style.

RIGHT: FIG 17.14
A span with a class.

8. View the page in Split view. We will modify the HTML code so that the *.headline class* will only be applied to the phrase "CSS Separates Form from Content." Cut (Command+X) the class="headline" portion of the code from the <body> tag and delete the space that was between the two words "body" and "class."

In other words, the tag
<body class = "headline">
becomes the tag
<body>

Replace the tag
 <p>CSS Separates Form from Content</p>

with this tag
<span class="headline">CSS Separates Form from Content</span>

Notice that the rest of the text, "Use the span tag to apply the class in specific areas," is now formatted in the default text. (Fig 17.14)

EXERCISE
04 Creating an external style sheet

So far, the CSS that we have created has been saved in the head area of the HTML page *index.html* and applied in the body area of the page. CSS code can also be saved in an external style sheet. Saving the CSS externally has three implications:

1. The HTML document will rely upon a second document with a .css extension for any formatting that has been applied with CSS code.
2. The external style sheet can be applied to multiple HTML documents.
3. The CSS code saved in an external sheet is easily modified in one location (as opposed to opening multiple HTML files). In this exercise we will create an external style sheet, a CSS file that is applied by being linked to an HTML document.

1. Choose File > New and select CSS from the page type list and click Create.

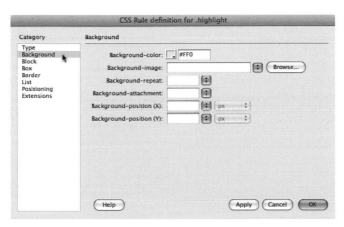

FIG 17.15 Background properties.

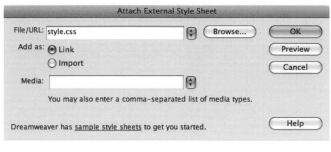

FIG 17.17 Attach External Style Sheet dialog box.

FIG 17.16 Attach Style Sheet.

2. In the CSS panel, add a new class called *.highlight* (leave the rest of the settings as we did in Exercise 3, Step 3). In the CSS Rule definition for the *.highlight* dialog box, click on Background from the Category list and set the Background-color field to bright yellow. We used #FF0. (Fig 17.15)

3. Click OK to exit the dialog box and choose File > Save As to save the CSS file. Name the CSS file *style.css* and save it in the same folder as the index.html file that you created in the previous exercises.

4. Click on the *index.html* tab or use File > Open to edit the page we created in the previous exercises.

5. Now we will link the new CSS document to *index.html*. Click the Attach Style Sheet icon on the bottom of the CSS Styles panel. (Fig 17.16)

6. You are prompted to browse for the CSS file that will be attached to *index.html*. You can press the Browse button, or if you know that you saved your CSS file as *style.css,* you can type the name of the file into the File field. We recommend browsing for the file to avoid typos. Make sure the Link radio button is selected and click OK. (Fig 17.17)

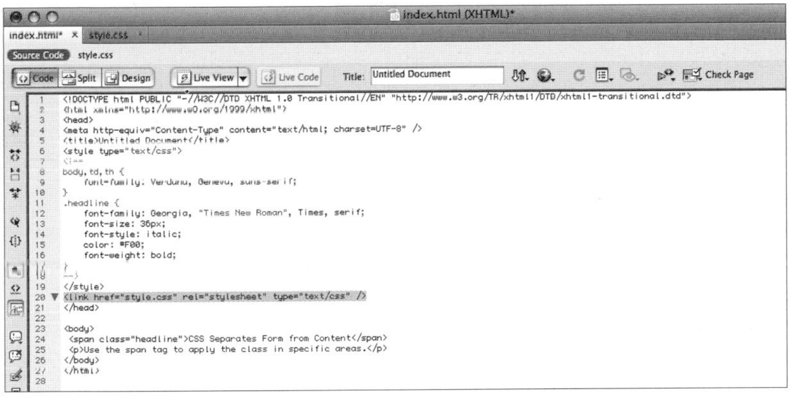

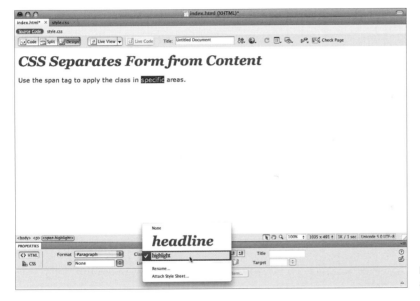

FIG 17.18 The code linking to the style sheet.

FIG 17.19 New styles appear.

7. Once you have linked the file using the CSS Styles panel, check the code in the *index.html* file to see how the CSS file is linked. You should see that Dreamweaver added the code <link href="style.css" rel="stylesheet" type="text/css" /> in the head area of the document. (Fig 17.18)

8. Now modify *index.html* in Design view. Select the word "specific" and use the Properties inspector to choose the class *.highlight*. (Fig 17.19)

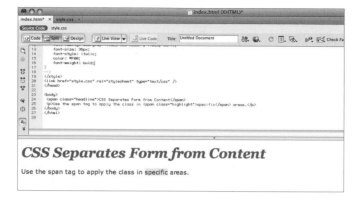

FIG 17.20 The span with background color.

9. View *index.html* in Split view and notice that the code includes the <span> tag around the word "specific." (Fig 17.20) This is because we selected the word individually before applying the style. The *.highlight* class applied to the <span> tag comes from the external style sheet.

10. Choose File > Save All. The Save All command saves all open documents.

11. Open the *index.html* file in a web browser to see the document with the styles applied. The red headline style is stored in the head area of the HTML document. The yellow highlight style is stored in the *style.css* document. Both documents should be saved in the same location. (Fig 17.21)

To see that the *style.css* document is affecting your index.html file, move the *style.css* to a new location on your hard drive. For instance, we had both files saved in a folder named *chapter17* on our Desktop. Move *style.css* out of the folder, to the Desktop. Refresh the *index.html* file in the web browser. (Fig 17.22) The style will not affect the HTML page if the page cannot find it. The linked file is pointing to the folder where the HTML file was stored. By moving the file, you are breaking the link between the CSS and HTML files. Move the CSS file back to the same location where the HTML file is stored and refresh the browser again. The link should be fixed.

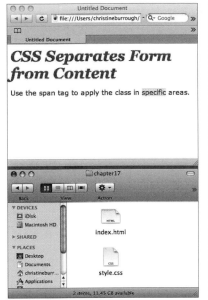

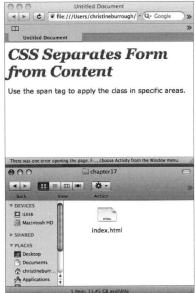

FIG 17.21 Linked browser.

FIG 17.22 Unlinked browser.

Note:

Visit http://www.csszengarden.com to see a gallery of CSS designs applied to one HTML page.

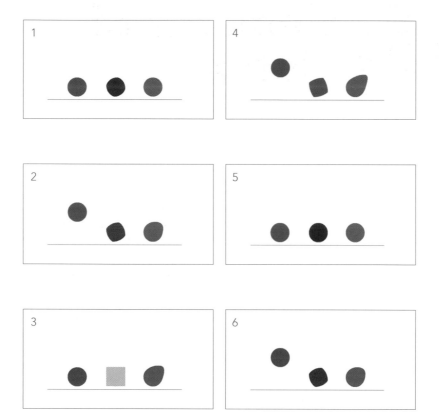

Frames from the final animation created during this chapter.

18 Elements of Motion

Rhythm is an essential consideration in the production of motion graphics. A common time signature is 4/4, where four even beats make up a bar. For example, House music has a 4/4 beat, with 90 beats per minute. In House music, the beat is counted in cycles of eight. The rhythm is established and peaks at the fourth beat. It reduces in the next four beats, in preparation for the next set of eight beats. This method of counting time can be applied to animation. Understanding animation becomes easier as you learn to visualize time. Whether you are keeping track of the musical score or graphic frames on a timeline, counting time is important, and "seeing" the count is a necessity.

Early experimental animation kept time visually with abstract shapes. Rhythm is the topic of Viking Eggeling's film *Symphonie Diagonale* (1924). (Fig 18.1) Lines, curves, and forms play in rhythm. Pay attention to the formal design relationships while watching this animation. Watch for balance and movement, form and negative space, and the expressiveness of a line. Notice how the formal balance changes over time and shapes change in size and value. Rhythm is used to create a sense of predictability within the abstraction, and departures from that predictability create drama and focus.

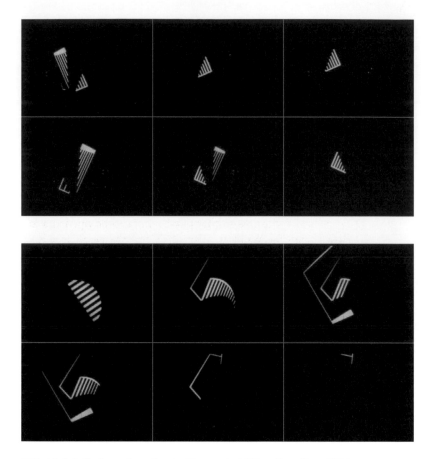

FIG 18.1 Stills from *Symphonie Diagonale*, Viking Eggeling, 1924.

In the following exercises, we will create Flash animations using basic geometric shapes. Keep the formal relationships that you viewed in Eggeling's film in mind while working through these exercises.

Note:

See Eggeling's film here:
http://www.youtube.com/watch?v=PxqqPiVDOQ4

01 Visualizing time, keyframes, shape tween

1. Click the Flash File (ActionScript 3.0) button in the Create New area of the Flash startup window to create a new document, or choose File > New > Flash File (ActionScript 3.0). (Fig 18.2)

2. Inside Flash you will see a Timeline, Tools panel, Properties and various other panels that can be opened and closed from the Window menu. In Flash, the work area is the Stage. Most of your work will take place on the Stage or within the frames of the Flash Timeline. A timeline allows us to control shapes over time. The Playhead is like the needle of a record player, playing the contents of a timeline as it moves across individual frames. You can manually move the Playhead with the mouse to run over shorter parts of a file, which can be convenient when timelines become long.

Note: Choose the Essentials workspace from the pull-down menu in the Application bar before working on the following exercises.

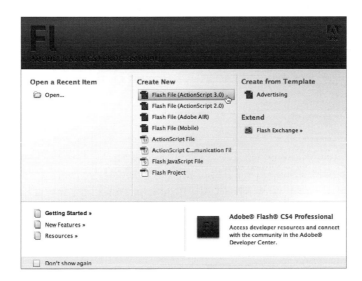

FIG 18.2 Flash startup window.

⋆ Finished exercise file available in the Download Materials area of the wiki.

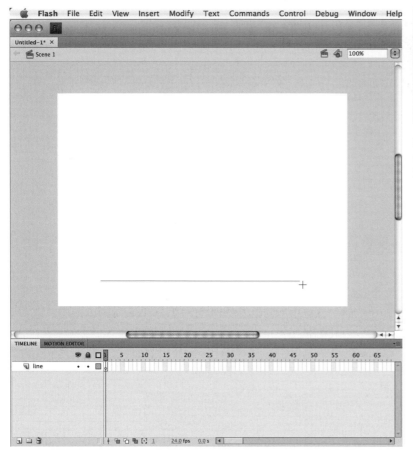

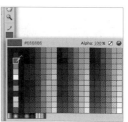

FIG 18.3 Stage with gray line and color picker.

Tip: Like all Adobe Creative Suite applications, the Shift key is used to constrain proportions. Hold the Shift key when using the Oval tool to create a perfectly proportioned circle.

The Timeline is located at the bottom of the screen. By default, there is one empty layer and one empty frame. Double-click on Layer 1 and name it *line*. In Flash, all of the art is made or placed on the Stage or Workspace while all of the instructions about how the art is animated are inserted into frames on the Timeline.

3. Draw a grey line in the bottom one-third of the stage. This line will serve as a visual baseline to anchor the animation. (Fig 18.3)

4. Apply a gray hex value to the stroke property of the line. We used #666666 in the Fill and Stroke area of the Properties panel.

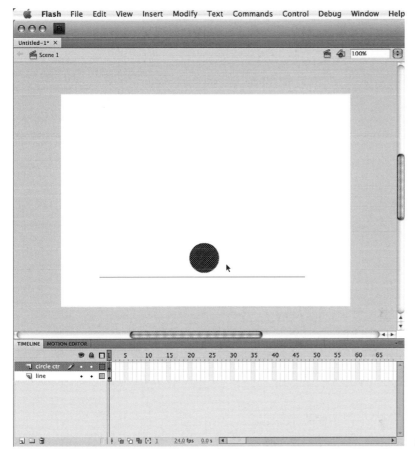

FIG 18.4 Stage with single circle.

5. Add a new layer by clicking on the Insert Layer button towards the bottom of the Timeline panel. Name it *circle ctr*. While the new layer is highlighted so you can tell it is active, draw a circle on the Stage using the Oval tool. (Fig 18.4) Position the circle above the center of the baseline. The stroke of a shape is the line around the outside. The fill is the color inside the outline of the shape.

6. Use the Selection tool to click on the stroke around the circle (in our example, the stroke is gray and the fill is dark red). Press Delete on the keypad so the shape is made by a fill with no stroke. (Fig 18.5)

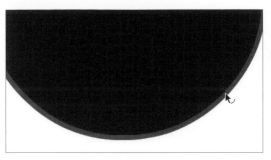 

FIG 18.5 Circle with red Fill and gray Stroke. Select the Stroke to delete it.

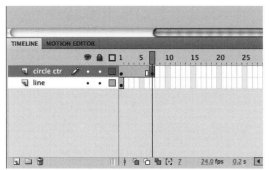 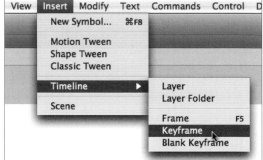

FIG 18.6 Insert > Timeline > Keyframe.

7. In the Timeline, click on Frame 7, then choose Insert > Timeline > Keyframe. (Fig 18.6) Keyframes are points on the timeline where we can control what our animation looks like. When we make a tween between two keyframes, Flash controls the manner in which the shapes are animated. "Tweening" is animation terminology for drawing the shapes between two keyframes so that it seems as if one morphs into another. We do have some control over how Flash makes the animation happen, but for the most part, our greatest control comes in changing keyframes.

Key Command: Click on the frame where you want to add a keyframe then press the F6 key.

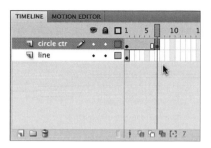

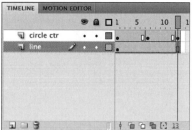

FIG 18.7 Insert > Timeline > Frame.

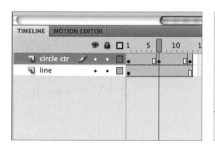

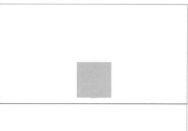

FIG 18.8 A new square at Keyframe 7.

8. Notice that a keyframe is indicated in the Timeline by a black circle where each keyframe is located. Frames between keyframes are gray. The last frame before a keyframe is a white rectangle. (Fig 18.7) The playback head is a red rectangle. It sits over the frame number indicator at the top of the Timeline, with an accompanying red line stretched through all layers. The frame number that the playback head rests upon is reported at the bottom of the Timeline panel (in our example, Frame 7).

9. Create another keyframe on Frame 13.

10. Add frames for the layer containing the baseline. We do not need to add another keyframe, as the baseline will not change for this animation. Click on Frame 12 on the *line layer* and select Insert > Timeline > Frame.

11. Click on Frame 7 on the *circle ctr* layer, then use the Rectangle tool to draw a square. Notice that we set the stroke color to None. (Fig 18.8) You can use the same color for the square as you used for the circle, or you can try a different hue.

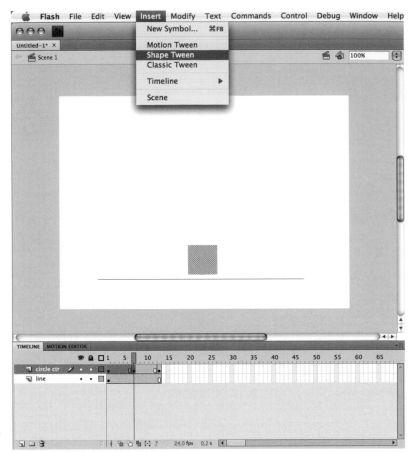

FIG 18.9 Insert > Shape Tween.

12. In the Timeline, click once on Frame 1, hold Shift and click once on Frame 7. This selects Frames 1–7. Now choose Tween > Shape Tween in the Properties panel. (Fig 18.9) Flash will construct all of the frames between the keyframes to animate the content. A shape tween changes one object into another in a smooth animation over a period of time. Flash can also tween the location, size, and color of shapes.

> **Note:**
>
> This concept is so important, we are going to restate it: you decide where the keyframes are placed, and Flash will take care of the animation between the keyframes.

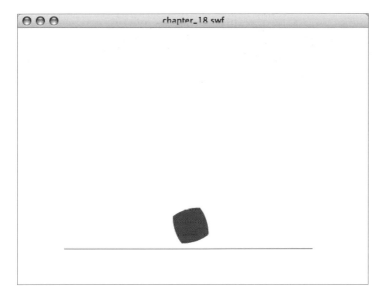

FIG 18.10 Animation preview.

13. In Flash, the .fla file is the master file. Click File > Save As and save the FLA file if you haven't done this already.

14. View the animation by pressing Command+Return or choosing Control > Test Movie. Testing the movie creates a SWF file. (Fig 18.10)

Note:

The difference between an FLA and a SWF is that the FLA is the editable master and the SWF is a non-editable web-ready movie. The SWF can be uploaded to a server, coded into an HTML page, and viewed in a browser.

EXERCISE 02 Adjusting the frame rate to the speed of the beat

FIG 18.11 Properties panel with the frames active.

FIG 18.12 Properties panel with the Stage active. Frame-rate adjustment.

The animation created in Exercise 1 is exactly one second long. The frame rate determines the length of time that each frame is played. Dividing the number of frames in the animation by the frame rate results in the duration of the animation. In Exercise 1, the frame rate is 12 frames per second (fps), so 12 frames divided by 12 frames per second = 1 second. Since the frame rate is the same for the entire timeline, it is a property of the document. This means the frame rate is consistent throughout the entire document. Changing the frame rate would affect the whole animation.

In this exercise we will modify the frame rate by using the Properties panel. (Fig 18.11)

1. Click on the Stage, and notice the properties displayed in the Properties panel on the right side of the screen. These properties are specific to the Stage. (Fig 18.12) If you click on the Timeline, you will see different properties. Use the box next to Frame rate to change the rate to 24 fps. Doubling the frame rate will make the animation move twice as fast.

1. Play music while watching your animation. Choose some House music from an online music source, your MP3 collection, or some of the classic House tracks on YouTube.

2. Try to synchronize the animation so it is in time with the music by adjusting the frame rate.

3. Adjust the frame rate up or down until you have the animation synched with the rhythm of the music.

03 Visualizing tempo

1. Click on the *circle ctr* layer to highlight it, then add a new layer above it. (Fig 18.13) Name it *circle rt*. Select the circle on the Stage. This is the circle located on the first layer. Copy it using Edit > Copy or Command+C. Click on the first frame of the new layer and paste the circle on the Stage using Command+V. Notice that the new layer also registers the new circle as a frame in the Timeline.

2. Hold the Shift key while clicking and dragging the new circle to the right of the first circle. (Fig 18.14)

Tip: Holding the Shift key while dragging an object restricts the movement to 90 and 45 degrees.

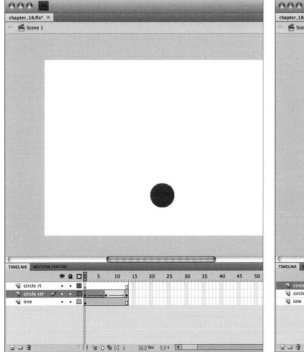

FIG 18.13 A new layer.

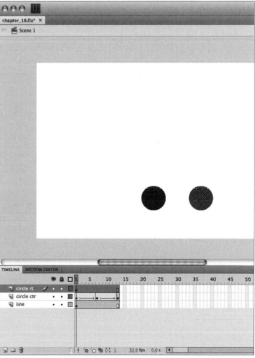

FIG 18.14 A new circle.

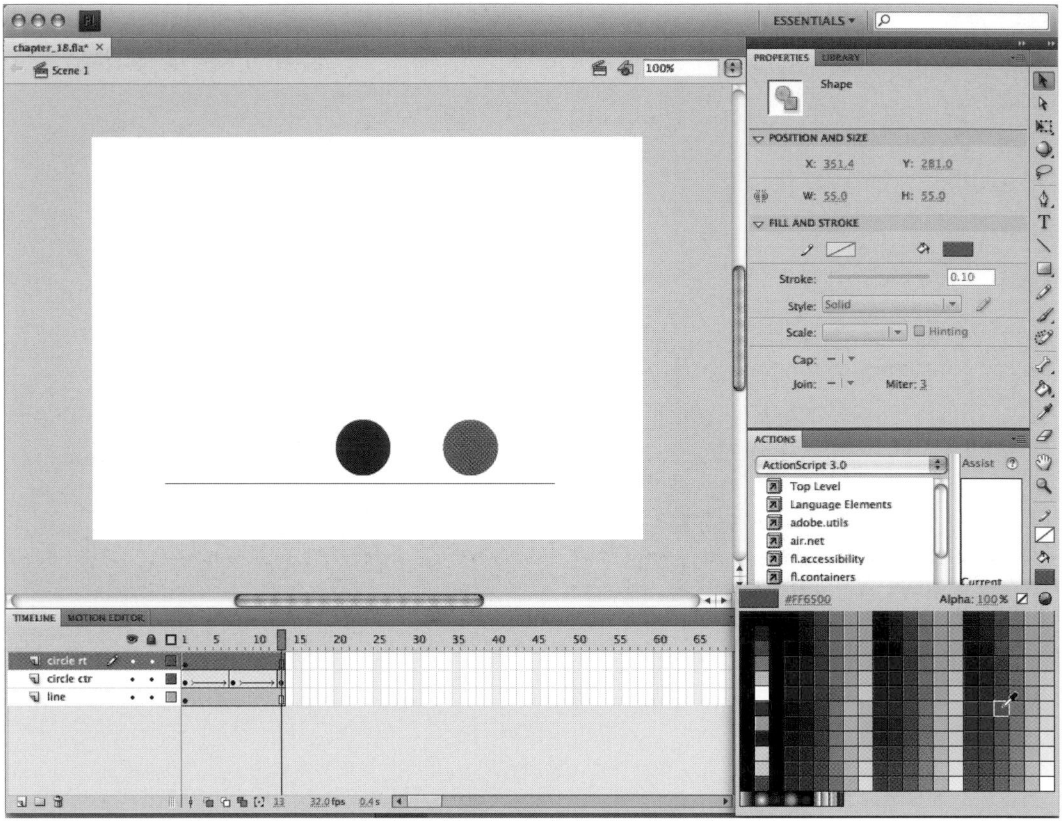

FIG 18.15 The color picker.

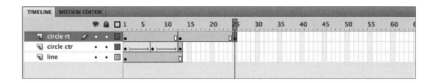

FIG 18.16 A new keyframe: function key F6.

3. Use the Color panel (Window > Color) or the Fill and Stroke area of the Properties panel to change the color of the new circle. (Fig 18.15)

4. Insert a new keyframe at Frame 13 on the *circle rt* layer. Click on Frame 25 and press the function key F6 to add another keyframe. (Fig 18.16)

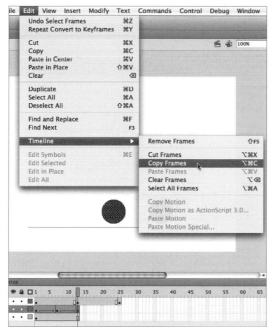 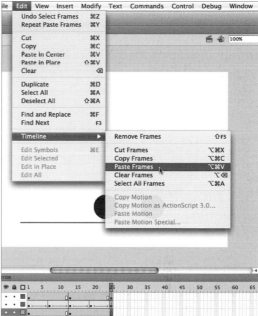

FIG 18.17 Edit > Timeline > Copy Frames.

FIG 18.18 Edit > Timeline > Paste Frames.

5. In order to see the original circle on the *circle ctr* layer after Frame 13, we will duplicate the first 13 frames. Select the frames you want to copy, by clicking on Frame 1 of the *circle ctr* layer and holding the Shift key while clicking the 13th frame. Choose Edit > Timeline > Copy Frames. Select the first destination frame, or Frame 13, and click Edit > Timeline > Paste Frames. (Fig 18.17 18) We are pasting on top of the second keyframe. On the *line* layer, click on Frame 25 and use Function Key F5 to insert frames, or choose Insert > Timeline > Frame.

Watch Out: There is a difference between Copy and Copy Frames. Edit > Copy will copy a shape or an object. Edit > Timeline > Copy Frames will copy the entire content of the selected frames, which is important to do when additional information needs to be included.

> Key Command: Command+Option+V is a shortcut for Edit > Timeline > Paste Frames.

6. Click on Frame 13 on the *circle rt* layer and mouse over the edge of the circle on the Stage with the Selection tool. The cursor changes into an arrow with a curved line. (Fig 18.19) This symbol means that you can pull the edge of the circle to reshape it. Change the shape of the circle using this technique.

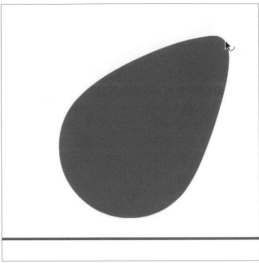

FIG 18.19 Distorting the new circle.

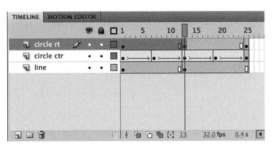
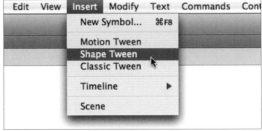

FIG 18.20 Insert > Shape Tween.

7. Select Frames 1 through 13 on the *circle rt* layer and apply the Shape Tween in the Properties panel. (Fig 18.20)

8. Test the new animation (Command+Return) and notice that the new tween takes twice as long as the tween in the first circle-to-square animation. The tempo of the new tween is slower than the tempo of the first circle.

04 Basic bouncing ball

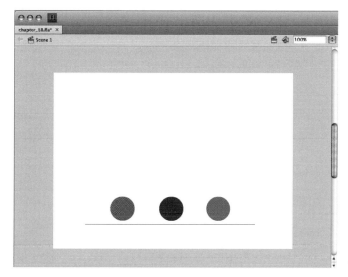

FIG 18.21 A new layer with a new circle.

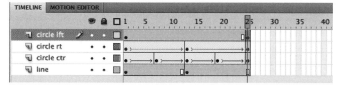

FIG 18.22 A new keyframe at the end.

1. Repeat the first steps in Exercise 3 to create a new layer above *circle rt* called *circle lft*. Add a third circle to the left of the original with a new hue. (Fig 18.21)

2. This circle is going to have a shorter cycle than both of the other shapes. This will result in the fastest tempo. Add a new keyframe on this layer at Frame 25 so the circle will end in the same position. (Fig 18.22) When an animation is supposed to cycle seamlessly, a keyframe should be placed at the end of the layer holding the same content as the first frame.

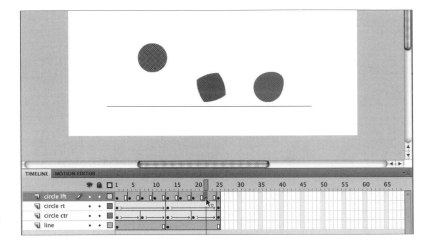

FIG 18.23 A keyframe
every 3 frames.

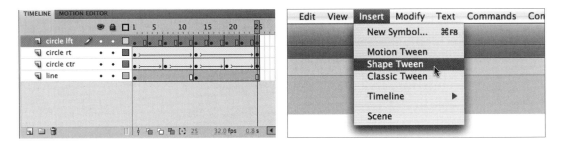

FIG 18.24 Insert > Shape Tween.

3. Insert a new keyframe (F6) every three frames. In each keyframe, move the circle up or down with the Selection tool.

We started on the second keyframe (Frame 4) and used Shift+Up Arrow three times (Shift + up + up + up) to move the circle 30 pixels higher than its starting point. On the next keyframe, we used Shift+Down Arrow. On the following keyframe, Shift+Up Arrow four times. On Frame 13, Shift + Down Arrow. We repeated this pattern throughout so the circle would look like a ball that bounces higher each time it hits the baseline when played. (Fig 18.23)

4. Create a shape tween between each keyframe. (Fig 18.24)

5. Use Command+Return to watch the new animation. (Fig 18.25)

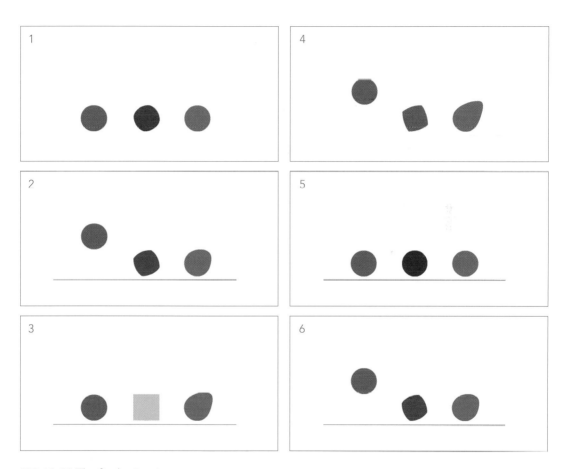

FIG 18.25 The final animation.

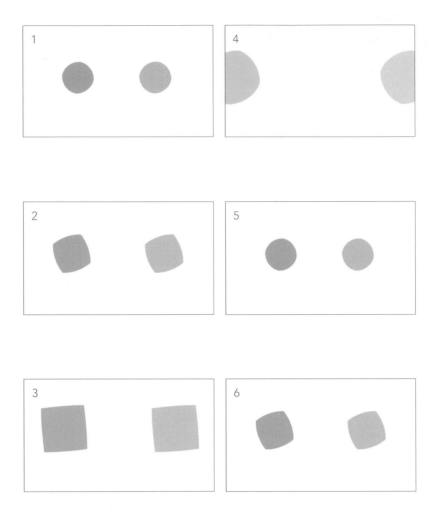

Frames from the final animation created during this chapter.

19 Pacing

The formal design relationships we have created in still compositions also exist in animations. Repetition, symmetry, asymmetry, balance, and rhythm become enveloped in a new formal element: time. In the visual examples, forms are reused to create unity between different moments in the animation. At the same time, transformations of scale, color, and value create contrast, which helps differentiate moments in the animation. Early experimental animation kept time visually with abstract shapes. Pacing is key to Hans Richter's film *Rhythmus 21* (1921). (Fig 19.1) With the most simple forms, Richter was able to explore the transformations of shapes over time through size. Everything is understood through an even, consistent pace, which leads to a contemplation of the purity of form. (Fig 19.1)

In the 1970s, Lillian Schwartz made cutting edge experimental computer animations at Bell Labs. She explained to us that most of the work she produced was created in the laboratory where she reshot 35mm black and white microfilm onto 16mm film, created colored filters and experimented with new editing techniques she devised to produce optical effects. Her work may look like the earlier Richter animation, but the video effects were programmed using a computer. She revealed to us that she wasn't aware of Richter's films until after she made her work, which is only more proof that great minds do think alike! Her process was similar to our exercises. In her 1971 animation UFO's, the introduction of the computer results in faster edits and elemental shapes. (Fig 19.2)

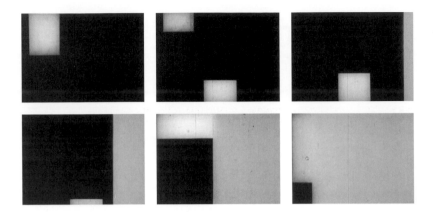

FIG 19.1 Stills from *Rhythmus 21*, Hans Richter, 1921.

FIG 19.2 Stills from *UFO'S*, Lillian Schwartz, Copyright ©1971 Lillian F. Schwartz. Courtesy of the Lillian Feldman Schwartz Collection, The Ohio State University Libraries. All rights reserved. Printed by permission.

Note:

See Hans Richter's film here:
http://www.ubu.com/film/richter_rhythmus.html

See Lillian Schwartz's video here:
http://www.lillian.com/

EXERCISE

01 Library and symbols

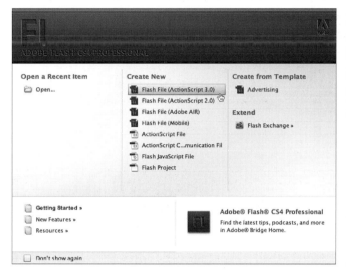

Note: Choose the Essentials work-space from the pull-down menu in the Application bar before working on the following exercises.

FIG 19.3 New Flash document.

1. Click the Flash File (ActionScript 3.0) button in the Create New area of the Flash startup window to create a new document, or choose File > New > Flash File (ActionScript 3.0). (Fig 19.3)

2. Using the Oval tool, hold the Shift key to draw a circle on the right side of the stage. The circle is added to the first frame of *Layer 1* in the Timeline. (Fig 19.4-5)

Tip: Holding the Shift key while drawing con-strains the ratio of the shape proportions to be equal.

3. Double-click *Layer 1* and rename it *right circle*.

Note:

Don't forget that whatever happens on the Stage corre-sponds to a frame in the Timeline.

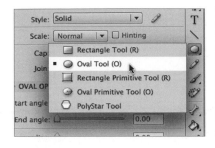

LEFT TO RIGHT:

FIG 19.4 Oval tool.

FIG 19.5 Oval: fill, no stroke.

FIG 19.6 Convert to Symbol dialog box.

LEFT TO RIGHT:

FIG 19.7 Library panel.

FIG 19.8 A new symbol.

4. In Chapter 18 we used shapes. Now we are going to convert our circle from a shape into a symbol. Symbols are reusable graphic or textual elements stored in the Library panel. When we drag a symbol to the Stage, we are actually using an "instance" of the symbol. For each instance, we can change certain properties of the original symbol, like color, size, transparency, position on the stage, etc. If we make a change to the symbol itself, such as changing its shape from a circle to a square, it will be reflected in all instances of the symbol. Select the circle with the Selection tool and then choose Modify > Convert to Symbol. Name the new symbol *circle* and choose Graphic from the Type pull-down menu. (Fig 19.6)

Tip: If the Library panel is not open, choose Window > Library. All panels are accessible from the Window menu.

5. Click on the Library tab behind the Properties panel to see the circle included in the Library as a symbol. (Fig 19.7)

6. Look on the Stage and notice the attributes of the symbol. The circle has a blue square around it, and there is no option to reshape the circle when you mouse over its edge. (Fig 19.8)

EXERCISE

02 Instances of symbols

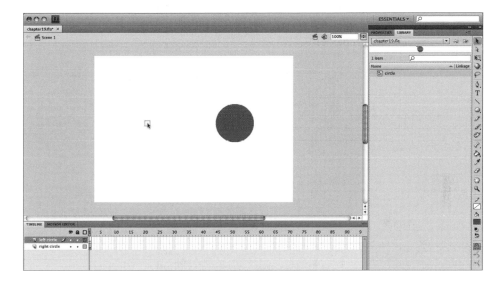

FIG 19.9 The next symbol goes on a new layer named *left circle*.

A symbol is saved in the Library so that it is always available to use on the Stage. The circle that is on the Stage is called an instance of the symbol. Instances can be modified independently from the saved symbol. We can delete the circle from the stage and make another instance by dragging the symbol out of the Library onto the Stage. We can also have several instances on the Stage at the same time and animate them without changing the original symbol in the Library window.

1. Add a new layer to the Timeline called *left circle*. (Fig 19.9)

2. Create a new instance of the circle by dragging the symbol from the Library to the left side of the Stage.

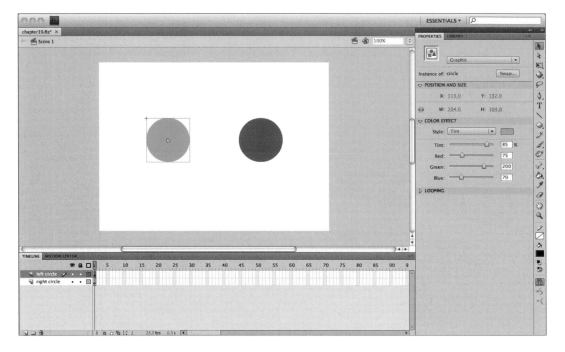

FIG 19.10 New symbol with a new fill.

3. Change the color of the new instance on the stage. If you try to change the color of the circle by double-clicking on it and filling the shape, you will change the color of the symbol so that every time it is used it will be the newly selected color. Instead, to change the color of the instance only once, use the Color Effect portion of the Properties panel. Select the left circle with the Selection tool then choose Tint from the Style menu beneath Color Effect. Modify the Tint, Red, Green, and Blue values. Our values were 85, 75, 200, 70, but you can make any modification you wish. (Fig 19.10)

EXERCISE
03 Classic Tween

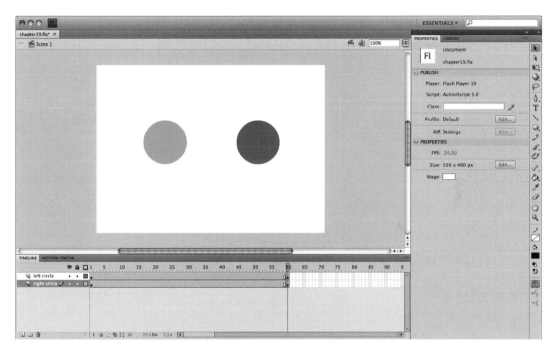

FIG 19.11 The exercise so far.

The word "tween" derives from "in between." Classic tweens are used to animate properties of symbols without changing their shapes. They create frame-by-frame animation for properties, such as changing the position, scale, color, or opacity of a symbol over time. Instead of having to draw 60 frames of one circle moving across the Stage, you can position the circle in one area of the Stage in Frame 1, in a different location or even off the Stage in Frame 60, and allow the computer to draw all of the frames between 1 and 60 so that the circle appears to move.

Watch Out: If you are using Flash CS3 or earlier, you will be doing a Motion Tween here. The Classic Tween was introduced in CS4.

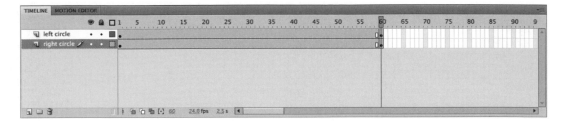

FIG 19.12 Keyframes inserted at Frame 60.

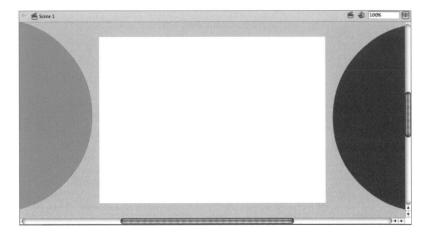

FIG 19.13 The circles scaled and moved.

1. Insert a new keyframe (F6) at Frame 60 in the Timeline on both of the layers. (Fig 19.12)

2. Start with either of the two layers. Click on the keyframe to make it active. Scale the instance of the circle so it is larger than the stage using the Free Transform or Scale tool. Hold Shift while transforming. Move the large circle off the Stage — move the left circle to the left and the right circle to the right. (Fig 19.13)

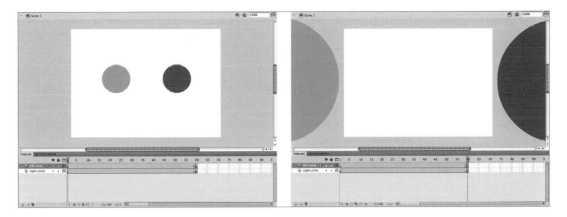

FIG 19.14 You should be able to toggle between Frame 1 and Frame 60 to see that you have two small circles on either side of the stage on Frame 1 and two large circles positioned off the stage at Frame 60.

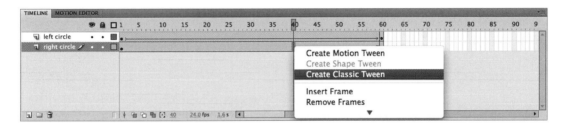

FIG 19.15 Create Classic Tween.

3. Click to activate the keyframe on the second layer and repeat the portions of Step 2 that scale and move the circle.

4. Add a Classic Tween between Frames 1 and 60 on each layer, one at a time. Position the mouse over any frame between 1 and 60 on one of the layers and use the contextual menu (Control-click or right-click) to choose Classic Tween. Repeat this on the second layer. Choose Play from the Control Menu. Now the circles move off the stage. The circles increase in size, but the shapes remain intact. (Fig 19.14 & 19.15)

04 Creating a fade

Classic tweens can also be used to change the transparency of a symbol, as this type of modification does not result in a change to the shape of the instance on the Stage. *Alpha* is a word used in Flash to mean transparency, much like an alpha mask controls transparency surrounding an image. We will modify the alpha values on Frame 60 of each layer, one at a time. Adding a keyframe for alpha on Frame 60 is the cinematic equivalent of fading out.

1. Start with one layer. With the Selection tool, click on Frame 60 in the Timeline then click on the instance of the symbol on the Stage. Change the alpha value of the circle instance to 0 percent by choosing Alpha from the Style pull-down menu in the Properties panel. (Fig 19.16)

2. Repeat this process for the other layer.

3. Test the movie and watch the frames fade out over time.

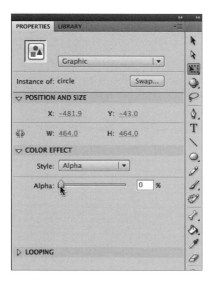

Note: Remember, the Properties panel displays property information for whatever is active. So if you click on a frame, you can see and edit properties for that frame. If you click on a symbol on the Stage, you can see and edit properties for the instance.

FIG 19.16 A new *alpha* value.

EXERCISE
05 Animating the symbol

Symbols can also be animations with independent timelines. For example, a circular symbol could morph between an oval and a circle in its Symbol Timeline. Then, the animated symbol could move across the Stage in the Document Timeline. The pace of the moving symbol across the Stage would be determined by the number of frames used in the Document Timeline, while the pace of the morph between the oval and the circle would be determined by the Symbol Timeline.

1. Create a new Movie Clip symbol and call it "circle animation." (Fig 19.17)

2. Double-click on the symbol in the Library and it will open in Symbol editing mode. This mode allows you to edit the symbol. Any edits made here will affect all instances of the symbol.

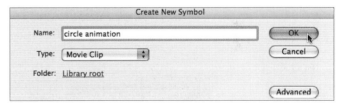

FIG 19.17 Create New Symbol.

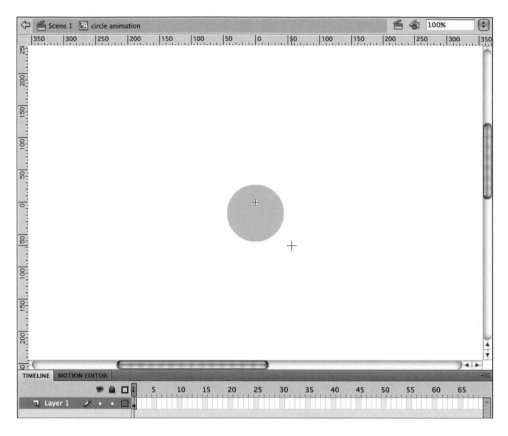

FIG 19.18 A new circle drawn with the Oval tool.

Note:

For Steps 3-8 we are working in the Movie Clip Timeline.

3. Use the Oval tool to draw a circle on the Stage in Frame 1 of the Timeline with any fill color and no stroke applied. (Fig 19.18)

4. Insert keyframes in the Timeline on Frames 13 and 25. (Fig 19.19)

5. Select Keyframe 13 and delete the circle from the Stage. Then draw a square in its place using the Rectangle tool. Now you have a square in Keyframe 13 where you used to have a circle. (Fig 19.20)

6. Control-click or right-click on a frame inbetween Keyframes 1 and 13 to select Create Shape Tween from the contextual menu. (Fig 19.21)

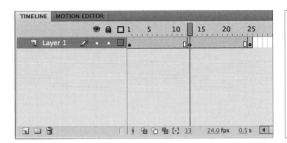

FIG 19.19 Keyframes at Frame 13 and 25.

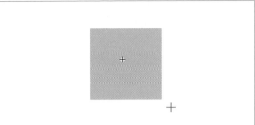

FIG 19.20 A square drawn on Keyframe 13.

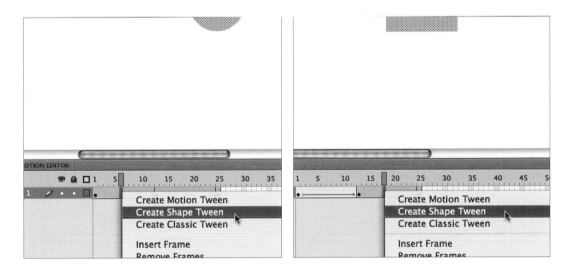

FIG 19.21 Create Shape Tween.

FIG 19.22 Create second Shape Tween.

7. Control-click or right-click on a frame inbetween Keyframes 13 and 25 and select Create Shape Tween from the contextual menu again. You can see the results of the shape tween by "scrubbing" over the timeline, or dragging the playback head from Frame 1 to Frame 25. (Fig 19.22)

8. Exit the Movie Clip Timeline and return to the Scene timeline using the Back button in the top left area of the Stage. (Fig 19.23)

FIG 19.23 Back button

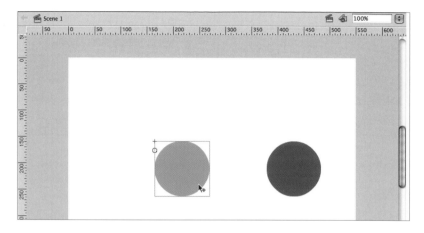

FIG 19.24 Select the left circle on the stage.

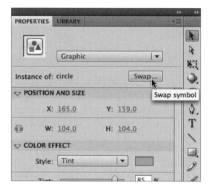

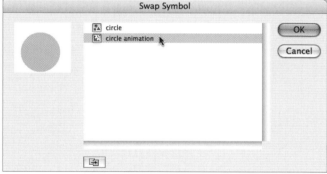

FIG 19.25 The Swap... button.   **FIG 19.26** Swap the old symbol with the new circle animation.

9. Use the Selection tool to select the left circle on the stage. (Fig 19.24)

10. Now we will trade the circles on the Stage for the movie clip animation we just created. In the Properties panel, click the Swap... button. (Fig 19.25) Choose *circle animation*, and click OK. (Fig 19.26)

11. Next, swap the right circle on the Stage for the movie clip animation. Notice that any effects you placed on the instance are still active when the symbol is swapped.

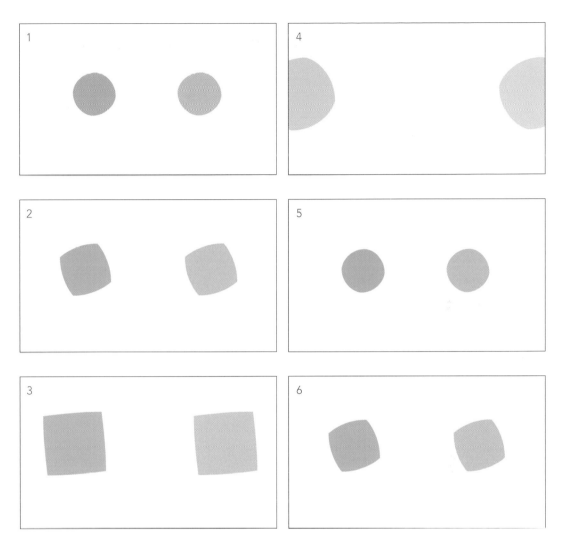

FIG 19.27 The final animation.

12. Test your movie (Command+Return), and you will see that the both the symbol and the scene animate according to different timelines. The symbol is an animation loop of a square turning into a circle and back again. The animation has a tween that makes it move out of the frame and increase in size.

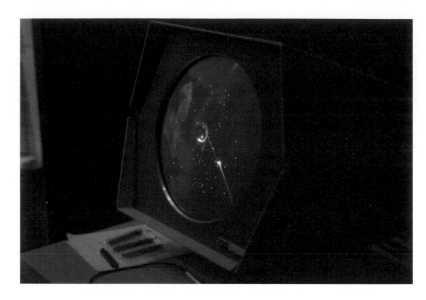

Spacewar!, 1961, Martin Graetz, Stephen Russell, and Wayne Wii-tanen, computer program for DEC PDP-1 computer. Photo credit: Joi Ito, http://joi.ito.com, CC-BY.

THOMSON & CRAIGHEAD

INSTALLATIONS & EXHIBITION HISTORY / ONLINE ARTWORKS / DOWNLOAD / CONTACT

TRIGGER HAPPY

 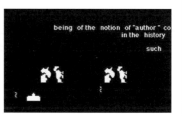

triggerhappy is a gallery installation whose format will be familiar to anyone who has encountered that early arcade game, Space Invaders combining an absurd quest for information with an old-fashioned shoot-em-up computer game. In this, it accurately reflects, and comments upon, the electronic environment in which we live, work and play. "In effect", the artists say, "triggerhappy becomes a folly. A self-defeating environment looking at the relationship between hypertext, authorship and the individual." They cleverly recontextualise existing representations and subject them to active manipulation on the part of the viewer, who becomes an unwitting participant in a meaningless game of "info-war".

Michael Gibbs. 1998.

Trigger Happy, 1998, Jon Thomson and Alison Craighead, computer program written in Macromedia Director, the predecessor to Flash, used by permission of the artist. Screen shot taken November 17, 2008, http://www.thomson-craighead.net/docs/thap.html/

20 ActionScript3.0

Interactivity is a much-ballyhooed concept of the late
20th and early 21st centuries. We walk around listening
to iPods while texting on our cell phones, drive according
to directions from a satellite spoken to us live in a calm
computerized voice, and are constantly reviewing our blogs,
Flickr pages, Google Alerts, and email.

Interactivity is not new. The archaeologist Alexander
Marschak has argued that the caves at Lascaux represented
an interactive site; that it was a place people visited to
leave reactive marks. From chess to basketball, mahjong to
tennis, games are ancient interactive forms of entertainment,
intellectual diversion, and fun.

In these exercises we will be asking you to copy and paste
code into your FLA Actions panel. Since it is easier to do this
on the screen than from a printed book, the exercises in this
chapter are all available on http://wiki.digital-foundations.
net/index.php?title=Chapter_20.

*Page numbers for images and
photos are set in italics.*